WORLD

FRANCIS KILVERT AND HIS WORLD

FRANCIS KILVERT AND HIS WORLD

Frederick Grice

with a contribution from

Rev D. T. W. Price

© CALIBAN BOOKS
c/o BIBLIOS, Glenside Industrial Estate,
Star Road, Partridge Green, Horsham,
Sussex.

Hardback ISBN 0 904573 52 4
Paperback ISBN 0 904573 78 8

Printed in Great Britain by A. Wheaton & Co. Ltd., Exeter

To my Dear Wife Gwen
and her new grandchildren
Laura and Luke

What I have come to like best in the whole of Russian literature is the childlike Russian quality of Pushkin and Chekhov, their shy unconcern with such high-sounding matters as the ultimate purpose of mankind or their own salvation. It isn't that they didn't think about these things, and to good effect, but they always felt that such important matters were not for them. While Gogol, Tolstoy and Dostoievsky worried and looked for the meaning of life and prepared for death and drew up balance-sheets, these two were distracted, right up to the end of their lives, by the current individual tasks imposed on them by their vocation as writers, and in the course of fulfilling these tasks they lived their lives, quietly, treating both their lives and their work as private, individual matters, of no concern to anyone else. And these individual things have since become of concern to all, their work has ripened of itself, like apples picked green from the trees, and has increasingly matured in sense and sweetness.

B. Pasternak. Dr Zhivago. Chap. 9. v. 7.

It often happens that the diarist, who in his lifetime has gone unnoticed or had been ridiculed by forgotten nonentities, emerges 200 years later as a first-rate writer, who knew how to immortalise, with a striggle of his old-fashioned pen, an airy landscape, the smell of a stage coach, or the oddities of an acquaintance.

Vladimir Nabokov. The Eye

i

Acknowledgments

The author and publishers would like to thank the following–
the Kilvert Society for permission to use their photographs;
Mrs E. Farmery for permission to draw upon her researches
into the Cholmeley and Heanley families, and Mr R. B. Taylor
for his cooperation; the Keeper of the Archives at Wadham
and the Librarian of Corpus Christi for information on Kilvert
at Oxford; the Librarian of the National Library of Wales, and
Lady Delia Dillwyn-Venables-Llewelyn for permission to quote from
the letters in the Venables Archive; the Keeper of Rare Books at
the University of Durham Library for permission to study the
Plomer papers in his keeping; Robin and Heather Tanner for
information on the Colemans and Kington Langley; Miss Lois
Lang-Sims for her letter on Kilvert's last poem, and her discovery
of Mrs Kilvert's letter to Bredwardine School; Mr and Mrs R. I.
Morgan for invaluable information on many aspects of Kilvert
studies; the Rev D. T. W. Price for his essay and advice on all
things to do with Kilvert and the Church; Mr A. Scott-Ashe for the
diary entries found among his late brother's papers and the letter
by Lucy Ashe; Sir Rupert Hart-Davis for rescuing the transcript
made by William Plomer of the unpublished sections of the
'Cornwall' notebook; the Librarian of the Hereford Public Library
for permission to read Mary Bevan's Diary; Mr P. Dawson for
additional information on Mary Bevan; Laurence Le Quesne for
his work in pioneering serious Kilvert studies and his stimulating

ii

After Kilvert; the Rev D. N. Lockwood for many interesting conversations on Kilvert and his background; Margaret Mathers, Edward West, Hugh and Guy Dearlove and many other members of the Kilvert Society for their constant help; Professor Mark Doughty for information on the pupils of Hardenhuish School; Mrs K. Hughes, Research Assistant at the National Library of Wales; Dr A. Walk for a note on Dr Clouston; Godfrey Davies, who took many of the photographs and provided the rest from the Kilvert Society collection; and especially Mrs Teresa Williams who has salvaged from nineteenth century newspapers and magazines innumerable invaluable items of information, and whose letters have been a constant source of inspiration and encouragement. lastly tribute must be paid to the late C. T. O. Prosser, for many years a dedicated servant of the Kilvert Society, and probably the best-informed Kilvertian of all.

iii

CONTENTS

page

iv

Chapter One
Forbears

Francis Kilvert, like most romantics, was given to speculation about his ancestry. On 14 October 1872 he took what he called his 'silver cup' to be engraved with the arms of the Kilvert family (sable, a fesse between six crosslets argent, three escallops of the first) and a motto to go with the scallop shells. The motto, which he invented, partly because of the shells, and partly because of its 'lovely, solemn melancholy sound' was PEREGRINAMUS. The choice is characteristic; it is poetic and fictional. And on other occasions when Kilvert was ruminating on his ancestry he exhibited the same tendency to let fancy outrun fact. On 10 April 1875 a friend of his, the Rev. Rhys Bishop, the curate of Moccas, was showing him around Moccas Church, and drew his attention to the tomb of Sir Reginald de Fresne. The name Fresne (Fraxinus = Ash) prompted him to imagine that he was related to Sir Reginald on his mother's side (his maternal grandmother was an Ashe). By New Year's Day 1878 the fancy had grown into a fact.

> I told (James Davies) that the knight in armour whose recumbent figure rests upon the tomb in the chancel in Moccas Church was an ancestor of mine, and that my forefathers owned the Moccas estate. The Churchwarden opened his grey eyes almost incredulously...

James Davies may well have looked incredulous because the only evidence to support Kilvert's claim was supposed to be in a book which Mrs Ashe of Langley House had mentioned to him but never produced.*

In most things connected with his ancestry Kilvert tended to rely less on fact than on intuition. On one occasion, enchanted by the good humour, high spirits and natural courtesy of the people whom he met in the little Brecon market town of Builth, and intrigued by the sense of kinship he felt with them, he wrote,

I believe I must have Welsh blood.

Unfortunately this claim is as unsubstantial as his assumption that the Ashes once owned Moccas. There is no evidence that either the Kilverts or the Colemans from whom he was descended ever lived in Wales.

The Kilverts

There were Kilverts in Shropshire in the 17th C., but to avoid confusion we shall pick up the story with Francis Kilvert (1757–1817), son of Thomas Kilvert and Elizabeth Caint. This Francis was one of two sons. The elder was Richard who became first of all Chaplain to Bishop Hurd of Hartlebury Castle, and then a Prebendary or Canon of Worcester Cathedral, and acquired a considerable fortune. His only daughter was Maria Frances, whose funeral the diarist attended and described (Vol. 1. 265 *et seq*). When Thomas Kilvert, father of the Canon, died in 1782, his widow and her younger son, Francis, moved to Bath and settled in Widcombe. This son, the diarist's grandfather, married Anna Parsons and had a large family (seven sons and one daughter). He set up as a coachmaker in 1787, but in 1794 was declared bankrupt. He died in 1817, leaving his numerous family in charge of his widow and his eldest son, the second Francis Kilvert.

*June Badeni says the Ashes came from Somerset *(Wiltshire Forefathers)*.

The plight of the family was so desperate that all the children had virtually to fend for themselves, and all who were of an age to work had to do so. One brother went into medicine, and another emigrated to Canada. Fortunately Francis, the eldest son, whom to avoid confusion it may be best to refer to as Francis Kilvert the Antiquary (a name by which he was commonly known) was a gifted and resourceful young man who had already graduated and become curate to the Rector of Claverton near Bath. He supplemented his stipend by acting as Second Master in the Grammar School at Bath, where he himself had been Head Boy, and then set up his own school in Claverton Lodge, a commodious house on the outskirts of the city. He did not only make a success of the school, but he also undertook the training of his younger brother, Robert, whom he educated so efficiently that he also was able to take on the tuition of young pupils; and the straitened nature of the family finances may be judged by the delight Robert took in bringing home his first fees (£20). It was again through the good offices of his brother Francis and two of his friends, a Mr Allfield and a Mr Stafford Smith (a friend of John Keble who was at that time a Fellow of Oriel) that the Provost of Oriel offered Robert an exhibition which enabled him to go up in 1822.

It is surprising that Kilvert, who was clearly anxious to let the world know of the honourable connections of his family, should have omitted to mention three links of which he could legitimately have been proud. When his uncle Francis, Francis Kilvert of Claverton Lodge, wrote his book on Bishop Hurd, the book that deeply offended Maria Kilvert and prompted her to cut his family out of her will, he mentioned that he had embarked upon it partly as an act of homage to a distinguished relative. The connection between the Kilverts and the Hurds was slight but real. In 1689 a William Parsons, from whom the Kilverts were descended on the distaff side, married a sister of Bishop Hurd's mother.

Kilvert does not mention this link, nor does he refer to the aristocratic lineage of his aunt, the wife of his uncle Francis. Mrs

4 FORBEARS

Kilvert, who before her marriage assumed the name of de Chièvre, was of very noble birth, being the only child of Count Leopold von Berchtold of Buchlau in Moravia, and Maria Catherine Josephine de Croy. The Count, who had come to England shortly after his marriage, was sent to France by his emperor to intercede for Marie Antoinette, the Emperor's sister. It was at Paris that Eleonora Adelaide Sophia Leopoldina was born in the fateful year of 1789. When her father was in danger of being arrested as a Royalist sympathiser the child was smuggled out of France in an open boat, and befriended in England by her guardian, Mr Woodruffe Smith, with whom she lived at Stockwell Park, Clapham, until her marriage to Kilvert's uncle on 10 December 1822 at Holy Trinity Church, Clapham. She was married from the house of Sir Robert Inglis.*

The third link is one which Kilvert may be referring to in an oblique way in a note in his Diary for 23 February 1875.

> At Kingston St Michael the good Vicar was busy in the village amongst his flock, so till he should come home I asked for the keys of the church and spent some time in the Church examining all the old monuments, and the new East Window, and musing and praying among the graves of my forefathers.
> Vol. 3. 152.

One Kingston St Michael monument that Kilvert may have had in mind is to the Sadlers (to whom the crazy Sadler Gale, the squire who tried to fly was related). The Sadlers, Stokes, Powers, Mascalls and Colemans were all descendants of the sisters of Sir Charles Snell (*fl.* late sixteenth and early seventeenth century), who died unmarried. Through his sisters part of his estate passed to the Coleman family, to which the diarist's mother belonged.*

*I am indebted to Mrs E. Farmery for this information, which was kindly communicated to her by Mr Norman Goodford Cholmeley, a descendant of Francis Kilvert, the Antiquary.
*See June Badeni: *Wiltshire Forefathers.*

It is strange that Kilvert, with his interest in the more romantic aspects of his own family history, makes no mention of these well-authenticated connections. Nor does Robert Kilvert refer to them in his memoirs, probably largely because they end long before he meets his wife.

The story of the career of Robert, the diarist's father, will be resumed in the next chapter.

The Colemans

The Colemans are first mentioned in the parish registers of Kingston St Michael in 1563, and the entries continue without a break to Walter Coleman, the diarist's great grand-father. Some time ago, Mr and Mrs R. Tanner of Kington Langley, starting from the name of the field in which they had built their house (the Old Chapel Field) and two references to this Walter Coleman in Kilvert's Diary, brought to light a forgotten item of local history and posed for themselves a few intriguing questions. The relevant diary entries are as follows:–

> 24 Sept 1874 . . . This afternoon I walked over to Kingston St Michael by Langley Burrell Church and Morrell Lane and the Old Mausoleum and Langley Ridge and the Plough Inn.
> (Vol. 3. 86)

> 18 March 1876 . . . I went on to the Plough and up to the Ridge . . . I went on past the head of the steep green lane in (Kilvert probably wrote 'into') the site of the old Chapel and burying place where my great-grandfather was laid to rest . . .
> (Vol. 3. 244)

The Walter Coleman in question did not marry till 1778, when he was 57. Shortly after his marriage he began to make plans for a private mausoleum, and the site he chose was a field called Batten's Patch, in his own village of Kington Langley. There was to be a chapel on the site, available daily for any three hours for

any group of Christian worshippers other than Roman Catholics.
Mysteriously Walter Coleman gave instructions that with him was
to lie the body, not of his lawful wife, but of a certain Sarah
Stephens, his wife's aunt. His widow, who survived him,
remarried and Kilvert refers to her in a short note in Vol. 3. 107.

My mother remembered her grandmother who married a
second time and became Mrs Reeves.

When Walter died in 1782 his chapel was still unfinished and
he was buried with his ancestors in the churchyard of Kington St
Michael, but as soon as the chapel was ready his body and that of
Sarah Stephens were re-interred in the chapel graveyard. It is not
surprising to learn that his widow refused to pay for the completion
of the chapel.

Mrs Heather Tanner, who unearthed the mystery of the
Mausoleum, still does not know what happened to the Chapel. By
the late 19th C. it had vanished from the Ordnance Survey maps,
and the only visible evidence of it is a six- or seven-stone course of
walling along the road running into Kington Langley. For all she
knows Walter and Sarah are still somewhere under her garden.

It was the second Walter Coleman, the son of the Mausoleum
builder, who, in spite of severe opposition from her parents,
married Thermuthis Ashe, the daughter of Robert Ashe, Squire of
Langley Burrell. This connection made Kilvert's mother cousin to
the Squire Ashe of the Diary; and it is important to remember this
connection because, in all probability, this was the reason for
Robert Kilvert's being at Langley Burrell in the first place.

For some reason Kilvert has far more to say in his Diary
about the early Colemans than any other branch of his family. He
twice tells the story of the occasion on which his great grandmother was shot at through the window of the Manor House at
Kington Langley by a mysterious gunman; and he twice mentions
the unhappy marriage between his grandmother and Squire
Walter Coleman. Carrie Britton, once a housemaid at Langley

House, told how on one occasion Kilvert's grandmother had come to help her mother (Madam Ashe, who in her later years was paralyzed) and repeated a conversation which showed how much the old woman still resented her daughter's rash marriage. (Vol. 2. 112); and Kilvert adds

> At another time when my grandmother had gone over to Langley House to see her parents, with her heart full of irrepressible sorrow because of her unhappy marriage, the old man said, 'My dear, we warned you. You made your bed and now you must lie on it.' He and his wife had been deeply averse to her marriage with my grandfather, Mr Coleman, and had done all they could to prevent it, but in vain.
> (Vol. 2. 400)

Robert Kilvert's account of Squire Coleman is an ambivalent one.

> He was a man of middle height, thin and spare. His hair was grizzled when I knew him. He had a good profile and fine nose, but his face was the colour of a kite's foot, yellow and unwholesome-looking, and his address was rendered unpleasant by a set un-meaning smile . . . He was a good and easy landlord, and an upright and honourable man in all his dealings. (Vol. 2. 402–3)

'Almost everyone in the countryside knew my grandfather by sight' said the diarist. 'Once seen he could never be forgotten'; and he goes on to speak of the deep impression the old man made on a lady who saw him when she was a child. The Fry's of Chieflands spoke of him as a good considerate landlord; and Isaac Giles said 'Old Squire Coleman, your grandfather, was a very plain man. When I was travelling with my pack past his house he would call out that he was going my way as far as Cold Harbour Forge and he would walk along with me. He would rail against the pride of the farmers nowadays . . .' (Vol. 2. 281)

It is easy to see, from accounts such as these, why it was that the Ashes with their imperious natures did not desire to have him

as a member of their family; perhaps it is just as easy to see where
Kilvert inherited his humility and friendliness. He was said to have
inherited too some of his grandfather's physical characteristics
(his darkness and sallowness); perhaps he had also something of
his unassuming nature; and the tension that always existed
between the Ashes and the Kilverts may have dated from the
family resentment against the Coleman who married their
daughter.

The Ashes

There is a shortage of information about the early pedigree of the
Ashe family, but June Badeni *(Wiltshire Forefathers)* says that
Samuel Ashe, who bought the Manor of Langley Burrell in about
1655, came from Somerset. The Manor House at that time stood a
little to the south of the present house in what is now the garden.
The present Langley House was built (in about 1750 according to
June Badeni and *c.* 1771 according to Pevsner) by Robert Ashe
who was both Squire and Parson of the parish. His son, also
Robert, had a very masterful wife who was still remembered in the
1870's as 'Madam Ashe'; and an old man told Kilvert that he
remembered Robert Ashe 'coming into church and sitting in his
pew in a black skull cap. He was a tall man – over six feet – and
stout . . . When he was High Sheriff of Wiltshire he had a large
coach built. In this coach Madam Ashe used to go out driving with
the footman, John Chambers, standing behind on the footboard.'
(Vol. 2. 286) Kilvert was also told that 'Madam Ashe was
popular, though very quaint and eccentric, self-willed and a little
tyrannical.' (Vol. 2. 297). It was, of course, the daughter of this
Squire and Madam Ashe who, against their wishes, married
Squire Coleman of Kington Langley, and became the grandmother of the diarist; and if Kilvert got his large frame from both
Squire Coleman and Squire Ashe, Robert Martin Ashe, the

Squire Ashe of the diary, seems to have inherited his mother's tyrannical and self-willed nature.

Robert Martin Ashe took holy orders (Kilvert refers to him on one occasion as an 'elderly clergyman') but apparently was never appointed to a living, preferring to assist his father who was both patron and incumbent of Langley Burrell. On the death of his father he resigned his clerical duties and devoted himself to the running of the estate. The living was given to Robert Kilvert, the diarist's father and husband to Thermuthis (née Coleman) the Squire's cousin.

Chapter Two

Hardenhuish

Cardinal Newman said of Robert Kilvert, the diarist's father, that 'he left a fragrant memory behind him at Oriel'; otherwise his years at Oxford seem to have gone uncommented on, and on his own confession they were undistinguished and uneventful.

> I have but little to record about my life at Oxford. It was very uneventful. Probably few undergraduates spent the three or four years in a more quiet or even course. I had one or two friends, very few acquaintances, no lounging in other men's rooms. There was the two hours' constitutional walk almost every day from two to four o'clock – in fine weather out in the country, when wet generally in the cloisters at Magdalen – besides a run before morning chapel . . . Singular to say, I never drank a glass of wine there throughout my residence nor any fermented liquor at all, only water . . .
>
> My reading was carried on steadily, but from lack of sufficient funds I had not the advantage of a private Tutor to put me on the right track for success in the public examinations. When the time came I had read a great many books, but had no-one to test me in my accurate knowledge of them, so I went before the examiners at a disadvantage. I was nearly a week in the Classical and Mathematical Schools, and before it was over I was quite worn out, sick in head and at heart, and broke down sadly before the last. The consequence was that

instead of being in the First Class, I was in the Third, to my
great disappointment and mortification.

Memoirs of Robert Kilvert
Kilvert Society. n.d. p. 60–61

He was eventually ordained at Salisbury, and then through
the intervention of a college friend who lived at Melksham was
offered a curacy in the parish of Keevil just outside Trowbridge at
£70 a year. He was almost as poor as he had been at Oxford, but
he managed to keep one servant and his sister came to live with
him and keep house for him; and 'having a house of my own and a
lady at the head of my establishment I was able to advertise for
pupils, and was not long in getting one or two at a fairly liberal rate
of remuneration... Here I spent five years of my life in great
happiness generally, with only the occasional drawback of having
an ill-conditioned or unruly pupil.'

In 1832, however, with the arrival of a new vicar, Robert
Kilvert was obliged to leave Keevil. He was offered a curacy at
Bradford, near Dorchester, and was tempted to go there since he
would be close to his friend, Henry Moule, later Vicar of
Fordington and father of one of Thomas Hardy's closest friends;
but he chose to serve under a Mr Hume, whom he knew closely, at
Melksham. It was an unfortunate choice, because the work proved
too much for him, and in three months his health broke down and
he was obliged to leave.

Not much is known about the next few years of Robert Kilvert's
life, but eventually through the kind offices of Mr T. Clutterbuck
of Hardenhuish House he was presented to the living of
Hardenhuish, and presumably then felt in a position to marry. His
marriage to Thermuthis Coleman took place in 1838.

For its position (Hardenhuish in the eighteenth century was
in open country) the church, built by John Wood the Younger in
1779, is a surprisingly elegant structure (Hare called it 'Wrenian');
and Mr Clutterbuck's residence, Hardenhuish House, boasted
work by Sir John Soane; but the living was a poor one, and

Kilvert's stipend little more than he had received as a curate at
Keevil. However Mr Clutterbuck enlarged the Rectory for him,
and enabled him to accommodate more pupils and, like his brother
at Claverton, build up a profitable school.

Robert Kilvert, for all his obscurity and lack of academic
distinction, never seems to have lacked influential connections.
Even before going to Oxford he had been invited by Sir William
Holtham to go with him on a tour of France and Switzerland as
tutor to his son, an offer which illness compelled him to decline,
and which was taken up by Henry Moule; and to his school at
Hardenhuish came the sons of the rich London banker, Mr Martin
(one was to become Sir Richard Martin of Overbury Court near
Bredon), the sons of Sir Walter and Lady Farquhar, and Augustus
Hare, who was at Hardenhuish from 1843–6. One cannot help
feeling that it was Robert's eldest brother, Francis, who brought
him to the notice of these influential connections. The Clutterbucks,
for example, came to Hardenhuish from Widcombe Manor, Bath,
and had been neighbours of Francis Kilvert of Claverton Lodge.

Although Hare kept in touch with his old schoolmaster long
after he had left school, the picture he paints of the Kilvert régime
is not a flattering one. The following passages are taken from his
autobiography, published by George Allen in 1896.·

My mother took me to Harnish Rectory on July 28th 1843.
The aspect of Mr Kilvert, his tall figure and red hair
encircling a high bald forehead was not reassuring, nor were
any temptations offered by my companions (who were
entirely of a rich middle class) or by the playground, which
was a little gravelled courtyard – the stable yard in fact – at
the back of the house. The Rectory itself was a small house,
pleasantly situated on a hill, near an odd little Wrenian
church which stood in a well-kept churchyard...

Mr Kilvert, as I have said, was deeply religious, but he
was very hot-tempered, and slashed our hands with a ruler
and our bodies with a cane most unmercifully for exceedingly

slight offences. So intense, so abject was our terror of him that we used to look forward as to an oasis the one afternoon he went on his parish duties, and Mrs Kilvert or her sister Miss Sarah Coleman attended to the school . . . The greater part of each day was spent in lessons, and oh what trash we were wearisomely taught; but from twelve to one we were taken out for a walk, when we employed the time in collecting all kinds of rubbish – bits of old tobacco pipe etc – to make museums . . . my mind dwells drearily on the long days of uninstructive lessons in the close hot classroom, or the monotonous confinement in the narrow court which was our usual playground, and my recollection shrinks from the reign of terror under which we lived.

Hare also comments, more obliquely, on what happened in the Rectory when the Headmaster was not present.

The first evening I was there, I was compelled to eat Eve's apple quite up – indeed the Tree of the Knowledge of Good and Evil was stripped absolutely bare; there was no fruit left to gather.'

And to this confession William Plomer just as obliquely added (in the introduction to Vol. 3 of Kilvert's Diary).

Although at that time Francis Kilvert was less than three years old, and although he himself looked back happily to his earliest years it seems possible that certain peculiarities of his character first germinated in the days when his father kept a school at Harnish.

Hare's is an uncomplimentary but probably distorted picture. The little school at Hardenhuish cannot have had a bad reputation. In addition to the two sons of Mr Martin, and the sons of Sir Walter Farquhar, there were two Bond brothers, sons of Lady Sophia Bond, and Winnington Lowder, son of a Mrs Lowder whose second husband was Sir Rutherford Alcock, and whose daughter

Amy married Sir Lewis Pelly. Nor did all the boys do badly in the
academic world. Walter Medlicott went to Wadham and his
brother to Christ Church. Nathaniel and Dennis Bond both went
to Oriel, Nathaniel subsequently marrying a daughter of the
second Earl of Eldon and becoming a canon of Sarum. Bengough
went to Oriel and became Rector of Hemingby in Lincolnshire.
Philip Scudamore Stanhope went to Magdalen and became
Rector of Humber in Herefordshire.*

Other less disagreeable aspects of life at Harnish are given in
the *Rambling Recollections* of the diarist's sister, Emily. (Kilvert
Soc. Publication. n.d.)

> The boys were a never-failing source of interest to us
> children... At first there was only room for eight or nine
> boys, but when Mr Clutterbuck of Harnish House enlarged
> the house by building a schoolroom out at the back and a
> room over it which became our nursery, this gave room for
> twelve boys and the tutor was taken into the house... Our
> music master was Mr Coombs who came from Chippenham,
> but the only boy I can remember having pianoforte lessons
> was Bengough... The French master we had was M.
> Lamousie who used to wipe his pen in his hair... Then there
> was Mr Alfred Keene, who used to gnaw his moustache, bite
> his lips, and then smile kindly at my feeble attempts at
> drawing a straight line... I must not forget Sergeant Reeves,
> the drill master, who used to come up on Saturdays and drill
> the boys in front of the house.
>
>   (Rambling Recollections. p. 92)

The six Kilvert children were all born at Hardenhuish –
Thermuthis (or Thersie) 1838: Robert Francis, the Diarist, 1840;
Emily, 1842: Frances, 1846; Sara Dorothea Anne (Dora) 1848;
Edward Newton (Ted or Perch) 1849. Kilvert refers mysterious-
ly to a fifth sister who seems to have died young (see Vol. 3. 443)

*Information from Professor Mark Doughty of Montreal.

and, more mysteriously, to the graves of two children who may
have been members of the family; but no trace of these is to be
found in the genealogy prepared by Brigadier Falkner, nor is there
any mention of them in the Hardenhuish parish registers.

Emily's memoir suggests that the Kilvert children were
educated with the other pupils her father engaged; but eventually
Robert Francis was sent to his uncle's school at Claverton Lodge.
Proof of this is to be found in a volume presented in 1851 by
seventeen of the Claverton Lodge pupils to their master. All
seventeen signed the book, and the eighth signature is that of
Francis Kilvert. Besides confirming the suspicion that Francis
was taught by his uncle (at least from the age of eleven) the
document is one more testimony of the high esteem in which the
Antiquary was held by all who knew him.

But before we follow Kilvert to Claverton Lodge, we must not
neglect the rare picture of the diarist as a boy, given by Emily in
her memoir.

A wonderful event in our childhood was Papa and Mama
taking us all up to London in 1851, the year of the Great
Exhibition... They took a house in Hans Place, Sloane
Street, and our servants went with us. I can see now the great
brass cage over the 'Kohinoor' and hear the policeman in
charge saying 'Move on, move on, please,' and can remember
Mary Strange (the servant) holding my hand and pointing up
to a gallery just above where Queen Victoria, Prince Albert
and some of the Royal children were standing, looking down
upon the crowds below. I remember Mama remarking
afterwards how very cross the Queen looked. Whilst we were
in London we were taken to see the Zoological Gardens,
Regents Park. The hippopotamus was a recent acquisition,
having been brought over to England in 1850. When he came
up dripping out of his tank, Frank naïvely inquired where his
bath-towel was, at which the people standing by tittered a
great deal.

Emily also provides us with a glimpse of Claverton Lodge, the
house where his uncle had his school and to which the young
Francis Kilvert was to go for the next phase in his education.

> In the winter we sometimes went to stay at Claverton Lodge
> on Bathwick Hill, Bath, where Papa's eldest brother, the Rev
> Francis Kilvert lived. How we loved and revered him, and in
> what awe we stood of our Aunt Sophia, his wife, who wore a
> black wig or front as it was then called. She was of French
> extraction, and was brought over from France in an open boat
> as a little child during the Reign of Terror.
>
> I used to think it (Claverton Lodge) such a grand house,
> and though it was so in a way, Mama used to dislike going
> there very much. Perhaps it was the horrid smell of gas,
> which, directly the hall door was opened, came out with a
> sickening puff to our nostrils from the great gas-stove which
> opened into the inner hall . . . Aunt Sophia always sat in what
> was called the bow or bay room, which had long glass
> windows opening on a lawn which sloped down to a field at
> the bottom of which Uncle Francis's cows grazed. A door in
> the recess of the wall opened into Uncle Francis's study,
> though a bookcase in front of the papered door prevented
> anyone from entering the bay-room from the study side. It
> was only used by my uncle when he wanted to speak to my
> Aunt, as it saved his leaving his study for this purpose.

Francis Kilvert the elder is described by the *Dictionary of
National Biography* (he is the only member of the family to be
found there) as an antiquary. History was clearly one of his main
interests. He published monographs on Ralph Allen and Prior
Park, and Robert Graves of Claverton, and wrote *The Memoirs of
the Life and Writings of Bishop Hurd* (whom he mentions as a
distant relative), a book which offended his cousin, Maria Kilvert
of Worcester and caused her to cut his family out of her will. But
both he and his wife seem to have been equally interested in

literature, and were among the earliest members of the Bath
Literary Club. Francis Kilvert read to its members many papers
on the literary associations of Bath, and his wife – Eleonora
Adelaide Sophia Leopoldina Kilvert (she loved to give her full
name) has recorded the pleasure the Literary Club gatherings gave
them in a poem to be found in the records of the Bath Reference
Library.

> They met around the Social Board,
> With Gracious mien and courteous word,
> And Learning, Wit and Science fair,
> Soon filled the every vacant chair,
> Each Viand and each Wine was placed
> With tempting shew and picquant taste,
> But Ah! what crowned the perfect Whole?
> The Feast of Reason and the Flow of Soul!

Francis was also a poet, and left behind him a series of essays and
verses which were edited by his friends the Rev W. L. Nichols
and Mr W. Long under the title of *Remains in Verse and Prose*.
Aunt Sophia also published in 1841 a book on *Home Discipline*
which was reissued twice later in the century before it went out of
print.

It seems then that the younger Francis Kilvert's most
formative years were passed in close association with his learned
and literary uncle, and this may be the explanation of his
remarkable familiarity with a wide range of English poets.
Kilvert's tastes in fiction are undistinguished. He enjoys a great
number of ephemeral novels but makes no mention of Jane
Austen, Dickens, Thackeray, the Brontës, George Eliot – or even
Fielding, Richardson or Smollett. Someone, however, had clearly
inspired him with a genuine passion for good poetry. The list of
poets whom he mentions and from whom he quotes is very
impressive. It includes William Barnes, Elizabeth Barrett Browning,
Robert Browning, John Clare, Robert Burns, Lord Byron,

Thomas Chatterton, John Milton, Bishop King, William Cowper,
S. T. Coleridge, Geoffrey Chaucer, George Crabbe, George
Herbert, James Hogg, William Shakespeare, Lord Tennyson,
William Wordsworth, Alexander Pope, John Keats and Oliver
Goldsmith; and to this list of native poets are to be added the
names of Lamartine, Virgil and Horace.

We know that Kilvert's father was a well-read man, and was
in the habit of reading aloud, especially from Shakespeare, to his
family. We know too that several of Kilvert's friends had literary
interests. He read the account of his visit to William Barnes, the
Dorset poet, to his college friend Anthony Mayhew. It was
'David' Laing, another Oxford friend, who introduced him to the
Jacobean poets, especially Bishop King. He had many conversations about William and Dorothy Wordsworth with Mrs Henry
Dew (who was the poet's niece), Elizabeth Hutchinson (another
niece to the poet), Mr George Stovin Venables (who had met
Wordsworth and discussed *The Prelude* with him), and others. At
Oxford, however, Kilvert does not seem to have been unduly
studious. He took a poor degree (worse than his father's) and he
makes no mention of any poetry he may have read or discussed
while he was there.

Who was it then that familiarised him with so many good
poets – living and dead? In all probability it was his sensitive and
literary uncle–tutor; and it was perhaps his influence that bred and
nourished in him that vein of poetry that gives to his best prose a
fluency, eloquence and literary grace that makes it more poetic
than his conventional and derivative verse.*

*W. Warde Fowler, who was a pupil at Claverton Lodge, and later became Rector of
Lincoln College, Oxford, writes appreciatively in his *Reminiscences* (privately
printed) of the austere but kindly Headmaster, and the liberal regime he allowed his
pupils to enjoy.
  'The two years (I spent at the school) were perhaps the happiest and most fruitful
of my life. It was an entirely new life of freedom that my brother and I lived there . . .
What I owe most to the school is the entire absence of pressure or cramming. It is
an astonishing fact that I cannot recollect ever doing a written examination all the
two years I was there. Perhaps we were what now would be called slack; my

brother and I played no games, went for no runs, shirked all the work we possibly could; and yet I cannot allow that we wasted our time altogether . . . But what did we do with our time?

In the first place we read all the books we could lay hands on in the house, and added to them many from the circulating libraries of the city; what they were I do not well remember, but they must have been well-written books, for we could both of us write good English in those same years . . . Then again we used to explore together the whole city of Bath, making the various churches the various points to aim at . . .

It must have been here that Kilvert first felt the stirrings of that curiosity that led him to wander, explore and record; and here too that his graceful and poetic style was first formed.

Chapter Three
Langley Burrell

In 1855 when Kilvert was fifteen and still at school in Bath, Robert Ashe, Squire and Rector and Patron of Langley Burrell, a few miles east of Hardenhuish, died, and was succeeded by his son, Robert Martyn Ashe. The new squire was, like his father, in Holy Orders, and although he could have assumed the living himself, being unable or unwilling to support the double role of Rector and Squire, he withdrew from clerical duties and devoted himself to the management of his estate.* Perhaps it would be more correct to say that he meant to withdraw from clerical duties, but he had been too long involved in the running of the parish to surrender them completely, and his tendency to interfere was a great embarrassment to his new incumbent.

Squire Ashe had married a Miss Letitia Daly, and by her he had three daughters, Lucy, Emily (generally known as Siddie) and Thermuthis (Thersie), but no male heir, his only son having died of convulsions in infancy; and since there was no likelihood of another male Ashe to take over the parish, he presented to the living Robert Kilvert, husband of his cousin, Thermuthis (née Coleman).

Robert Kilvert must have felt some reluctance at leaving Hardenhuish. He was on good terms with the patron of the living, Thomas Clutterbuck. Mr Clutterbuck, who had married a daughter of David Ricardo, the great economist (Ricardo was buried in Hardenhuish churchyard and an elaborate monument to

---

*A newspaper notice says ill-health compelled him to spend some time abroad.

him still stands there), is always mentioned in the Diary with
affection.

> All the cry (at Hardenhuish) seems to be
> for the old family, the beloved and honoured
> family, the Clutterbucks, to come back to
> their own again.
>
> (Vol. 3. 241)

Besides, the school which Robert Kilvert had set up in the Rectory
was apparently a success. There was no shortage of pupils, and the
school was so large that the Rector had to employ a number of
assistants; but, since the stipend of Langley Burrell was over £350
a year, compared with the niggardly £90–100 that Hardenhuish
was worth, he must have thought it worthwhile to sacrifice the
society of Mr Clutterbuck and the relatively lucrative school.

Some time, however, after appointing Robert Kilvert to the
parish, Mr Ashe demolished the old Rectory in which presumably
he had lived, and which stood near the church (and therefore near
Langley House into which he had moved on the death of his
father) and installed the new Rector in another house, a pleasant
mid-eighteenth century house, nearer to the village and about a
quarter of a mile away from the church. It is difficult to see why he
did this; but his was an autocratic and possessive nature, and it
may not have suited him to have a stranger, although that stranger
was his cousin's husband, on his doorstep. There is no reason to
interpret his action as a deliberate slight, but perhaps it was meant
to hint that relations between the Rectory and Langley House
were not to be too intimate. Robert Kilvert, until his fortunes
prospered with his long stay at Langley Burrell and the money he
inherited on the death of his cousin, Maria Kilvert of Worcester,
was very much a poor relation; and the disparity between him and
the Squire can be gauged by the entries in the 1871 Langley
Burrell census. There were no less than eight servants employed at
Langley House and one governess; Robert Kilvert, even after

several years at Langley Burrell employed only one, and no
governess.

But, as far as we know, the new Rector had no reason to be
dissatisfied with his accommodation. The Ashes had a reputation
for keeping their estate houses in good condition, and the new
Rectory was a pleasant house, stone-built, with the date 1739 cut
on the keystone over the door, elegantly proportioned and
surrounded by fine trees. The present owner has renamed it
Kilvert's Parsonage, keeps it in excellent condition, and has
refurnished it in dazzling taste.

Langley House, from the proximity of which Robert Kilvert
was banished, does not rank among the show houses of Wiltshire.
Professor Pevsner, who assigns to it the date *c.* 1771, finds it
'dignified but uneventful'; but the hall, staircase and principal
rooms are well-proportioned and not without grace. If privacy was
a desideratum for Squire Ashe, he certainly achieved it, for not a
single cottage or farmbuilding is visible from the house.

The church (St Peter) is accurately described by Professor
Pevsner as 'delightful, not neglected but also not over restored . . .
a picturesque church externally as well as internally'; and it is a
matter for regret that Kilvert, in the published parts of his diary,
leaves us virtually no detailed description of the church as he knew
it, except perhaps for these fine evocative passages:–

> I went to church early, soon after ten o'clock, across the
> quiet sunny meadows. There was scarcely anyone about –
> only one boy loitering by the stile in Becks by the road under
> the elms. The trees are in their most exquisite and perfect
> loveliness . . . I went into the churchyard under the feathering
> larch which sweeps over the gate. The ivy-grown old church
> with its noble tower stood beautiful and silent among the elms
> with its graves at its feet. Everything was still. No one was
> about or moving and the only sound was the singing of birds.
> The place was all in a charm of singing, full of peace and quiet
> sunshine. It seemed to be given up to the birds and their

morning hymns. It was the bird church, the church among the
birds . . . The hour for service drew on. The clerk coughed in
the church. Two girls in grey dresses passed quietly through
the church and moved about among the graves on the N. Side
bending over a grave beneath the elm. Then a woman in deep
mourning moved slowly down the path of the churchyard and
the clerk began to ring the bell for service . . .

(Vol. 1. 328–30)

I have rarely seen Langley Church and Churchyard look
more beautiful than they did this morning. The weather was
lovely and round the quiet church the trees were gorgeous, the
elms dazzling golden and the beeches burning crimson. The
golden elms illuminated the Church and Churchyard with
strong yellow light and the beeches flamed and glowed with
scarlet and crimson fire like the Burning Bush . . . Then the
latch of the wicket gate tinkled and pretty Karen Wood
appeared coming along the Church path and under the
spreading boughs of the wide larch, and in the glare of yellow
light the bell broke solemnly through the golden elms that
stood stately round the Church.

(Vol. 2. 284)

The rectory stands approximately half way between Langley
House and the village of Langley Burrell. The village itself is
straggling, and lacks unity and focus, but it contains several
interesting houses such as Langley Lodge where Kilvert's friends,
the Dallins lived, the Old Brewery House, the Home Farm, the
house where Keren or Karen Woods lived, and the village school
which the Ashes had built and was their property. Between the end
of the village and the charming little eighteenth century church of
Kellaways runs Brunel's Paddington–Bristol railway line, and at
an angle to the line lies what remains of that remarkable
thoroughfare built in the late fifteenth or early sixteenth century to
give villagers free and dry access across the Avon to the market at

Chippenham – Maud Heath's Causeway. Maud Heath herself surveys the scene from the top of her column on Bremhill Down. Nearby is the village of East Tytherton with its Moravian chapel and the school to which Kilvert's mother rode every day on her donkey. Among the other parishes that surround Langley Burrell are Kington Langley or Langley Fitzurse as it was sometimes called, where there can still be seen the two manor houses occupied at times by the Colemans, Kilvert's forbears on his mother's side, (one is now a Cheshire Home), and at the opposite end of the village the site of the Mausoleum which Mr and Mrs Tanner have identified. Almost opposite is the Ridge, where Ettie Meredith Brown's brother lived, and nearby a field gate restored by Mr and Mrs Tanner and equipped with a memorial plaque, overlooking the tract of wild land that still reaches down to Langley Burrell and is known as the Marsh or Birds Marsh. The rhododendrons planted there in the nineteenth century are almost smothered now by the wild trees that have grown up around them, but they are still to be seen, and, along the lanes and footways that thread the Marsh, the briar roses that Kilvert noticed.

A little farther afield are the parishes of Seagry with its woods, but now without its mill; Draycot where Kilvert went skating in 1870, now alas without its great house; Kington St Michael where the egregious Mrs Prodgers lived; and beyond them in one direction the ancient country town of Malmesbury, and another the vast estate of Lord Lansdowne, Bowood, and the parish of Chittoe, with the beautiful stone house in which Ettie Meredith Brown lived, Nonsuch. From the railway station at Chippenham there were frequent trains to Bristol, Bath and London.

This part of Wiltshire, the home of many of Kilvert's friends and fellow-clergymen – Mr Daniell, Vicar of Langley Fitzurse, Charles Awdry, Rector of Draycot St James, the other Charles Awdry, Vicar of Kington St Michael, Sir John Awdry of Notton House, the Dallins of Langley Lodge, and Ettie Meredith Brown's brother, is a peaceful pastoral land of great beauty. Kilvert loved it and it inspired some of his finest descriptive writing. But of his relations with the Ashes, the Awdrys and the Meredith Browns, it will be more appropriate to speak in a later chapter.

*Neither Langley House nor Kilvert's Parsonage is open to the public.

Chapter Four

Kilvert at Oxford

As far as we know Francis Kilvert was the fourth member of his family to go to Oxford. His uncle Francis was at Worcester, his uncle Edward, his father's younger brother, was at St Alban's Hall (which was later incorporated into Merton), and his father was at Oriel. Kilvert went up to Wadham on 29 June 1859, and was there till Michaelmas 1862.

He always speaks of Oxford with affection, and the diary records two return visits there. The first was to stay with Mr Charles Symonds, father of Mrs Dallin of Langley Lodge, Langley Burrell, who was a livery stables proprietor and lived in various houses in Holywell Street. In that section of the diary that deals with this visit Kilvert recalls Wadham as it was when he first saw it in 1859.

Thursday 21 May

Rose early, missed the New College Matins at 7.30 by being a minute too late. Walked round the gardens in the green light of the great lime cloister, and wandered round to Wadham gardens. All was as usual, the copper beech still spread a purple gloom in the corner, the three glorious limes swept their luxuriant foliage flat upon the sward, the great poplars towered like a steeple, the laburnum showered its golden rain by the quiet cloisters, and the Wisteria still hung its blue

flower clusters upon the garden wall. The fabric of the college
was unchanged, the grey chapel walls rose fair and peaceful
from the green turf . . .

(Vol. 3. 22–23)

When Kilvert paid his second return visit in 1876 he stayed
with his friend Anthony Lawson Mayhew, and while he is there he
mentions meeting 'David' Laing, who introduces him to some
Jacobean poets whom he has not read, notably Henry King,* the
seventeenth century divine who wrote the memorable *Exequy on
His Dead Wife;* Dr Griffiths the then Warden of Wadham; Mr
Thorley, one of the Fellows of the college; and a Mr Spurling
whom he had known as a junior scholar of Wadham and was now a
tutor at Keble. A scrutiny of the *Registers of Wadham College*
throws some light on these friends and acquaintances.

Anthony Lawson Mayhew, whose name appears frequently
in the diary, entered Wadham a year after Kilvert. Kilvert first
mentions him in Vol. 2, p. 136, when he describes him as one of
the owners of the *Times,* and living with his family near Rochester,
where he is in charge of a mission school chapel. Some time later
Mayhew comes to stay with him at Langley Burrell and it is when
he is there that Kilvert lets him read parts of his diaries (Vol. 3,
P. 213). He was not yet Chaplain of Wadham but he was soon to
be given that office (1880). Later he visited Kilvert at Bredwardine.
The new information which the Registers reveal about Mayhew is
that he, like so many of Kilvert's acquaintances, was also an
author. In addition to a *Glossary to The Book of Common Prayer,*
he compiled a *Dictionary of Middle English.* He was clearly
interested in philology; it was he to whom Kilvert sent his list of
Some Radnorshire Words which appeared in *Notes and Queries*
and subsequently in the *Hereford Journal.* Was it from Mayhew
the philologist that Kilvert got those fanciful names he used on
occasions for the names of the months – Wind Monat, Barn

*Kilvert writes incorrectly, Richard King.

Monat, Trimilki, etc? It was to him that Hopewell Morrell offered
the living of Moulsford, a perpetual curacy worth only £60 a year.
Mayhew did not accept it.

Kilvert also fell in with the only man in his college year who
finds his way into the diary.

Monday 22 May 1876

In Morton *(sic)* Meadows we overtook 'David' Laing, now
fellow of Corpus, and we came upon him again on board the
barge. David was in an odd excitable defiant mood and whilst
walking backwards like a 'peacock in his pride' and declaring
that he would rather be a drunkard than a teetotaller, because
there would be some pleasure and satisfaction out of drink
and drunkenness, he was very like to have got enough to drink
and to have put his paradox to the test for he suddenly
staggered as if he were really intoxicated, overbalanced
himself and nearly fell into the river. Then David suddenly
became hospitable and invited us to breakfast on Saturday,
but, shortening his notice of invitation like a telescope he
gradually brought us nearer to his view and heart, and at last it
was settled that we should breakfast with our old college
friend in his rooms in Corpus tomorrow.

(Vol. 3. 310)

Tuesday 23 May 1876

. . . Mayhew and I went this morning to Corpus to breakfast
with Laing. . . We had a merry laughing breakfast spiced with
many college stories and recollections of old days. David
read us some of his own poetry describing the solitude of a
mountain in the Highlands of Scotland, a pretty poem, and
treated us also to a selection from the Jacobean poets, and the
beautiful noble lines to his dead wife by Richard King, Bishop

of Chichester. These were quite new to me and they impressed me greatly.

(Vol. 3. 311)

All that is implied in Kilvert's portrait of Laing is borne out by what we now know about him. The following account of him comes from G. B. Grundy, *Fifty Five Years at Oxford.*

> Cuthbert Shields, who was a colleague during my earlier years at Corpus, was in a way a remarkable man, and also was a recognised character in Oxford. He was a mystic. His real name was Robert Laing, but he had abandoned that for one which signified that he regarded himself as under the protection of St Cuthbert of Durham. He had founded a society which he called the Society of the Grain of Mustard Seed, of which friends and acquaintances were liable to find themselves members. He was also a firm believer in the reincarnation of those who had lived in the past. Save for these fantasies he was sane during the years that I knew him. It is true that on one occasion he was reported to have shown signs of a coming breakdown, and Plummer (Grundy's colleague) warned us all that we must be careful how we talked to him . . . At the time of his previous breakdown many years before Shields had made a bonfire in his room which had fortunately been discovered by Plummer, who lived opposite to him, and extinguished before serious harm was done . . .
>
> *Fifty Years at Oxford.* p. 115–6

Kilvert speaks of Laing with his habitual tolerance, the kind of sympathetic understanding he later displays towards Father Ignatius and the Solitary of Llanbedr. His friend was clearly a very unstable person, but he was also gifted. He took a first class honours in Law and Modern History (Kilvert read the same and took a fourth), and wrote at least one book, *Some Dreams of a*

Constitution Monger, and so enrols himself among the long list of
authors whom Kilvert knew.

Dr John Griffiths, whom Kilvert describes as 'a kind and
courteous old gentleman' had succeeded Dr Symons as Warden of
Wadham in 1871. George Earlham Thorley, next to whom
Kilvert sat when he dined with the Fellows, was elected a Fellow
of Wadham in 1854 and eventually succeeded Dr Griffiths as
Warden in 1881. Frederick Spurling, whom Kilvert met when he
was out walking with Mayhew, he remembered as 'a very junior
scholar when I took my degree'. Spurling was also a very able
scholar. He took a first class in Classics Mods, and a first in Litt.
Hum. in 1866. He became a lecturer at Wadham in 1870 and a
tutor at Keble in 1875.

Thorley is the only Fellow Kilvert mentions, but it is possible
that he may have been influenced by Charles Douglas Ross who
was Dean of Wadham from 1855 to 1867. Ross was a man of
outstanding ability with a special gift for languages 'with which his
acquaintance, even to obscure dialects, was extraordinarily wide'.
It may have been Ross who stimulated Kilvert's interest in the
Welsh language, and the dialect of Radnorshire.

Kilvert says little about his years at Oxford, and there is little
in his diary (begun many years after he had gone down) to suggest
that he brought away any strong interest in sport (other than
pleasant memories of boat-races and an ability to join in the milder
social diversions of archery and croquet) or in the religious
controversies of his time. He appears to have left Oxford with no
strong vocational convictions or prejudices, except perhaps a
dislike of Oxford Movement ritual.

By the time he went up to Wadham the great stir made by the
movement had begun to die down, although it was still strong
enough to persuade G. M. Hopkins to become a Jesuit in 1868;
and the kind of ritual it advocated was still being practised.
Kilvert's attitude is clearly expressed in an account he wrote in his

diary of a service held at St Barnabas on 24 May 1876, which he
attended with his friend Mayhew.

The account is detailed and telling. St Barnabas is in its own
way quite an impressive church, but Kilvert seems to have been
too impatient with the ritual to take in its particular excellences.
He takes little pains to hide his mounting dislike of the ornate
vestments, the stifling incense and the pretentious attitudinising of
the priests in charge. It was a dislike shared by Mayhew, who said,
as they came out of the church, '*Well*, did you ever see such a
function as that?' Kilvert's answer was, 'No, I never did, and I
don't care if I never do again'.

Kilvert's father's stay at Oxford had been quiet and
uneventful. To the extract already quoted from his memoirs may
be added this passage.

> I may mention here that before I left home my eldest
> brother asked me one or two point blank questions. One was,
> "Can you swim?" and when I said "No", the order he gave
> me was, "Then never get into a boat till you have learnt to
> swim". The consequence was, since I did not learn to swim, I
> never entered a boat while I was at Oxford. Another thing he
> asked me was, "Can you afford wine parties? If not, don't
> give them". So in making my purchases of china, etc., I rather
> overacted his instructions, omitting to buy either decanters or
> glasses, and singular to say, I never drank a glass of wine
> there throughout my residence, nor any fermented liquor at
> all, only water. It certainly agreed with me; I was in excellent
> health all the time, and weighed heavier than at any other time
> in my life. At one period of my course it may have been that I
> carried this total abstinence too far, and a glass or two of wine
> might have done me good when I went up for my examination.

His son's years there probably followed the same pattern.
The likelihood is that he was too poor to live a very full social life.

Until Kilvert's father inherited a few thousand pounds from Maria
Kilvert, the Kilvert family were not especially well-to-do. In
addition, his studies (he read Law and Modern History, and
though he remained interested in History he reveals in his Diary
not the slightest interest in Law) may well have seemed humdrum
after his literary studies at Claverton Lodge under his enlightened
uncle. William Plomer says in his introduction to the first volume
of the Diary that he met Lewis Carroll at Oxford, but I have found
no evidence for such a meeting.* It is perhaps characteristic of
Kilvert that in addition to Mayhew, Laing, Spurling, Thorley and
Dr Griffiths the only other Oxford acquaintance he mentions by
name is George Hawks, who was his scout at Wadham, and who,
by a strange coincidence, had also been scout to his father at Oriel.

*Mr Le Quesne has pointed out to me that Carroll knew the Mayhews, but
quarrelled with them in 1879 when Mrs Mayhew refused him permission to
photograph her eleven year old daughter in the nude.

Chapter Five

Ordination

Kilvert graduated (with a disappointing fourth) in 1862. In the Wadham College registers he is enrolled B. A. on 4 December 1862 and M.A. on 21 June 1866. In 1863 he was made a deacon, and late in 1864 was ordained priest by Dr E. J. Ellicott in Bristol Cathedral.

We have it on the evidence of William Plomer, and Mr Venables, that after ordination he served as curate to his father at Langley Burrell, and that he remained there until going to Clyro early in 1865. Mr Venables records in his diary that he interviewed Kilvert at Clyro in November 1864 (Kilvert was there from November 8 to 11); and on 10 November he wrote to his brother George Stovin Venables

> I have got a young fellow here named Kilvert about the curacy and I believe it is settled. He seems to be a gentleman and I like what I have seen. He is quite young and will not be in Priest's Orders till Christmas. The Bishop of Gloucester and Bristol has agreed to his leaving his present curacy, which is his father's, after the ordination, and from the tone of the Bishop's letter which he sent me it is evident that he is respectable. However he has referred me to a Canon Shirley at Christchurch, and I have written to him as a matter of precaution. He is tall with a black beard and moustache. It will be a great satisfaction to have got this matter hopefully settled.

Later Mr Venables tells his brother that his new curate ('I am very glad to have a university man') arrived early in January. He had in the meanwhile had 'a most satisfactory character' from Canon Shirley. But there is one little puzzle about Kilvert's movements in the last few months of 1864 that remains to be cleared up.

There are three references in the Diary to a period in his life when he lived at Lanhill, near Kington St Michael.

> Wednesday 10 January 1872
> After dinner I went to see old Jacob Smith, who used to be head-carter at Sheldon when I was at Lanhill.
>
> (Vol. 2. 113)
>
> Thursday 24 September 1874
> Near the entrance to the village (of Kington St Michael) I fell in with a team of red oxen, harnessed, coming home from the plough, with chains rattling, and the old ploughman riding the fore-ox, reminding me vividly of the time when I used to ride the oxen home from plough at Lanhill.
>
> (Vol. 3. 87)

This almost implies that he is recalling his boyhood, for it is difficult to imagine a deacon of the Church of England riding plough oxen; but the third reference gives an exact date.

> Tuesday 23 February 1875
> At Kington St Michael the good Vicar was busy in the village amongst his flock, so till he should come home I asked for the keys of the church and spent some time in the Church examining all the old monuments and the new East window, and musing and praying among the graves of my forefathers. Am I better or worse, have I gone forward or backward, than I was when I lived here at Kington St Michael ten years ago?
>
> (Vol. 3. 152)

What was Kilvert doing in Kington St Michael in 1865? The parish registers of Langley Burrell, Kington St Michael and

possibly Clyro, suggest an answer. The last mention of Kilvert at
Langley Burrell is 2 October 1864, when he baptised two children.
In November of that year, however, he conducted a funeral and
two baptisms at Kington St Michael, whereas all the services at
Langley Burrell in late 1864 and early 1865 were taken by his
father. Then on 2 March 1865 we find the first Kilvert entry in the
Clyro registers.

We know that Edward Awdry, Vicar of Kington St Michael,
was a particular friend of Kilvert's. Mr Awdry remained his friend
long after he had left Wiltshire, and on one occasion visited him at
Bredwardine. We know too that he was liable to attacks of
lumbago. It may be that towards the end of 1864 (maybe up to the
end of the first week in January 1865) Mr Awdry was for some
reason or other unable to carry out his duties at Kington, and
Kilvert stood in for him, and he was there long enough for him to
take up temporary residence in the parish.

No one knows for certain why Kilvert elected to leave
Wiltshire for the comparatively remote and apparently obscure
parish of Clyro in Radnorshire, but the link between the two
parishes may have been the Clutterbuck family. It was Thomas
Clutterbuck who had been responsible for presenting Robert
Kilvert to the living of Hardenhuish. Another Mr Clutterbuck
lived at Boughrood, not far from Clyro. He was the uncle of Mr
Crichton of Wye Cliff, near Hay, who was, in turn, a friend of Mr
Venables, the Vicar of Clyro. There is just the possibility that
Crichton, hearing that Mr Venables was looking for a curate,
mentioned this to his uncle in Boughrood, who in turn passed it on
to his relatives at Hardenhuish. Why Mr Venables was referred by
his prospective curate to Canon Shirley of Christ Church rather
than to Wadham is another mystery; but as we have seen Canon
Shirley recommended Kilvert, who moved to Clyro early in 1865,
in time for an exceptionally cold winter. He went into lodgings
with a Mrs Chaloner, a widow, at Ashbrook, and stayed there for
the whole of his time in Clyro. The second Mrs Venables, in a

letter to her husband complained that Kilvert was being
overcharged.

> The more I think of it considering that Kilvert has neither
> plate nor linen provided by Mrs C. and that his sheets and
> towels are charged to him, the more I am convinced that his
> 12/- is very dear, and that 2 guineas is more than enough for
> neither plate, linen or attendance, these are always the
> regular find in lodgings.
>
> (undated letter)

Whatever the exact nature of Mrs V's complaint (her letter is a
little incoherent), and however much he disliked Mrs Chaloner's
servant and her carpet, Kilvert was prepared to put up with his
accommodation. At some day in the first fortnight of January
1865 he began his parochial duties at Clyro.

Chapter Six

Clyro

The Land and the People

Clyro, a smallish village of rather more inhabitants than it had in Kilvert's day (the 1871 Census gives the total parish population as 842), and the centre of a scattered parish, stands on the north side of the River Wye, about a mile and a half from Hay-on-Wye. It is just on the Welsh side of the border which runs, as it ran in the 1870's, between the picturesque English-looking inn of Rhydspence, and the more severe dark stone house which in Kilvert's day was the Welsh inn. The parish has two outliers, the hamlet of Bronydd, (spelt Bronith by Kilvert) to the east, and the hamlet of Bettws to the north. The village houses are mainly grouped around the church, but of late a new housing estate has sprung up on the west side of the Painscastle road. Many buildings have survived from the 1870's – the church itself, slightly altered since Kilvert knew it, the Baskerville Arms (known to him as The Swan), Ashbrook House (his lodgings), the vicarage, and many of the old cottages. The surrounding countryside has changed even less. Cae Mawr, the home of Kilvert's friend, Hopewell Morrell, and Clyro Court, the residence of the Baskervilles, have both undergone severe internal alterations, but their external appearance has changed little; and most of the farms that are scattered over the parish are much as they were when Kilvert described them more than a century ago.

Behind Clyro, to the north and the west rise the first ranges of the great Radnor Forest, crossed by steep roads leading to Painscastle and Rhosgoch. From the top of these roads there is access to thrilling upland country, traversed by paths that lead northeast to the Little Mountain and Newchurch, or westward to the Begwns, crowned with the Roundabout, and on towards Bychllyn Pool and the Rocks of Aberedw. These are the mountain paths that Kilvert especially loved, the Wordsworthian heights that uplifted and refreshed him.

About a mile and a half from Clyro, to the south, is the little border township of Hay-on-Wye, known to Kilvert simply as Hay. It is smaller now than it was in his day (1200 as opposed to 2000 inhabitants), but little changed in appearance, except that the railway that once skirted the river has been taken up. The castle, which Kilvert knew so well, still dominates the town. Part of it had been converted into a residence in Jacobean times, and this part, which has unfortunately been damaged recently by fires, was the home of the Vicar of Hay, the Rev W. L. Bevan, and the gift of his wealthy uncle, Sir Joseph Bailey, ironmaster, of Glanusk.

Just as Clyro is cut off from the north by Radnor Forest, so Hay is cut off from the south by the great Black Mountains, now crossed by a narrow road, with passing places, which runs from near Cusop over the Gospel Pass down to Capel-y-Ffin and Llanthony to Abergavenny; but in the 1870's only rough tracks crossed from Hay to the head of the Honddu, where Father Ignatius, that eccentric visionary, was trying to set up his new monastic establishment.

But, if movement north and south from Clyro and Hay was difficult, movement east and west was easier than it had ever been, thanks to the new railway from Hereford to Brecon, and the two junctions of Three Cocks and Llechryd, which between them gave access to the rest of Wales. To the east lay the parishes of

Winforton, Whitney and Kinnersley, and deeper into Hereford-
shire, Moccas and Bredwardine; to the north, Glascwm,
Newchurch and Gladestry; to the west Llowes, Glasbury and
Boughrood. Near Glasbury stood the massive new castle of
Maesllwch, the home of the De Wintons, largely built in the early
nineteenth century; Lady Jocelyn Percy lived in a large house,
now demolished, at Llanstephan; farther up the valley stood
Llysdinam, the home of the Venables; and near Clifford, east of
Hay, was Clifford Priory, a large Victorian mansion that was not a
priory in any sense and was owned by Mr Haigh Allen. Clifford
Priory, like Llanstephan and Llanthomas, the home of Daisy
Thomas's father, the Vicar of Llanigon, has vanished since the
1870's.

The whole area is one of outstanding beauty. From Rhayader
to Hay the Wye is at its most enchanting – 'the sylvan Wye, the
wanderer through the woods', that Wordsworth loved. It must
have been even more beautiful in the 1870's, for, as Laurence Le
Quesne points out in his perceptive book, *After Kilvert*, 'Kilvert
had extraordinary luck. What he was given to describe was a
wholly rural England which had been gardened to the pitch of
visual perfection at the very moment before the wave of modern
industrialism crashed down over it and left it strewn with bricks,
cars, overhead wires, concrete blocks and old prams'.

The journey up-river by the little railway that followed the
Wye for so much of the way must have been one of the most
picturesque in the country, and Kilvert has left several accounts of
the impression it made upon him; and for those for whom the river
landscape is too tame, there are the vast uninhabited heights of the
Black Mountains and Radnor Forest, and the secret romantic
appeal of such places as Craig-pwll-du (or Grappledee as it is
known in the hybrid border tongue). This, more than any other
place, typifies for me the elusive fascination of this land.
Grappledee is not easy to find, and all who go in search of it ought
to be warned that the descent to the waterfall down the steep

slopes of the gorge of the Bach Howey can be dangerous; but when you find it you come upon a spectacular fall, discoverable only, as the best secrets are, to those who are prepared to take a risk. Kilvert found it twice, and a vivid account of his first visit is to be found in the description that Essex Smith incorporated into her *Radnorshire Legends and Superstitions* (reprinted in the Kilvert Society's *Miscellany Two*).

Kilvert's decision to leave Langley Burrell for Clyro, picturesque though his new parish was, must have appeared to his family and friends almost like an act of self-imposed exile. But he never looked upon his years in Radnorshire as years of banishment. On the contrary they were the most exciting years of his life, a time of extraordinary happiness and fulfilment. In the hills and valleys of this Welsh borderland he found himself in a landscape with which he was in immediate and deep sympathy, and which he was never tired of extolling. It was land which, in an unexpected way, answered the deepest needs of his nature. Remote, romantic, secret and undisturbed by most of the changes that were transforming and defacing Britain, Radnorshire was to Kilvert what Lakeland had been to Wordsworth and what the Aran Islands were to be to Synge.

In the first place it was, as it remains today, a border region par excellence. East of Clyro the land falls away abruptly. As one moves into Herefordshire the hills dwindle and diminish and give way to a rich pastoral landscape of lush pastures, picturesque villages, herds of placid fat cattle, cider orchards and half-timbered farmsteads. Even the weather seems to alter. Clouds lift and skies clear.

But west of Clyro lies another landscape, the Welsh landscape of massive hills, sombre brown mountains, small fields, hidden waterfalls, impoverished hill-farms with herds of lean and hardy cattle and flocks of small-boned sheep; and the sounds that fill the air are the rushing of fast-flowing brooks, the calling of curlews, plovers and ravens, the bleating of ewes and lambs. Here the landmarks have mostly retained their difficult Welsh names, and Whitney and Clifford and Peterchurch have given way to Aberedw, Builth, Glascwm, Bryngwyn and Llanbedr; and the way of life is not that of lowland farmers with centuries of prosperity behind them, but of mountain people who have known oppression and poverty, clinging to their ancient racial pride, their un-mercenary way of living, their stubborn unfashionable eccen-tricities. Here England and Wales met, in a colourful fusion of culture, language and behaviour that fascinated Kilvert.

In many ways his new parishioners were stubborn and backward. With humour and self-deprecation he often records his failure to make plain to them even the most elementary lessons of his religion. His inveterate truthfulness impels him also to record, even in his most idyllic mood, the elements of violence and vindictiveness that lie close to the surface, the acts of gratuitous savagery, of cruelty towards the young, the unfortunate, the deranged; but his general attitude to his parishioners is not one of censure but of admiration and affection. In an interesting passage to be found, not in his diary, but in a collection of observations he made when he was thinking of writing a book about Radnorshire, used by Essex Smith in her *Radnorshire Legends and Super-stitions* article, he wrote

> The people of Clyro are still sufficiently Welsh to be suspicious of strangers, and an Englishman would probably not be thoroughly liked and trusted till he had lived for some years in the country. But there is not in Radnorshire the same hostility and bitterness of feeling that is still shown towards the Saxon in many parts of Wales. In fact the people, as a whole, are singularly civil, courteous and obliging, and this pleasant characteristic is not merely superficial, for to those who are kind to them they are demonstrative and really affectionate.

One of the most remarkable features of Clyro, (and, as far as one can see, of the neighbouring parishes) was the absence of social friction. That is not to say that it was a totally homogeneous society, for the divisions, in terms of wealth, leisure, influence and privilege, were real enough. The poor were often badly fed, badly housed and badly clothed. Parents were often cruel, children died young, premarital pregnancy was a real social stigma and drove many young women to desperate actions. But the rich were not overbearing and oppressive, and the poor were remarkably free from rancour and envy. Even the religion that they all embraced, although only partially understood, seemed a sweeter faith than the harsh oppressive code that brought so much unhappiness to young Edmund Gosse, Jane Eyre and Ernest Pontifex. The gloom and darkness of Victorian puritanism are largely unknown. Sadistic clergymen such as Mr Brocklehurst in *Jane Eyre*, canting dissenters such a Mr Bulstrode in *Middlemarch*, hypocrites such as the Pecksniffs and Chadbands, and predators such as the Squeers and Murdstones, do not find a place in Kilvert's pages. Religious dissension is no serious threat to the Church. There is no insistence on the urgent necessity for moral regeneration, no hell-fire sermons or threats of horrific penalties awaiting the sinner and the backslider; and no militant proletariat has yet begun to question the rightness of the social order. It was not, to our way of thinking, in any sense a just society, nor was it wholly that Eden which Kilvert, in his more euphoric moments, conceived it to be. Even he tells stories of cupidity, greed, violence, selfishness and criminality; but more often than not he was aware of the privilege of living in a remarkably stable and contented community, one in which, as he wrote in his Diary, it was 'a positive luxury to be alive'. 'Lady Joscelyn Percy', he adds, 'says that in this neighbourhood she never hears people speaking unkindly of each other'. When he had to leave Clyro and suffer under the petty tyrannies of Squire Ashe at Langley Burrell, he realised more than ever the extraordinary social harmony that the people of Clyro enjoyed.

The Religious Renaissance

Kilvert arrived in Clyro at an auspicious time. The industrialisation of South Wales was going ahead fast, and the growth of a new industrial proletariat meant a growing demand for the kind of food that counties such as Radnorshire were well fitted to provide. Radnorshire had had for many centuries the reputation for being a poor county. An old rhyme went

Radnorsheer, poor Radnorsheer,
Never a park and never a deer,
Never a squire of 500 a year
But Richard Fowler of Abbey Cwm Hir.

But although the county had nothing to compare with the Earl of Lansdowne's vast estate at Bowood near Langley Burrell, the De Wintons had built Maesllwch; and even Mr Venables had far more than his five hundred a year. It was true that the poor of Clyro were still badly paid and badly housed and badly cared for, but they must have shared in some measure in the mid-century prosperity. If the lowest in the social scale – the agricultural labourers – had their miseries, the small farmers were relatively affluent. Kilvert records no Luddite activity (even the Rebecca rioters seem to have been halted at the border) and class resentment seems to have been unknown.

More importantly for Kilvert, the mid nineteenth century was a time of revival and progress for the Anglican church. For many years St David's had been a neglected and impoverished diocese. This is how E. Jones (*The Methodist Revival. Wales Through the Ages.* Vol. 2) summarises *Erasmus Saunders's View of the Diocese of St David's in 1721.*

Church buildings were in a ruinous state, some churches had become the habitations of owls and jackdaws, one had even been rented to dissenters, others were only half-served, prayers being only partly said, and the means of preaching, catechising and communion rarely exercised. Many of the incumbents were reduced to the lowest degree of poverty and meanness. Curates' stipends were so low that they had to serve three or four churches to secure a living of ten or twelve pounds a year. These churches were many miles distant so that the Sunday round was a kind of perpetual motion for the curate, hurrying from place to place like a hasty itinerant with little opportunity for refreshment or rest. The times of services depended largely upon his ability to manage his rounds. The clergy, many of them in circumstances worse than beggary, had neither the means for their work to be accomplished, nor the leisure to attend to it. They could hardly be expected to acquire the learning that was necessary to make them efficient guides for their flocks. They were too poor to afford hospitality to their neighbours or to strangers. Hardly able to get essential articles of clothing, they could not possibly keep themselves conformable to the canons of the church in dress and habits . . . The economic situation was not the only cause of decay. Erasmus Saunders devotes a chapter to the injuries done to the church by the inability of the Bishops to use the Welsh language, by non-residence, pluralism and the ordination of inferior candidates. Griffiths Jones of Llandowror went even further, accusing the clergy of immorality, drunkenness, neglect of domestic worship, and common swearing.

Erasmus Saunders's *View* has, in the opinion of some scholars, been too readily used to condemn the eighteenth century Church, especially by Methodist historians such as E. Jones; and visitation returns, in the opinion of the Rev D. T. W. Price of Lampeter, show that the picture was not quite as black as Jones maintains; but, although parochial neglect was not unknown in other parts of the country (Kilvert quotes many instances in the later Wiltshire sections of his diary), one is reminded of the Vicar of Painscastle who had preceded Mr Price, the drunken and quarrelsome Parson Button; of the good-natured but feckless Mr

Thomas of Disserth; of Kilvert's mention of the ruined church at
Llanbedr, and the old church at Boughrood when Mr Crichton
lived there with his uncle –

> 'A most miserable place. The choir sat upon the altar and
> played a drum.'

– his dismay at seeing the wretched condition of St Harmon's
church –

> 'My heart sank within me like a stone when I entered. A bare
> cold squalid interior and high ugly square boxes for seats, a
> three-decker pulpit and desk, no stove, a flimsy altar rail, a
> ragged faded altar cloth, a singing gallery with a broken
> organ, a dark little box for a vestry, and a roof in bad repair,
> admitting the rain.'

(Vol. 3. 289)

his vivid description of the ruinous state of Llanlionfel church

> The ruined church tottered lone upon a hill in desolate
> silence. The old tombstones stood knee-deep in the coarse
> long grass and white and purple flowers nodded over the
> graves... The window and frames and seats were gone.
> Nothing was left but the high painted deal pulpit bearing the
> sacred monogram in yellow letters... the place was utterly
> deserted... It was a place for owls to dwell in and satyrs to
> dance in...

(Vol. 2. 362–33)

and of the account of the visit he made with Mr Venables to look at
the church and vicarage of Bryngwyn

> 2 April 1869.
> Walked with Kilvert to Bryngwyn to certify that the Rectory
> is unfit for residence. Church in a disgraceful state. Nothing
> done in the last 4 years – not even Chancel window glazed.
> (Venables Diaries. K. S. Miscellany Two. p. 54)

But, first under Bishop Burgess and then Bishop Thirlwall, (the first bishop of St David's for centuries to be able to preach and conduct confirmations in Welsh) a vast programme of restoration and rebuilding was inaugurated in the diocese.

In many cases the restorations were clumsy and tasteless, but they must have seemed an enormous improvement on the dilapidated structures they replaced; and it is a sign of the genuineness of the renaissance of religious faith that a great deal of the money for the rebuilding or restoration or even the building of new churches came from the pockets of private individuals. According to the *History of Brecknock*, Mr Venables and his brother spent over £5000 on their new church at Newbridge-on-Wye, the De Wintons built All Saints, Glasbury in memory of Walter De Winton, whose illness and death in 1882 Kilvert mentions; and the remarkable Miss Thomas built no less than five new churches, including Abergwesyn, Eglwys Oen Duw, Cwmbach Llechryd and Llanlionfel.

The Bishop of St David's (and the Bishop of the neighbouring diocese of Hereford) were fortunate to be able to find that the men necessary for the furtherance of the religious revival they were inaugurating were available; and it is to the greatest credit of the Venables, Bevans, Marsdens, Vaughans, Dews and Stanhopes* and Webbs that they gave such faithful support to their bishop's lead.

The achievement of the Church of England in the latter half of the nineteenth century, not only in Wales, is summed up in the opening paragraphs of a book paradoxically entitled, for our purpose, *The Victorian Church in Decline* (P. T. Marsh. Kegan Paul 1969).

In the first half of Queen Victoria's reign, until Gladstone's electoral victory of 1868, the Church of England enjoyed its

*The Hon and Rev Berkeley Lionel Scudamore Stanhope had been a Fellow of All Souls before coming to Byford; and the 'lackadaisical' Mr Welby a Fellow of Magdalen.

last comparatively secure period of national strength. On the negative side, the Church's enemies, though newly invigorated, were held in check. Protestant nonconformists who were aware that their following was approaching the size of that of the established church, and were therefore determined to end religious discrimination by the State, found themselves, to their disappointment, pushed back into the political wilderness. Roman Catholicism, awakened out of a century of sleep by the conversion of Newman and Manning, was disappointed that the subsequent flow of defections from the Church of England never amounted to more than a trickle. Free thought muffled its voice for fear of undermining popular morality.

Positively the established Church displayed almost prodigious energy . . . (It) proved most unexpectedly that it was capable of thorough administrative reform. By spreading elementary schools over the country, the Church sought to reassert its social and intellectual grip on the country. Throughout the middle years of the nineteenth century, to an extent unprecedented at least since the thirteenth, members of the Church, alive to its failures and inadequacies, dug into their pockets, gave of their time, and devised fresh methods to make its institutions effective . . .

'For centuries' (wrote Gladstone to the Queen on 22 January 1874) 'there has not been a time of so much practical and hearty work, so much earnest preaching, so much instruction and consolation given, so much affectionate care for the poor and young'.

Gladstone might have been writing with Radnorshire in mind. In spite of long years of spiritual neglect, the people of Mid-Wales seem to have preserved a sincere hunger for the kind of religion that the Anglican Church was now ready to provide. Kilvert on occasions speaks disparagingly of Dissenters (and on one or two occasions with uncharacteristic insensitivity) but he never seems to have looked upon them as a serious threat to his ministry. Like most of his fellow-clergymen he is assured that the work he is doing is just and worthwhile; and the conviction that he is fulfilling a real need gives him a sense of confidence, the awareness of being part of a worthwhile movement, of belonging to a church that has found itself again, and rededicated itself to the true christian principles of tolerance, fellow-feeling and charity, and in so doing has recovered poise and buoyancy. Unfortunately we do not possess any of Kilvert's sermons, but on many occasions in the Diary he mentions the texts from which he preached, and a study of these texts is very revealing. Some of the sermons preached by his uncle, Francis Kilvert of Claverton Lodge, are available;* and a comparison between his themes and those chosen by his nephew shows the difference not only between the two men, but two ages. Francis Kilvert the elder is frequently didactic, censorious and puritanical. He does not scruple to remind his flock over and over again of their spiritual backslidings, of their failure to show proper reverence towards their pastors and betters, and of the dreadful punishments that await those who fail to observe the ordinances of the Lord's anointed. Judging from the texts which Francis Kilvert the younger chose, and from the slight indications we have of the content of his sermons, such a censorious de-haut-en-bas approach was alien to him. One has constantly the feeling that, far from setting out to convince his parishioners of their sins and to remind them of the punishments that could be visited upon them for their shortcomings, he preferred to speak of love and kindness and charity, and of his concern for their welfare.

In Wiltshire this confidence is a little impaired by his relations with Mr Ashe, and, from time to time, by the misdemeanours of his parishioners. An uncharacteristic note of doubt and misgiving about his role in society creeps into his voice,

*Sermons. Francis Kilvert. John Taylor. London, no date.

but it disappears as soon as he returns to his beloved Welsh Border country. There is little doubt that one of the factors that made for his happiness in Clyro, and gives a note of bouyancy and exhilaration to his Diary, was the assurance that he was part of a great and successful movement that was fulfilling God's purpose in a way that was wholly satisfying and rewarding.

The Wordsworthian Dream

Above all, Radnorshire was a land where Kilvert could act out his Wordsworthian dream, although to describe his experiences there as 'acting out' is to impute to them an element of artifice and pretence which they never possessed. Mr R. I. Morgan, in his interesting monograph *Kilvert and the Wordsworth Circle* (Kilvert Society. n.d.) has shown the many links between Kilvert and the Kilvert Country and the Poet Laureate. Wordsworth was not only Kilvert's favourite poet; he was one of his spiritual mentors, and one to whom, in Clyro, through the medium of Mrs Dew, Wordsworth's niece, and George Stovin Venables, his friend, he felt physically close. Wordsworth had known and admired this part of Britain, and Kilvert often felt that he was not only walking in the footsteps of his great teacher, but, on occasions, almost listening to his voice.

There is no doubt that Kilvert in many ways modelled himself upon the Lakeland poet. He made pilgrimages to scenes that Wordsworth had visited – Brinsop Court, Tintern Abbey, the field in which the poet had paused to admire the view of the Shropshire Hills, and the stone near Old Leycesters Church on which his friend Mr Miller had carved his initials and those of his wife and the date of their visit, the Gospel Pass which Wordsworth and his sister crossed on their walk from Llyswen to Llanthony. Although he could not have known Dorothy's *Grasmere Journal*, which was not published till after his death, the resemblances between his diary and hers are remarkable.

Kilvert's faith in the orthodox religion he had imbibed from his forbears and tutors was sincere, but one might say that his Wordsworthian trust in the uplifting and edifying power of Nature and his admiration for the dignity and wisdom of the untaught peasant was even stronger. He responded to the scenery of Wales as Wordsworth had responded to the scenery of Lakeland; and his feelings towards the affectionate and imaginative peasantry of Clyro were akin to the admiration that Wordsworth had felt for his Cumbrian shepherds and farmers. He had the same good fortune as had fallen to his great predecessor – the luck to find himself in a land that fulfilled the deepest needs of his poetic nature, and woke his latent creative spirit.

Chapter Seven

The First Years at Clyro

According to William Plomer, one of the few privileged to see the whole of Kilvert's Diary in manuscript, the journal was begun on New Year's Day 1870, although the first published entry is for January 18 of that year. It begins abruptly. It looks as if there were no prefatory remarks such as those made by Fanny Burney ('to have some account of my thoughts, manners, acquaintances and actions, when the hour arrives in which time is more nimble than memory'), or by Dorothy Wordsworth who said she was keeping her Grasmere Journal to fill up the time till her dear brother returned, and to make for him a record of happenings at Grasmere while he was away. It seems inconceivable that, if Kilvert did declare his motives for keeping so detailed a diary, Plomer should have omitted them, especially since he took care to include in a later volume this passage –

> Why do I keep this voluminous journal? ... Partly because life seems to me such a curious and wonderful thing that it seems almost a pity that even such a humble and uneventful life as mine should pass away altogether without some such record as this, and partly too because I think the record may amuse and interest those who come after me.
>
> (Vol. 3. 107)

In January 1870 Kilvert plunges *in medias res*, and right from the beginning shows an astonishing mastery of his medium.

The assurance of the opening entries, coupled with the fact that by 1870 Kilvert had already been in Clyro for five years, and must have had many experiences similar to those which, after 1870, he felt impelled to record in detail, has led some readers to suspect that the diary must have been begun before that date, and that earlier entries have been lost or suppressed.

However there is no evidence to support that view. In fact the evidence that does exist implies the opposite. Of the two surviving notebooks, that given by Mrs Essex Hope to Jeremy Sandford and recently bought by the National Library of Wales, the volume that covers the period 27 April to 9 June 1870, is clearly marked in Kilvert's own hand *Notebook No. 2*; and the Plomer notebook, now in the University Library, Durham, which covers his holiday in Cornwall with his friends the Hockins, and begins 19 July 1870, is also labelled in Kilvert's hand *Notebook No. 4*. Presumably Notebook No. 3 ran from 9 June to 19 July. If, as Plomer said, the first entry was made on 1 January 1870, Kilvert filled his first notebook in just under four months, took less than two months over the second, about the same period over the third and filled the fourth in a month. This, the Cornwall notebook, is probably exceptional. To begin with it is not completely full (there are a few blank pages at the back), and the daily entries are presumably longer than usual, because he is in a part of the world that is new to him, and each day brings fresh experiences. One can only explain the unusual length of time taken over the first notebook by the fact that either he started slowly and took some time to get into his stride, or that the first notebook he used was bigger than those he used later. Plomer did say that the notebooks submitted to him were 'variously shaped and bound'. It seems reasonable to assume that Notebook No. 1 was started early in January 1870, perhaps as the result of a New Year Resolution, although there is no doubt that before that Kilvert did keep written records of a kind, and the accounts that Mrs Essex Hope drew upon in her article on *Radnorshire Legends and Superstitions* (reprinted by K. S. in *Miscellany Two*. 1978), of his visit to Craig Pwll Du and the Mari Llwyd ceremony he witnessed in Clyro look like extracts from some kind of diary. Perhaps it was only in 1870 that he began to keep a systematic journal.

Why did Kilvert wait until 1870 before beginning his diary, especially since, having started it, he continued it so consistently and patiently for so many years? It is difficult to find a convincing explanation. It is just possible that after Mr Venables's second marriage, to Agnes Minna Pearson, he may have found himself with more time on his hands. When Mr Venables was a widower he and his curate spent a great deal of time in each other's company. Now that there was once more a Mrs Venables in the vicarage, although clearly he was very welcome there and on good terms with the new Mrs Venables, he may have found that he had lost a confidante, and all those hopes and fears and impressions he had once shared with his vicar he now began to put down on paper. His diary became his new confidante.

What happened to him between his first coming to Clyro and beginning his journal? It is difficult to build up anything approaching a complete picture, but one may assume that he was quickly taken into Mr Venables's confidence. During the years before the vicar married again Kilvert dined with him approximately once a week; and after the marriage which took place in August 1867 (Kilvert was in Clyro in September to welcome them home) he seems to have been just as frequent a guest at the vicarage. He seems too to have been quickly accepted into what one might call the Hay Circle. By 1870 he was on friendly terms with the Bevans, Crichtons, Dews, Morrells, Thomases and Haigh Allens. He spent a great deal of time with Hopewell Morrell of Cae Mawr, and went with him on one occasion to Craig Pwll Du (he made a second visit to it in the company of an old mole-catcher. See *Miscellany Two*. K.S.). In 1869 he went on a picnic

to Wen Allt with some members – including Daisy – of the
Thomas family

> 5 April 1872 (the day of the ball at Clifford Priory) (Daisy)
> was telling me that her brother John had come home, and that
> she had been for a walk with him down to the Wye this
> afternoon. Yesterday their whole party and some of the Dews
> accompanied by Sailor (the dog) to make a fourteenth made
> an expedition to the top of the Wen Allt. Daisy was quite
> enthusiastic about the dear old Wen Allt. 'I should never get
> tired of it', she said heartily. And I have one happy sunny
> memory at least connected with it and her, the picnic in
> August 1869 when I first began to know her and love her.
>
> (Vol. 2. 173)

He must have forgotten the entry he made earlier in
September 1871

> Today I fell in love with Fanny Thomas.
>
> (Vol. 2. 29)

Another red-letter day was 29 May 1865, to which in his
diary he returns twice. In Vol. 3. 162, he speaks of a journey he
made on foot to Aberedw 'on that lovely 29 May 1865' when he first
saw 'Sarah Bryan, then a little girl with dark hair and clear wild
eyes helping the tall grey-moustached man her father to cut turves
on the hill to roof his little keeper's hut in the woods'; and a few
pages later he writes

> I had not been to Builth since that memorable day to me, May
> 29th 1865, when I walked alone over the hills from Clyro to
> Builth and first saw the Rocks of Aberedw, the day I first saw
> Painscastle and the ruined church of Llanbedr, and
> descended from the great moor upon the vale of Edw and saw,
> in the orchard of the newly yellow thatched cottage near the
> Court Mills, the beautiful chestnut-haired girls at play with
> the children under the apple boughs. Then every step was

through an enchanted land... Oh Aberedw, Aberedw. I
never pass thy enchanted gorge without seeming for a
moment to be looking in at the gates of Paradise just left ajar.
But there stands the angel with the flaming sword and I may
not enter and only look in as I pass by the Gate.

(Vol. 3. 168)

On more than one count this is an intriguing entry (how for
instance is it that he remembers the date so precisely?); but we
shall probably never know exactly what happened to him at
Aberedw to revive in him, so many years later, such vivid mingled
feelings of guilt, and remembered ecstasy.

For the rest of his life during these years we can only use odd
notes in his own diary, a few entries in Mr Venables's journal, and
some newspaper reports. We know that by 1865 he had begun to
write poetry (one poem is dated 1865) and many others were in all
probability completed before 1870. Retrospective remarks in the
Diary reveal that in his first year he visited the Lloyds at
Vernywawr, called on Mrs Thomas and found her son, whom he
reproved himself for neglecting, already dead; visited the
Zoological Gardens at Clifton and cut from a sleeping lion a lock
of hair which he subsequently exhibited with great éclat to the
children of Clyro; attended the funeral of Mr Venables's first wife
in October, and later went skating at Draycot. In 1866 he took his
first walk to Capel-y-Ffin, attended a Choral Society Concert in
Hay, and went twice on holiday to Langley Burrell (from then on he
generally took a summer break and a Christmas break at home).
On August 1 1867 he attended the wedding of Mr Venables and
his second wife Agnes Minna and went on frequent excursions
with the Venables family, in spite of the heavy snow in March of
that year; was given a despatch box by his Vicar, and took his
customary breaks at Langley Burrell. In 1868 he attended with Mr
Venables the Archdeacon's Visitation at Brecon; went twice with
Walter Baskerville to the Assizes at Presteign; discussed with his
Vicar his plan to write a book about Radnorshire, and attended the

funeral of Mrs Sophia Venables, the Vicar's mother. (Kilvert had befriended her and she speaks in a letter of his kindness in helping her to get to church – she found difficulty in getting up steps.) In the following year, 1869 he preached at the funeral of old Mrs Webb at Hardwick; called in May on the Dewings just after their marriage; visited and inspected Bryngwyn Church and Vicarage with the Vicar of Clyro; and then in June, instead of going to Langley Burrell spent six weeks in Switzerland, Germany and France. In August came the picnic to Wen Allt which has already been mentioned. Earlier in the year he had been to Kinnersley Church with Mr Venables and Haigh Allen; in October he preached the Harvest Festival Sermon at Llwynmadoc.

Perhaps the most exciting of all these events was the continental holiday. There are many references to it in the Diary, and from them we can reconstruct in rough outline his itinerary. He seems to have gone first to Paris. He kept for many years a souvenir of Notre Dame which he eventually gave to little Eveline Savournin. He saw Strasbourg, for which he retained a particular affection, Baden and Heidelberg. Many years later, seeing the hills near Clyro reflected in the Wye, he was reminded of the sight of Mont Blanc reflected in the waters of Lake Geneva. In addition to his Notre Dame souvenir he bought a musical box in Geneva, with which he amused countless children in later years. This was a long holiday for him. Mr Venables records that he left for Switzerland on 19 June and did not return till 24 July.

Apart, however, from these scattered snippets of information, we know surprisingly little about Kilvert's early years in Clyro. Only one letter from this period of his life has survived, no sermons, no notes; but in Jan 1870 he begins to keep his diary in earnest. The dry bones of his career are clothed in life, and from then on the whole pattern of his existence is brought to life for us.

It is not surprising to find Kilvert turning for emotional satisfaction to writing. The Kilverts were a gifted family, with an undoubted, but, until Kilvert himself, not dominant creative strain in their make-up. The memoir left behind by Robert Kilvert, though stiff and formal in comparison with his son's diary, is not without interest and merit. Edward, Robert's younger brother, was a competent artist, and the Kilvert Society possesses two of his sketchbooks of delicate monochromes of English and Welsh landscapes; and in 1867 he published in Bath *Eight Papers on Ritualism*. Emily, the Diarist's younger sister, also wrote a memoir of her early life. His brother, Edward (Perch) was a fellow member of the Harrow Weald Poetical Society. Dora, the youngest of all, wrote a lively journal of her honeymoon in the Lakes. Mention has already been made of the impressive literary out-put of the elder Francis Kilvert of Claverton Lodge (in addition to the books already mentioned he also published *The Literary Remains of Bishop Warburton* and *Pinocothecae Historicae Specimen* – a book of Latin inscriptions of the most remarkable men he had met in his literary studies). In addition to the poem by his wife, Adelaide Sophia, found among the Plomer papers in Durham University Library, four more are kept in the Bath Reference Library; and mention has already been made of her book on *Home Discipline*. Thersie was a more than competent water-colourist, and her daughter, Essex, later Mrs Essex Hope, won a certain reputation for herself as a novelist in the 1920's.

It seems as if this creative strain, which found only partial expression in the critical prose of Francis Kilvert the Antiquary, and the occasional jottings of Robert Kilvert, Emily and Dora, finally came to fruition in the younger Francis Kilvert. In him the family at last found its writer.

Chapter Eight
The Golden Years

When the published diary opens, on 18 January 1870, Kilvert is
staying at Cranmers, a house in Mitcham belonging to friends of
his, a Mr and Mrs Thomas, probably related to the Thomases of
Llanthomas; but William Plomer has stated that it was begun on
the first of that month. It looks as if Kilvert had begun to keep his
journal as the consequence of a New Year's resolution, and that he
bought his notebook from Horden the Hay stationer and took it
with him to London. It is not until 8 February that we find him in
Clyro.

Immediately we are caught up in the Clyro scene. From then
on, stroke by stroke, Kilvert completes the picture of this, his
favourite land.

> The morning spread upon the mountains, beautiful Clyro
> rising from the valley and stretching away northward, dotted
> with white houses and shining with gleams of green on hills
> and dingle sides.   (Vol. 1. 33)

> A lovely evening and the Black Mountain lighted up grandly,
> all the furrows and water courses clear and brilliant. People
> coming home from market, birds singing, buds bursting, and
> the spring air full of beauty, life and hope. (Vol. 1. 40–1)

> The mountains were very silent and desolate. No human
> being in sight, not a tree. No living thing moving except a few

mountain sheep, some of them with long curling horns . . .
The only sounds were the sighing of the wind through the
rushes and the rushing of distant streams in the watercourses
with which the mountain sides were seamed and scarred . . .

(Vol. 1. 51)

The Clyro women . . . stride about the village like storks. The
industrious blacksmith chinks away at his forge night and
morning late and early, and the maidens and mothers go up
and down the water steps with their pitchers continually.

(Vol. 1. 63)

Vignette follows vignette until we feel we know this landscape
as intimately as Dorothy Wordsworth's Grasmere or Gilbert
White's Selborne. It is one of our memorable literary landscapes;
and against this magnificently realised background Kilvert unfolds
the story of a whole community. The pages of his Diary are as
crowded as the pages of a Dickens novel with great eccentrics such
as Father Ignatius and the Solitary of Llanbedr, impressive
bourgeois families such as the Thomases, Dews and Bevans, less
privileged but equally memorable figures such as Hannah
Whitney, and John Morgan the veteran of the Peninsular
Campaign, beautiful children and sick and demented villagers.

Of many of these men and women who people the pages of the
Diary, we now know a great deal, and can supplement Kilvert's
account.

Father Ignatius

The general facts about the strange career of the Rev Joseph
Leycester Lyne, who preferred to be known as Father Ignatius,
can be found in the *Dictionary of National Biography** – his
unpopular desire to revive the monastic life for men in the Church

*For a fuller account see 'The Enthusiast'. A. Calder Marshall. Faber. 1962.

of England, the refusal of all the orthodox bishops to ordain him
priest, his ultimate ordination by the bogus Archbishop Mar
Timotheos (Joseph Rene Vilatte), his highly successful fund-
raising tours and his less successful attempts to found and
maintain his monastery, Llanthony Tertia, at Capel-y-Ffin, which
eventually, contrary to his intention, passed into the hands of the
Roman Catholic Church.

   Kilvert's account of his meeting with Father Ignatius is
remarkably objective and unprejudiced. He had little intellectual
sympathy with Lyne's views on monasticism, and could see little
sense in the way of life he had formulated for his monks.

> They allow no woman to come near them, and do their own
> washing. Probably, however, there is little of that to do. They
> may wear linen but they don't show any and perhaps they did
> not take off their habits when at work because they had
> nothing under. They looked very much like old women at
> work in the garden. It does seem very odd at this age of the
> world in the latter part of the nineteenth century to see monks
> gravely wearing such dresses and at work in them in broad
> day. One could not help thinking how much more sensible
> and really religious was the dress and occupation of the
> masons and the hearty healthy girl washing at the Chapel
> House, living naturally in the world and taking their share of
> its work, cares and pleasures, than the morbid unnatural life
> of these monks going back into the errors of the dark ages . . .
>   (Vol. 1. 78)

But this passage was written before he had met Father
Ignatius. It is clear that once he has come face to face with him
Kilvert falls under his spell, or at any rate responds to the charisma
of his personality.

> His head and brow are very fine, the forehead beautifully
> rounded and highly imaginative. The face is a very saintly one

and the eyes extremely beautiful, earnest and expressive, a
dark soft brown. When excited they seem absolutely to
flame... His manner gives you the impression of great
earnestness and single-mindedness. Father Ignatius thinks
every one is as good as himself, and is perfectly unworldly,
innocent and unsuspicious.

(Vol. 1. 220/222)

This was the only occasion when Kilvert and Father Ignatius
came face to face, and the meeting ends on a moving note.

When we had parted a little way and our roads had diverged
he called out through the half screen of a hazel hedge, 'Father!
Will you remember us the next time you celebrate the Holy
Communion?' 'Yes,' I replied, 'I will'.

Father Ignatius was of course still only a deacon and not
permitted to celebrate Holy Communion himself.
There are several other references to Father Ignatius in the
Diary, but few are in any way censorious. S. G. A. Luff, in an
article in *The Clergy Review* for December 1979 says 'Kilvert's
sympathy for things catholic amounts to a nostalgia'. There are
passages in the Diary, such as the account of the High Church
service at St Barnabas, Oxford, which seem to refute this; but he
certainly paints an undoctrinaire and tolerant picture of the
irregular Mr Lyne, and reveals himself as more receptive of ideas
which, in the end, the twentieth century will embrace than even the
official leaders of the Victorian Church.

The Solitary of Llanbedr – Painscastle

Kilvert reveals the same sympathy with the outsider when he
comes to speak of that other eccentric, the Rev John Price of
Llanbedr–Painscastle.
Kilvert's picture of Mr Price has been filled out by the
Reverend David Edmondes-Owen in an article originally pub-

lished in the July (1907) number of the *Treasury*, a now defunct Church magazine. The parish of Llanbedr–Painscastle had been without a vicar for nine years when Mr Price came from Lancashire to care for it. There was scarcely one churchman in the parish, and the few who had any religious convictions were dissenters. There was no vicarage house, and Mr Price, after living for a while in a cottage from which he was turned out when the accommodation was needed for farm servants, contented himself for many years by living in three bathing machines, presumably brought from Aberystwyth, until they were accidentally burnt down, and he was forced to take refuge in the squalid hut in which Kilvert found him when, with his friend Tom Williams, the Vicar of Llowes, he visited him in July 1872.

The church was in a ruinous state, and the services, though regularly held, were scantily attended, until the Vicar hit upon the idea of holding a special Sunday service for the many tramps and vagabonds who passed through the parish. To encourage attendance he gave sixpence to each member of the congregation, and even installed a portable oil-stove in each pew. The tramps brought whatever food they had begged from neighbouring farms to the service and cooked it on the stoves. At the end of the service, often with their pastor, they adjourned to a neighbouring barn to eat the meal they had cooked during the sermon.

One thing distressed the saintly vicar greatly; so many tramps ignored the form of marriage simply to save the fee. The Church, he thought, was at fault in demanding payment fees from the poor for administering any ordinance. One Sunday he preached on this question, and then announced that in future he would not only marry the tramps for nothing, but would start each couple in life with five shillings. This promise led to results both humorous and tragic. It is on record that he married the same couple five times under different names, and through failing eyesight violated some of

the Church marriage laws which he himself regarded as
sacred and vital.

> (D. Edmondes-Owen. Reprinted in *Miscellany Two*.
> *K.S. p. 9*)

Kilvert tells us that towards the end of his life he had a seizure
and fell into the fire burning himself badly. Mr Edmondes-Owen
does not confirm this, but says that in the end he was persuaded to
abandon his hut and take lodgings in Talgarth. He had neglected
himself for so long that his clothing had to be cut away from his
skin before he could be bathed.

> He was at last placed in a bed in an exhausted state, but
> beaming benedictions on all for their great kindness to him, and
> wondering what he had done in his life to merit such attention
> and so many blessings. He slept in peace that night. He never
> woke.
>
> *(Miscellany Two. p. 13)*

Kilvert was appalled at the squalor in which the poor Solitary
lived, and his account of the inside of his cottage is one of the
most memorable descriptive passages in the Diary.

> 'The house' was a sight when once seen never to be forgotten.
> I sat in amazement taking mental notes of the strangest
> interior I ever saw. Inside the hut there was a wild confusion
> of litter and rubbish almost choking and filling up all available
> space. The floor had once been of stone but was covered thick
> and deep with an accumulation of the dirt and peat dust of
> years . . . No table cloth. No grate. The hearth foul with cold
> peat ashes, broken bricks and dust, under the great wide open
> chimney through which stole down a faint ghastly sickly
> light . . . The squalor, the dirt, the dust, the foulness and
> wretchedness of the place were indescribable, almost incon-
> ceivable.

And in this cabin thus lives the Solitary of Llanbedr, The Revd John Price, Master of Arts of Cambridge University, and Vicar of Llanbedr–Painscastle.

(Vol. 2. 226–7)

But, just as he was perceptive enough to see behind the eccentricities of Father Ignatius a true visionary, so Kilvert can recognise behind the squalor of Mr Price's life the existence of a man who approached saintliness.

The Solitary ... showed us the way down the lanes to the Church. The people who met him touched their hats to his reverence with great respect. They recognised him as a very holy man, and if the Solitary had lived a thousand years ago he would have been revered as a hermit and perhaps canonized as a saint.

(Vol. 2. 231)

Friends

The circle in which Kilvert moved during his years in Clyro was made up of a handful of families – the Dews, Bevans, Crichtons, Venables, Thomases, Baskervilles and Morrells, many of whom were very interesting and gifted people in their own right.

The Venables Family

Richard Lister Venables, Vicar of Clyro, was a gifted member of a gifted family. He was not only a conscientious churchman, and an able administrator and highly valued chairman of the Quarter Sessions (he performed the duties which would now fall to a County Council Chairman); he had written a book about his experiences in Russia, which he had visited in the company of his first wife, the daughter of a Russian General. (*Domestic Scenes in Russia*. Murray, 1839.) It had been reprinted during the years of

the Crimean War. His brother, who frequently visited Clyro and
the seat of the Venables family, Llysdinam, was George Stovin
Venables, a distinguished London man of letters, who had known
Wordsworth, was a friend of Thackeray (whose nose he had
broken in a fight at school), and of Tennyson, and may have been
in part responsible for the offer of the Laureateship to the latter.
But he was not above giving lectures to country audiences, and
Kilvert tells how impressed he was by a lecture he gave on 5
December 1871 in Hay schoolroom on the German Empire. (The
lecture lasted two and a half hours and the lecturer did not use a
single note.) Mrs Venables (the second Mrs Venables, the first
having died in Kilvert's first year in Clyro) had no such intellectual
pretensions but she was responsible for introducing her curate to a
great number of interesting and influential friends.

The Bevans of Hay Castle

William Latham Bevan owed his advancement in the Church to
his uncle, Sir Joseph Bailey of Glanusk, a wealthy iron-master. Sir
Joseph purchased in 1833 both the manor and the advowson of
Hay, and to these he added in 1844 the Castle. As soon as he had
purchased the Castle he installed his nephew in it, and presented
him to the living. Such generous patronage might have robbed a
weaker personality of his independence and enterprise; but
William Latham's integrity and intelligence were proof against the
temptation to rely solely on his uncle's benevolence. He became a
devoted parish priest and an illustrious educationalist. Under his
guidance the Hay National School became one of the finest in
Wales. He was responsible for reviving the Hay Mechanics'
Institute as the Hay Literary Institution; and the reports in the
local newspapers of the concerts, lectures and Penny Readings he
organised reveal what a potent force he was in the lively cultural
life of the town. He contributed to *Smith's Dictionary of the Bible*,
and wrote a *Student's Manual of Ancient and Modern History*.
He was a friend of Dr Livingstone. His son, Edward, succeeded

him as Archdeacon of Brecon in 1907, and in 1923 became the first Bishop of the newly-formed Diocese of Swansea and Brecon. His daughter Mary, one of whose diaries is deposited in the Hereford Public Library, and who also clearly inherited her father's intellectual gifts, wrote in later life a series of monographs on the history of Wales, was a friend of Edward Lear (she is said to have helped him to write *How Pleasant to Know Mr Lear*), and had a son who became a distinguished theological scholar and Professor of Catholic Studies at Harvard.

The Bevans moved in distinguished circles. From Mary's diary we learn that Mrs Bevan and her daughters frequently wintered in Weymouth, sometimes spending six or seven months there. Mary in her early twenties seems to live in a constant social whirl, mixing on fairly easy terms with people of high rank – Lord and Lady Hereford, Sir Henry Croft and others. But perhaps her closest friends were the Thomases of Llanthomas (especially the sons), and the other families whom Kilvert also knew. One gets the impression that the Dews, Venables, Thomases, Haigh Allens, Crichtons and Baskervilles formed a circle of close and loyal friends, and that Kilvert was perhaps more of a fringe member than his Diary suggests. On the several occasions on which the two diaries overlap (the Ball at Clifford Priory, the concert in the Hay schools, the visit to Weymouth to see the Fleet) Kilvert mentions Mary but she does not mention him. The name Kilvert occurs only twice in her three-year record.

How much ought we to read into this lack of reference to Kilvert? It is fairly clear that he is of far less interest to her than the young men of Llanthomas, or the army and navy officers whom she meets at Weymouth; but, in her early twenties, Mary, in spite of her great gifts and superior intelligence, bears a certain resemblance to the younger Bennett girls of *Pride and Prejudice*, with little time for an obscure and impecunious curate of thirty odd years.

Mary's record mentions one or two events that Kilvert

merely notes *en passant* or does not (as far as we know) report at
all. She adds details to the sad story of the death of little Lily
Crichton from tuberculosis, and of Charles Thomas of typhoid in
Rome, and of the accident to Mr Haigh Allen that cost him one of
his arms. On the whole it is a diary with an underlying note of
sadness. She lives what looks a full social life, with balls, croquet
and archery meetings at Ludlow, Kinnersley Castle, Clifford
Priory and Stoneleigh Abbey in Warwickshire; she goes to
London to see plays (she saw Henry Irving in *Charles the First*),
visits friends in Windsor etc. But her friendships with Henry
Thomas and others do not ripen into an engagement. She longs for
some happy love-affair to give zest and fulfilment to her life; but by
1875 when her diary ends and she is in her 23rd year it still has not
come to her.

Eventually when she was thirty-six, she married Col H. P.
Dawson of Hartlington Hall, Burnsall, Yorks.

The Dews of Whitney

There were two branches of the Dew family at Whitney. Tomkyns
Dew lived at Whitney Court, not the present house which stands
on the hill above the railway station, but a more modest building,
now demolished, which overlooked the river. His brother, Henry
Dew, was Rector of the parish from 1843 to 1901. The Rector's
wife, Mary (née Monkhouse) was related to the Hutchinsons into
whose family William Wordsworth had married. She was in fact
the subject of the Wordsworth sonnet *To the Infant M. M.* She
spoke frequently to Kilvert about the Wordsworth family and
showed him letters from Dorothy Wordsworth. It was Miss
Elizabeth Hutchinson, who was related to Mrs Dew, who gave
Kilvert a holograph poem by Dorothy Wordsworth.

The Baskervilles, Morrells, Haigh Allens, Dr Clouston and the Crichtons

Of these families less has been recorded. Walter Baskerville seems to have been a kindly and hospitable squire. The celebrations which marked his marriage to Miss Bertha Maria Hopton of Canon Frome Court near Ledbury, and which will be described later, culminated in a lavish ball at Clyro in January 1876. Hopewell Morrell seems to have left Clyro under a cloud, and, in spite of the style in which he lived at Cae Mawr, died relatively poor. He was probably related to the brewing family of Morrells of Moulsford. It is rather surprising to find that he had in his gift the living of Moulsford. Of Dr Clouston, who was Kilvert's doctor, we know a little more. Although he was quite a young man, he was a Medical Officer for Health for the Hay District, and had published two papers on *Short Rules for Disinfection*, and *Acute Rheumatism and its Treatment with Salicyates*. He was seven years younger than Kilvert. Benjamin Haigh Allen, who was a D.L. and a J.P. had built Clifford Priory, a Gothic mansion which Kilvert admired, in 1860, and was still there in 1902. Mary Bevan in her diary says he lost an arm in a farm accident.

Of Mrs Crichton, whom Kilvert greatly admired, a detailed picture has survived in an unexpected place. In Vol. 1 of the Diary (p. 260) Kilvert says, 'In the *Saturday Review* for last week there was a paper on *Great Girls* which described Mrs Crichton to the life'. Mrs Teresa Williams has unearthed the passage, which reads as follows.

> Nothing is more distinctive among woman than the difference of relative age between them. Two women of the same number of years will be substantially of different epochs of life – the one faded in person, wearied in mind, fossilized in sympathy; the other fresh both in face and feeling, with sympathies as broad and keen as they were when she was in

her first youth, and perhaps even more so; with a brain still as receptive, a temper still as easy to be amused, as ready to love, as quick to learn, as when she emerged from the schoolroom to the drawing-room . . .

This kind of woman, so fresh and active, so intellectually as well as emotionally alive, is never anything but a girl, never loses some of the sweetest characteristics of girlhood. You see her first as a young wife and mother, and you imagine she has left the schoolroom for about as many months as she has been married years . . . Brisk and airy, braving all weathers, ready for any amusement, interested in the current questions of history or society, by some wonderful faculty of organising seeming to have all her time to herself as if she had no house cares and no nursery duties, yet these somehow not neglected, she is the very ideal of a happy girl roving through life as through a daisy field, on whom sorrow has not yet laid his hand, and to whose lot has fallen no Dead Sea apple. And when one hears her name and style for the first time as a matron, and sees with her two or three sturdy little fellows hanging about her slender neck and calling her mamma, one feels as if nature had somehow made a mistake, and our slim and simple-mannered damsel had only made-believe to have taken up the serious burdens of life, and was nothing but a great girl after all.

All that Kilvert tells us about Mrs Crichton in the Diary, her love of sport, her artistic pursuits, her natural charm, bears out this picture which he so cleverly recognised in the *Saturday Review.*

The Thomas Family of Llanigon

Daisy Thomas (her proper name was Frances Eleanor Jane, and Kilvert may have called her 'Daisy' to avoid confusing her with Fanny Bevan) was the youngest daughter of the Rev William Jones

Thomas, third son of David Thomas of Wellfield (now known under its old name of Cefndyrys) and Annie Elizabeth, daughter of the Rev John Jones of Hereford. Before coming to Llanigon (a small parish a mile or so out of Hay) Mr Thomas had been Vicar of Gladestry, and had lived, not in the vicarage, but in a much larger house, Newcastle Court, and it was there that his many children were born. The Thomases had a large family, six sons and five daughters – the whole family were photographed together in a very impressive group in the 1870's. By this time Mr Thomas had changed livings with Mr Dowell of Llanigon and purchased Llanthomas, a substantial country house on the other side of the road from the church. Mr Thomas, like Mr Venables, must have enjoyed a considerable private income. Llanthomas was a large establishment, and from what we learn from the Diary of Mary Bevan the sons lived mostly like gentlemen of leisure, mixing freely with the most highly placed members of Herefordshire and Radnorshire society. One of the sons became a Colonel in the Third Battalion of the South Wales Borderers; a second died of cholera in Ceylon in 1878; and a third, the high-spirited Charlie, much lamented by Mary Bevan died of typhoid in Rome in 1873 while on holiday there. Kilvert records the death of Lechmere at Colombo on 3 Sept., 1878, but surprisingly makes no mention of Charlie's death (unless the record was not included by Plomer). Mary Bevan felt his loss deeply and refers constantly to his sad and early death.

Mr Thomas seems to have been an excessively possessive father, and probably felt that if his daughters were to marry they were entitled to hold out for what might be called 'good' marriages. There is a tradition that he not only refused to entertain Kilvert for a son-in-law, but forbade another curate to pay court to a second daughter. If Mr Thomas was indeed a second Mr Barrett of Wimpole Street, jealous of any rival in the affections of his daughters, he was extraordinarily successful, because in the event not one of his daughters, charming and talented though they were, ever married.

The story of Kilvert's unsuccessful courtship of Daisy is told in some detail by Kilvert himself, and there is little one can add to it, except perhaps a few words by way of sequel. Mr Thomas's decision clearly put Kilvert in a dilemma. Up to this point he had given Daisy to believe that he was more than fond of her, and she had grown to be fond of him (in spite of the fact that he was 12 years her senior). But once Mr Thomas had forbidden him to think of an engagement, there was nothing left for him but to disobey the father or cease to pay any attention to the daughter. He chose the latter course, and left Daisy confused and unhappy. Among the Plomer papers in the University Library at Durham is a letter from a Miss Garnett who taught at the St Helen's school which was housed at Llanthomas during the Second World War.

> Her (Daisy's) sitting room when an old lady was the Bow Room which looked into the garden and facing the Mountains, but had a delightful bow window facing the upstairs passage. The pathos of Daisy's life was told me by Mrs Sandys Thomas who heard it from a cousin in whom she confided. 'I thought Mr Kilvert passionately loved me, but I suppose I was mistaken'.

Clearly Mr Thomas never told Daisy what had passed between him and Kilvert, and the rejected suitor very honourably kept his part of the agreement, although his sudden withdrawal must have been very baffling to Daisy.

As for Kilvert, it seems to have taken him some time to recover from his disappointment. It is all the more surprising therefore that when he had been given the living, first of St Harmon, and then of Bredwardine, and was presumably in the eyes of Mr Thomas an eligible match, he did not return to Daisy. By that time, however several other love affairs had claimed him, and not even the knowledge that Daisy was still unattached and still young (she was only 22 when he went to St Harmon) encouraged him to renew his suit.

The last glimpse we have of Daisy in her old age is of a lady devoted to good works, filling her time with painting pottery, entering competitions at Eistedfodds, running a Temperance Society in the parish etc. She died in her 76th year in 1928.

The Webbs of Hardwick

Hardwick lies at some distance from Clyro but is close enough for Mr Webb to have been one of what one might call 'the Kilvert Circle'. Thomas William Webb, Vicar of Hardwick, combined in his person, priest, artist and scientist. With the aid of a simple observatory of wood and canvas, which he set up a few yards to the south-east of the vicarage door, he conducted an important series of astronomical experiments which were first published in 1859 under the title of *Celestial Objects for Common Telescopes*. This book is a key work for amateur astronomers and is still (1980) in print. Kilvert records seeing what he calls the Great Meteor from Mr Webb's observatory. Mrs Webb, who was, like her husband a talented artist, lectured on Switzerland to village audiences.

Andrew Pope

Andrew Pope, who was for a time curate of Cusop, and one of Kilvert's closest friends at Clyro, emerges from the early pages of the Diary as a rather feckless young man. When faced with a runaway horse in the streets of Hay all he could do was throw his umbrella at it, an action that did more harm than good; and of course he will be remembered for ever as the curate who got himself confirmed at that ludicrous service at Whitney-on-Wye. But Andrew Pope was almost certainly a more sensible and resourceful young man than Kilvert makes him out to be.

Although he was only a curate, his curacy was a more responsible one than Kilvert's. He was in sole charge of the parish of Cusop; and if we can trust the account given in the *Hereford Times* of the events that marked his departure for Preston-on-Wye, he served that parish with exemplary zeal.

> This picturesque and remote parish . . . ordinarily so quiet in its mountain seclusion, has lately been the scene of most interesting events. The occasion was the retirement of the curate of the parish, the Rev A. Pope, after a 'sole charge' of five and a half years. He has been lately appointed to the united livings of Preston and Blakemere, and had so endeared himself by his exemplary conduct to his parishioners that they part with him with deep regret. As one instance of the way in which he fulfilled the duties of his sacred office, we may mention that he established a mission service during the summer months in a remote part of his parish, when, at the foot of the Black Mountains, and in a rude cart shed, he held every other Sunday evening, a service for the benefit of the dwellers in that sequestered locality, although he had two full services at the parish church every Sunday . . .
>
>   It is in ways such as these that Mr Pope has endeared himself to the inhabitants of Cusop and its neighbourhood, and it is not to be wondered that his leaving has caused a deep feeling of regret amongst all ranks.
>
> *(Hereford Times.* 9 Aug. 1873)

Pope was almost certainly in better circumstances than Kilvert. When Kilvert went to Llanthomas to speak to Mr Thomas about his affection for Daisy, he tells us that he had but one sovereign in his pocket – and he owed that; but Pope, when he left Cusop, was able to provide out of his own pocket, tea and cakes for the schoolchildren, a 'comfortable tea' (whatever that was) for the matrons, and supper of beef and beer for the men. Pope also left a new alms-dish for the church but Kilvert does not seem to have been able to leave a similar gift to Clyro.

By 1873 the young man who had imprudently taken his dog with him to a confirmation service, had not had strength of mind to stand up to an over-bearing bishop, and who had rashly not been able to think of anything better to do to a runaway horse in the streets of Hay than throw his umbrella at it, had clearly matured. When he met Miss Harriet Mary Ernle Money-Kyrle of Homme House, Much Marcle, and asked for her hand, Colonel Money-Kyrle raised none of the objections that Mr Thomas raised against Kilvert. Pope was certainly better connected than the Diary implies (one of his forbears had been Mayor of Bristol in 1776, and Archdeacon Waring of Salop, who helped with the wedding service, was his uncle). It was generally thought at Clyro that Pope had married an heiress. Certainly her father was an important man, not only in Herefordshire, but Wiltshire (he was on visiting terms with the Marquis of Lansdowne of Bowood).

It was a grand wedding with a tent for the tenants, the Herefordshire Militia Band to play through the wedding breakfast, and four postilions in scarlet to drive the bride and bridegroom to Cheltenham on the first leg of their journey to Paris. The *Hereford Times* (12 Sept. 1874) prints a full and charming account of the wedding, contradicting Kilvert's statement that the bride was late, but adding one charming detail. When the happy couple left the church they were showered with *scented* rice.

After the Paris honeymoon Pope and his wife set to work to build the vicarage at Preston, decorating it with a plaque bearing their initials and the date of rebuilding, and at one time Pope had the grandiose idea of pulling down the church and moving it nearer the centre of the village.

When he was eventually presented to the living of Upton Bishop, the *Hereford Times* printed the following complimentary notice, which Mrs Teresa Williams has very kindly shown me.

Preferments in Herefordshire.

This week the Dean and Chapter of Hereford had to appoint clergymen to three important vicarages in the County of Herefordshire and one in the diocese of Oxford... For Upton Bishop they chose the Reverend Andrew Pope. Mr Pope was ordained priest in 1868 by the Bishop of Hereford and served for six years the curacy of Cusop, a straggling parish lying between Hereford and Hay.

In 1873 he was presented by the Dean and Chapter to the Vicarage of Preston-on-Wye with Blakemere. Here he (in addition to some vigorous parish work) built the vicarage house and rebuilt Blakemere Church. In 1880 he was promoted by the Dean and Chapter to the more important living of Diddlesbury near Ludlow, where he found that the vicarage house was a mile from the church. He immediately set to work and built a new house and subsequently carried out a second restoration of the church. Undoubtedly this appointment will be very gratifying to the inhabitants of Upton Bishop.

(*Hereford Times.* 22 November 1890)

By a singular coincidence Pope's last living was Langley Burrell, where he continued to live for some time after his retirement in 1910. He died at The Chestnuts, Ross-on-Wye in October 1924. When Kilvert died his estate was valued at less than £400. Pope left the considerable sum of over £22,000.

Humble Parishioners

As might be expected Kilvert deals at less length with the more humble of his parishioners, but although they are seen only in vignettes, such is the depth of his sympathy with them, and the power and vividness of his writing that in comparison, some of his close friends – Haigh Allen, Walter Baskerville, Hopewell Morrell – remain shadowy and vague figures. The first two volumes of the Diary are a gallery of brilliant pen-portraits of the poor of Clyro.

> From Cwmbythog I crossed the dingle and the brook and the little meadow and so up the path by the quarries to John Morgan's, the old soldier's. He and Mary his wife were cosily at tea. And after the veteran had done and pocketed his clasp knife he covered his face with his hand and whispered his long grace audibly.   (Vol. 1. 85)

> I found the old soldier sitting by his black fireplace and the door open, but soon a spark of fire showed and the flame leapt up and we soon had a glowing fire. We talked about the War and he amused me by telling me his remembrances of the wolves in Spain . . . 'We frightened them', he said, 'By making a flash of powder in the pan of our muskets . . . They did not like to see that.'   (Vol. 1. 247–8)

> I went to see old Sackville Thomas . . . He was lying in a bed in a corner of the dark hovel hole which serves as a bedroom almost underground. A crimson coverlet was on the bed and he had a red cloth or handkerchief wrapped about his head. There were two beds in the room and on the other bed lay a rosy fair-haired little girl of four years old flushed and just awaking from sleep . . .   (Vol. 1. 168)

> Next to visit old Laver (W. Price). He was all in confusion and excitement, not able to splutter out his words fast enough, all up on end, dancing first on one leg and then on another. It was his washing day (the first I should think that had occurred to afflict him for a very long time). His hovel had just been washed out and goodness knows not before that operation was needed, so I promised to call another day, and Price much relieved, yet fearing to be rude and inhospitable,

assented in great excitement, hopping on alternate legs, and
swarming with lice.   (Vol. 1. 251–2)

Turned in to old Hannah Whitney's. The old woman, cloaked
and with her rusty black bonnet fiercely cocked and pointed,
crown uppermost, on the top of her head, was standing in the
doorway taking an observation of the weather, the world, and
the stream of water flowing fast down the gutter before her
door . . . But, turning her withered grey face and white hair,
the fine delicate features whose ancient beauty is still
discernible, she looked earnestly at me, and her eyes shone as
she . . . spoke of the blessings of being cheerful and contented
and of being able to sit down by her own fireside and eat her
crust of bread in peace and quietness.

(Vol. 1. 251–2)

'You are of a better family than many of the gentlemen round
here,' I said. 'I know it,' said the old woman proudly . . .
'Thank God for my bit of breed.'   (Vol. 2. 92)

Visited Edward Evans, and the stench of the hovel bedroom
almost insupportable. The room below was occupied by 12
bushels of potatoes just brought home from Cabalva Farm
where they were set. The gaunt ghastly black and white cat
was still sitting on a box at the bedhead waiting for the sick
man to die.   (Vol. 1. 245)

Old John Lloyd of Cwmganon . . . told me that his sister Mrs
Watkins had gone mad and was living with them at
Cwmganon, and they did not know what to do with her . . .
They keep her locked up in a bedroom alone, for she will
come down amongst them stark naked. She has broken the
window and all the crockery in the room, amused herself by
dancing naked around the room, and threatens to wring her
daughter-in-law's neck.   (Vol. 1. 372)

Called on Old Whitcombe. The old man, ninety years old,
helpless, deaf, blind almost, and childish, leaned on me and
fondled my hand, talking earnestly but incoherently and
repeating himself almost every moment... I repeated some
of the Church prayers for him and he joined in eagerly at the
end or wherever the old familiar words struck a chord in his
memory. Then, putting his hands together reverently like a
child he repeated, speaking in a low voice as if to himself,
'Thank you for hearing my prayers'. It was very touching.

(Vol. 2. 119–20)

It is difficult to over-praise the charm of Kilvert's portrait of
Clyro, but Kate O'Brien in her *English Diaries and Journals*
(Collins. 1943. p. 40–3) gives a very good summary of the variety
and appeal of his account.

He gives us, like a painter, not the flat actuality, but his own
composition of it. He gives us all the 'properties' of his kind of
life indeed, all the things that we know are almost 'stock' now,
and that we have encountered over and over again in period
novels and family albums, but he gives them *as he feels them*,
and as partaking of his vitality: walks, sermons, frosty
mornings, visits to parishioners: toothache, confirmation
caps, talk of the Franco–Prussian war, 'a letter from my
mother', girls and kisses and 'mischievous saucy glances from
beautiful grey eyes' – a very great deal about girls and
glances; croquet parties, chubby babies, news from India...
archery, dances, kisses... prayers by the bedside of dying
children; a great deal of scenery; visits to Oxford; pious
reflections and sudden 'romps'; talks with Mr Barton, 'a
clever well-read man' about the Holy Grail; 'sun on the
lawn... claret cup iced'...

It is the unevenness, the eccentricity and the sheer
naturalness of the writer which distinguish this diary. Kilvert

puts down everything and anything, a landscape, a joke, a prayer or a rhapsody about yet another girl; and whatever it is, he lights it up; by some curious trick of his vitality and his innocence he makes everything *live* that he touches.

Chapter Nine

1870   A Memorable Year

1870 was a fateful year, for Kilvert and for Europe. In many ways it repeated the pattern of all his other years in Clyro, and to follow him from day to day throughout the year is to familiarise oneself with the tenor and texture of his life in Wales. In another respect, however, it was unique. This was the year in which he began his diary, the literary work that was to bring him in the end a reputation greater than anything he had dared to hope for when he was alive. It was also a year in which a foreign empire collapsed, and a new and serious threat to the peace of Europe began to emerge.

The year began uneventfully. More often than not Kilvert spent Christmas and New Year not in his parish but at home with his parents at Langley Burrell. Christmas in Clyro in the 1870's was not as important a Christian festival as it is for us today. For the people of Radnorshire the real climaxes of the Christian year seem to have been Easter and Harvest Thanksgiving. In 1866 Kilvert left Clyro on Dec. 24, not even staying for the Christmas services, and did not return till Jan 18. In 1867 he went home on Dec 16 and in 1868 on Dec 21. In 1870, however, he seems to have been at Clyro for the New Year, and perhaps it was on the first day of that year that he went to the stationer's, Horden's, in Hay, and bought himself his first notebook. What those first diary entries consisted of we shall unfortunately never know. By Jan 18, when the first published entries begin, Kilvert has left Clyro and, after a short stay in Langley Burrell, has gone to London.

Most of the time he spent in London (he stayed first at Mitcham and then at 3 Hobart Place, the home of the Pearsons, the parents of Mrs Venables), was taken up with going to services, concerts, pantomimes, plays, and especially Art Exhibitions. He was deeply interested in Art, and when he was in London he never failed to visit the exhibitions of the Royal Academy, on some occasions going to see them more than once. The full scope of Kilvert's interest in Art has been intriguingly explored by Rosalind Billingham in her Kilvert Society pamphlet, *Kilvert and the Visual Arts*.

There is no suggestion in these early London entries that the winter is abnormally severe; but as soon as he returned to Clyro he was forcibly reminded of the realities of a Radnorshire winter. By Feb 9 the mountains were covered in snow, and by St Valentine's Eve, the cold was intense.

> Very few people in Church, the weather fearful, violent deadly E. wind and the hardest frost we have had yet. Went to Bettws in the afternoon wrapped in two waistcoats, a muffler and a mackintosh, and was not at all too warm. Heard the Chapel Bell pealing strongly for the second time since I have been here and when I got to the Chapel my beard, moustaches and whiskers were so stiff with ice that I could hardly open my mouth and my beard was frozen on to my mackintosh. There was a large christening party from Llwyn Gwilym. The clerk (Wilding) thrust a tallow candle between the bars of the stove grate and lighted it and set it upon the table that once probably did duty for a Communion table. I had it put out again as the daylight was sufficient. The baby was baptized in ice which was broken and swimming about in the font.
>
> (Vol. 1. 34–5)

But the beleaguered parishioners of Clyro were not without their diversions. The Clyro Choir Supper was held a few days before St Valentine's Day, and must have been a success, because Kilvert's landlady, Mrs Chaloner, did not come home till 2.30 a.m. Then on St Valentine's Day itself there was a happy exchange of cards, and a Volunteer Concert in Hay. There were dinners for the gentry at Clyro Court and Llysdinam, and no doubt Penny Readings at Hay (though none were reported in the local papers).

Whatever the weather Kilvert spent a great deal of his time 'villaging' – paying pastoral calls. He was a conscientious parish visitor. We know from one of his parishioners that when he was at Bredwardine some years later he tried to see everyone in his parish at least once a fortnight, and there is every indication that this was also his practice at Clyro. Out of approximately 130 families listed in the census of 1871 for the mother parish he mentions no less than ninety, and out of thirty four in the hamlet of Bettws, twenty four. If we take into consideration that only about one third of the full diary has ever been published, and that in all probability he made many other calls which he did not bother to enter, we may assume that Kilvert made a pastoral call at every house in the parish – a very impressive record.

His concern for the welfare of the parishioners was especially welcome in the early months of 1870. The poor suffered badly in the severe weather. Edward Evans and his family had no blankets; Mrs Corfield had a house full of children and only one blanket. The Sackville Thomases of Dol-y-Canney were equally ill-provided. Mr Venables decided to spend some of the surplus communion alms on bedding for the poor, and it was Kilvert's responsibility to distribute the free sheets and blankets to the deserving.

By the end of the month, however, the weather was improving, and Kilvert was able to embark on those long walks over the hills that he loved – to the top of Drum Dhu with his vicar, to Colva in search of some folk songs he had heard of, and to Capel-y-Ffin with his walking companion, Hopewell Morrell of

Cae Mawr. Just before the excursion to Capel-y-Ffin the weather took a last vicious turn, and one storm brought with it an extraordinary incident at Clyro Court. Kilvert makes only a brief mention of it, but the *Hereford Times* of 15 Jan 1870 supplements his account in its own style. The journalism has a wonderful period flavour to it.

> *Clyro – Singular and Providential Escape at Clyro Court*
> Between seven and eight o'clock on Saturday morning an accident of a very alarming nature happened at Clyro Court, the residence of W. T. M. Baskerville Esq., and which will long be remembered in the locality for the remarkable escape from instantaneous death or very serious injury of the venerable housekeeper, Mrs Mills, and another domestic of the establishment. It was, we are informed, built in 1839 by the late proprietor of the Clyro Court estate, T. M. Baskerville Esq., who was for some years one of the Conservative members for this county, in conjunction with the father of Sir Joseph Bailey, one of our present members; and, either at the time of its erection, or soon afterwards, there were constructed over the servants' part of the mansion six false or imitation gables . . . The gables were erected on the top of the outer stone wall, east and west. Each gable is several feet in extent at the base and rises in graceful form to the height of perhaps about nine feet, the terminal of four out of the six being a stone ball, weighing, we should imagine, considerably more than one cwt. At the time named on Saturday morning the wind was blowing 'great guns' as it had been all night, when a terrific crash was heard, and in an instant the servants' hall was filled with the debris of the more southerly gable on the west side, together with the whole of the flooring of the housekeeper's bedroom, a massive oak beam about twelve inches by ten inches, the bedstead, and bedclothes of the housekeeper, the furniture of the chamber and the old lady herself alive and without broken bones,

but, as will readily be conceived, in a state of alarm bordering
upon unconsciousness, and a good deal bruised.

The violence of the wind had blown away the gable of the
outer wall, and the whole mass of masonry, many of the
stones being of great weight, had fallen through the roof, and
thence, carrying everything with it, into the servants' hall
beneath . . . That an incident of so alarming a nature should
have happened without serious injury to the domestics of the
establishment may with great propriety be said to be almost
miraculous . . .

In April Kilvert and his friends and parishioners began to
prepare for the great festival of the Christian year – Easter. On
Good Friday he got up early to write his special Easter sermon,
and then went out to distribute hot cross buns in the village. On
Easter Eve the people began to assemble to decorate the church
and to 'flower the graves'. The decorations were very elaborate –
flowers in and around the stem of the font, *Christ Is Risen* worked
in primroses on moss on a board for the window sill; and for the
'flowering of the graves' roots of wild flowers were dug up and
replanted in holes cut in the turf. Kilvert was immensely moved by
the sight of the whole community cooperating in a work of
devotion and beauty, and recorded the last moments of the day in a
passage of extraordinary beauty.

At eight o'clock there was a gathering of the Choir in the
Church to practise the two anthems for tomorrow, and the
young people came flocking in from the graves where they
had been at work or watching others working, or talking to
their friends, for the Churchyard on Easter Eve is a place
where a great many people meet. The clerk's wife had been
cleaning the Church for Easter Day and the clerk had kept the
church jealously locked as there were so many strangers
about in the churchyard. He now unlocked the steeple door
and let us in that way. There was a large gathering of the

Choir and two or three people stole in from the churchyard afterwards to hear the anthems practised. The anthems went very nicely and sounded especially well from the chancel. The moonlight came streaming in broadly through the chancel windows. When the choir had gone and the lights were out and the church quiet again, as the schoolmaster and his friend stood with me at the Church door in the moonlight we were remarking on the curious fact that this year Good Friday like the Passover has fallen on the fifteenth day of the month and the full moon. As I walked down the Churchyard alone the decked graves had a strange effect in the moonlight and looked as if the people had laid down to sleep for the night out of doors, ready dressed to rise early on Easter morning. The air was as soft and warm as a summer night, and the broad moonlight made the quiet village almost as light as day. Everyone seemed to have gone to rest and there was not a sound except the clink and trickle of the brook.

(Vol. 1. 95)

It was a happy Easter, and it marked the end of the long Welsh winter. After that the weather was fair enough for men to attend the many open-air ceremonies such as the laying of the foundation stone of the new Mission Chapel at Hysfa not far from Abbey Cwm Hir, a ceremony which for its mixture of earnest ritual and unpredicted mishaps was not unlike the famous funeral of Maria Kilvert.

But by now another more personal event was impending. Mrs Venables was expecting her first baby, and Mr Venables, presumably preferring not to rely on local medical services, took her to London to a house he had taken in Eaton Square. Since Kilvert normally took his summer break in May or June, and Mr Venables, who was unfailingly considerate to him presumably did not wish to miss it, he engaged a locum, the lackadaisical Mr Welby, who came to live in the Vicarage. A few days before Mr and Mrs Venables went to London, the first archery meeting of the year was held; there soon followed a sequence of croquet and archery parties.

On May 16 Kilvert went off to his parents' home at Langley Burrell for his summer break, but by the 28th he was back at Clyro waiting anxiously for news of Mrs Venables's confinement. Very charmingly, possibly in compliment to her, he used for his diary entry the special name for Sunday 29 May – *Expectation Sunday*. On 1 June the baby, a daughter, was safely delivered, and its birth was an occasion for long and noisy rejoicing. The people of both Clyro and Hay were clearly fond of Mr Venables. In 1867 his parishioners had celebrated his return after his marriage.

A few weeks back we noticed the marriage of the Rev R. Lister Venables of Clyro, and on Saturday last the Reverend gentleman, with his bride, returned home. All public demonstration was, however, avoided, owing to the known objection of Mr Venables to anything of the kind; but if garlands, bunting and revelry were dispensed with, the parishioners had taken a means of welcoming their vicar which must have been gratifying. Early in the day a committee of farmers and others residing in the parish met at Clyro, and distributed between 400 and 500 lbs of excellent beef amongst the poor, after which they adjourned to the Baskerville Arms Inn, and there partook of a social dinner in honour of the occasion, the chair being ably filled by Mr Griffiths of Portway. About six o'clock the arrival of the happy pair at the Vicarage was hailed by a salute on the bells of Clyro Church, which continued right merrily during the remainder of the evening.
In the course of the evening a deputation from the committee, consisting of Messrs Griffiths, Hamar, W. Price, D. Morgan and R. Chaloner, proceeded to the Vicarage for the purpose of presenting to Mrs Venables a very chaste and handsome silver inkstand bearing the inscription, 'A

Wedding Present to Mrs R. Lister Venables from the
Tenantry and Parishioners of Clyro, 1867'. An address of
congratulations was also read and presented.

Brecon County Times. Sept 21 1867

A similar welcome had been given him by the people of Hay and
was reported in the *Hereford Times* of the same day.

On Tuesday morning one of those agreeable incidents so
common, we are happy to state, amongst us, that they seem to
form part of our social life, took place at Clyro, in the county
of Radnor. On that day a committee, consisting of the
following gentlemen – Trumper Esq., H. Proctor Esq., J. E.
Smith Esq., Mr Charles Griffiths, Mr Horden, Mr J. L.
Davies, Mr Stokoe, Mr Rastell and Mr Thomas Pritchard,
presented the Rev Richard Lister Venables with a handsome
silver salver on the occasion of his marriage, which took place
on the 1st August last . . . H. Proctor Esq., being the oldest
member, opened the subject by stating that they had called
there simply to express their high sense of his character as a
gentleman who devoted his life to the duties of his station, and
to congratulate him on his recent marriage, and to give their
heartiest welcome to his bride, for whom and for himself they
all wished a long life of happiness . . . Mr C. Griffiths then
read the following address:–

To the Rev R. Lister Venables
The inhabitants of Hay desire to offer you their hearty
congratulations on the auspicious event of your marriage,
which they fervently trust will be conducive to your future
happiness. In offering you the accompanying present, they
beg you to accept it as a small token of their respect and
esteem for yourself personally, and also as an acknowledg-
ment of the various important services you have so ably and
so impartially rendered to the public during a long series of

years. They heartily welcome amongst them the lady you have selected as your bride, and hope that many years of uninterrupted happiness may be in reserve for you both, and that you may have health and strength to continue your course of public usefulness in this neighbourhood.

Now the people of Clyro went out of their way to show their delight at the birth of his first child. The church bells rang all day – the landlord of the Swan sent the ringers a gallon of ale and Kilvert contributed a second; and a bonfire was lit on the Bron, the hill behind Clyro.

By now the summer season was well under way for the gentlemen and ladies of Hay and Clyro. There were frequent picnics, croquet and archery parties and contests at Pont Vaen, the home of Captain Bridges, Clyro Court (the Baskervilles), Wye Cliff (the Crichtons) and Cae Mawr (the Morrells); and Kilvert was able to take another holiday, this time in Cornwall with his friends the Hockins whom he had known when they lived in Langley Lodge at Langley Burrell. Mr Hockin, who drew part of his income from Railway shares, was a seedsman and nursery gardener. He lived in a house called Tullimaar (still very much as it was when he lived there), and had a son who rowed in the Cambridge boat in 1876. The full record of this holiday is preserved in the Plomer notebook.

Just before he set off for Cornwall, however, a shadow had fallen over Europe. Without any real justification (except perhaps a reasonable resentment against the machinations of Bismarck) France declared war on Germany in mid-July; and the stage was set for the fall of Louis Napoleon and the Second Empire. At first Kilvert's sympathies were all with the Germans, but as the conflict moved towards its astonishing climax his natural sympathy with the afflicted made him more sympathetic towards France. When it was all over he met, on one occasion, a wounded veteran of Sedan, whose story of defeat, destruction and exile moved him very deeply, and one of his favourite books was the story of the sufferings of the Kromer family in *Max Kromer and the Siege of Strasbourg* by Hesba Stretton. On one fatal night when the exiled Empress Eugénie was on her way across the Channel the fate of the Imperial Family and one of Kilvert's dearest friends crossed. It was on the same night when the turret ship *Captain* went down with Captain Cowper Coles and all his crew. Captain Cowper Coles was the brother-in-law of Mrs Venables.

Hay Fair – an occasion Kilvert dreaded as some now dread local football derbies – was held on 15 September, but on this occasion Kilvert was preoccupied with preparations for the second great festival of the Christian year, the Harvest Festival service. As at Easter the Church was elaborately decorated with ferns, moss, hop vines, grapes, apples, pears and an impressive display of wheat ears and wild fruits. The Harvest Festival service must have had exceptional importance in Kilvert's eyes, for in the following year he and the schoolmaster, Mr Evans, wrote an account for the *Hereford Times*. It is perhaps worth quoting as a supplement to Kilvert's diary account, and an example of his 'official' prose.

Harvest Thanksgiving

A harvest thanksgiving festival was held at the parish church of Clyro on Tuesday, the 26th ultimo. The service, which commenced at 11 a.m. was read by the vicar, the Rev R. L. Venables, and the lessons by the Rev R. F. Kilvert, curate of the parish. An able and impressive sermon was delivered to a large congregation by the Rev W. L. Bevan, Vicar of Hay, from a portion of Our Saviour's Sermon on the Mount – St Matthew vi. 26. A collection was made at the end of the service in aid of Home Missions, when the sum of £10 17s. 9d. was contributed. The church was very tastefully and elaborately decorated for the occasion by the ladies of the parish. At the entrance of the porch was the appropriate text taken from the 100th psalm, 'Enter into his gates with thanksgiving'.

On either side of the east window hung a green banner,
bearing a white cross; upon the east window sill lay a bank of
moss, relieved by brilliant flowers, and beneath the sill
extended a text, exquisitely written in letters of white wool upon
a red ground. 'Thou crownest the year with thy goodness'.
Upon the altar stood a sheaf of wheat, barley and oats mixed,
and from the sheaf hung a bunch of purple grapes. A narrow
carpet of moss, brilliant with dahlias, bordered the higher altar
step at the foot of the rails; and the rails were surmounted by a
tastefully mixed ending of flowers, ferns and corn. Rare and
magnificent ferns lined the altar step. The font was dressed in
exquisite taste with moss, white geraniums and white
petunias, while a cross of white flowers floated in the water.

The *widows* (this was the misprint that caused so much fun)
were decorated with Latin and St Andrew's crosses, and
other beautiful devices in moss with dazzling flowers. The
pillars were wreathed with ferns and bunches of scarlet
berries, and the capitals with Spanish chestnuts, blackberries,
elderberries and brightly coloured leaves. Upon the walls
between the windows hung St Andrew's crosses of barley
sheaves, the butts looped across with wild hop sprays. The
chancel walls and the west wall were adorned with texts of
white letters on a scarlet ground, 'Thou visitest the earth and
blesseth it.'; 'O all ye works of the Lord, bless ye the Lord.'.

The reading desk and the pulpit were hung with violet
hangings, ornamented with a deep fringe of oats and flax,
looped up with fruit and embroidered with flowers. Upon the
violet hangings appeared the sacred monogram I H S, and a
sickle and sheaf and anchor, a cross and a heart, representing
faith, hope and charity, worked in corn with great taste and
beautiful effect. The service was short and hearty. The
Harvest Hymns from the Ancient and Modern hymn book,
and a beautiful anthem, composed for the occasion by Mr
Evans, the schoolmaster, was admirably sung by the choir

with great power, sweetness and precision. This is the third Harvest Thanksgiving that has been held in the parish, and in point of choral effect, tasteful decoration and liberal contribution, is the most successful festival which has yet been celebrated.

In October as the year drew to a close Kilvert observed the children, who had been given leave from school, collecting acorns to sell to local farmers for pig food at two to four shillings a bushel; and later the poor of the parish going round the farms for their free milk. By December the Winter diversions were in full swing – concerts and Penny Readings. Men went around cutting mistletoe to sell in the towns, charity was distributed from Cae Mawr, and Kilvert prepared to endure once more the rigours of the hill-winter.

Christmas Eve.
An intense frost in the night . . . When I went to my bath I sat down amongst a shoal of fragments of broken floating ice as sharp as glass. Every-thing was frozen stiff and stark, sponge, brushes and all.   (Vol. 1. 286)

Christmas Day.
I sat down in my bath upon a sheet of thick ice which broke in the middle into large pieces whilst sharp points and jagged edges stuck all round the sides of the tub like chevaux de frise, not particularly comforting to the naked thighs and loins, for the keen ice cut like broken glass.   (Vol. 1. 286)

The Church was decorated, but once more Christmas was celebrated in an offhand way. On Boxing Day the ceremonies were all over and Kilvert left for his winter break. The year ended for him with skating parties at Draycot.

Wednesday 28 December.
An inch of snow fell last night and as we walked to Draycot to skate the snow storm began again. As we passed Langley

Burrell Church we heard the strains of the quadrille band on
the ice at Draycot. The afternoon grew murky and when we
began to skate the air was thick with falling snow. But it soon
stopped and gangs of labourers were at work immediately
sweeping away the new fallen snow . . . The Lancers was
beautifully skated. When it grew dark the ice was lighted with
Chinese lanterns, and the intense glare of blue, green and
crimson lights and magnesium riband made the whole place
as light as day. Then people skated with torches.

(Vol. 1. 287–8)

At Clyro they were once more burning the bushes to celebrate the
New Year, but Kilvert was not there to enjoy the sight. He was in
Langley Burrell Rectory, sitting up with his mother and brother to
see the New Year in, opening the window, as he had learnt to do at
Clyro, to let the year in.

It had been a fateful year – his last full year at Clyro, the year
in which he had started his diary and kept it with exemplary
diligence, and the year in which a new and sinister power had
arisen in Europe.

Interlude   The Funeral of Maria Kilvert

In December 1870 Kilvert travelled from Clyro to Worcester to
attend the funeral of his father's cousin, Maria Kilvert. His father
and mother had already been summoned there by Mr Hooper, Miss
Kilvert's lawyer, and, against the wishes of the servants, who had
clearly been spoilt and were acting in a high-handed manner, were
staying in her house. Since Maria Kilvert had never married,
Robert Kilvert was a probable legatee, although he was afraid that
she might have left the bulk of her property to the Cathedral, of
which she was a great benefactor. She had generously supported
the fund for the restoration of the Cathedral (the results of which
Kilvert noticed as he crossed College Green), having given, in

several instalments, £600 to the main fund and £300 to the Clock
and Bells fund.

Miss Kilvert's life had, of course, been closely linked with the
Cathedral. Her father, Richard Kilvert, had been at one time
chaplain to Bishop Hurd, the friend of George the Third, and had
eventually been given one of the canonries. He died in 1817,
leaving behind him a considerable fortune (he had held several
livings in addition to his canonry) and was buried in the Cathedral
Garth. Miss Kilvert and her mother lived for some time in the
Tything, Worcester, but eventually she bought No. 10 College
Green, and she remained there for the rest of her life.

From what Kilvert heard of her, she was an eccentric figure.

> She used to come rapidly into Church (into the Cathedral) to
> receive the sacrament two or three times a month, but for the
> last three years she had not attended the other services. She
> used to come in a respirator... The House looked melan-
> choly and dreary, like a house of the dead, no movement, the
> blinds never drawn up, no carriage ever stopping at the gate,
> scarcely anyone ever going in or out at the door.
>
> (Vol. 1. 284)

Before arriving in Worcester Kilvert had been warned by his
mother that the provisions of Miss Kilvert's will might contain
some surprises. His father's fears that the chief beneficiary might
be the Cathedral were not wholly justified, but a considerable part
of her fortune had been set aside for charities. The sum of £10,000
was left to the Fund for the Relief of Widows and Orphans of the
Clergy in the Diocese of Worcester; £2,000 went to the Home
Mission Society for the provision of additional curates; another
£2,000 was left to the Society for the Propagation of the Gospel in
Foreign Parts; and there were several legacies to her servants. Mrs
Kilvert was left the deceased's furs and laces (Kilvert also
specifies her rose trees, but they are not mentioned in the actual
will). What remained of the estate was to be divided between three

relatives, one of whom was Robert Kilvert. Nothing was left to the
family of her other cousin, Francis Kilvert of Claverton Lodge,
and this was the omission that infuriated the diarist.

> A most iniquitous will, not a shilling left to any of the Francis
> Kilverts, the old grudge and malice against Uncle Francis
> for writing Bishop Hurd's life ruling strong in death.
> (Vol. 1. 266)

It is not entirely easy to see why Maria Kilvert resented
Francis Kilvert's writing his *Memoirs of the Life and Writings of
Bishop Hurd*, unless she considered that her cousin had poached
upon her father's preserves, and that if anyone had been entitled to
write the life of the Bishop it was his chaplain. Perhaps too she
may have considered that he had improperly used information to
which her father had innocently, and in confidence, afforded him
access. Whatever the reason, the wilful Maria had cut her
scholarly cousin (or rather his heirs, for he had died in 1863)
totally out of her will. Kilvert took his revenge in a very
unchristian manner. After the reading of the will, Mr Hobbs, the
Worcester auctioneer, was sent to weigh the plate.

> When he arrived we discovered that the plate ought not to be
> weighed now. But the scales were solemnly produced to
> weigh a silver seal which Hobbs pronounced worth 2/6 and
> which I immediately stole from the estate in consideration of
> my having come from Clyro to lend my support and
> countenance to the occasion. I should like to have stolen a
> great many things, books, plate etc., but I did not dare.
> (Vol. 1. 274)

The books in question went to her executors, and her prints
and engravings, which Kilvert had previously admired, were left
to the Bishop of Worcester, Bishop Philpott.

Kilvert's account of the days leading up to the funeral, the
bizarre funeral itself, the reading of the will, and the rest of his

experiences in Worcester constitute one of the highlights of the
Diary. Anyone looking for a conventional account of a Victorian
funeral will be surprised at the detachment and irony of Kilvert's
account of the ceremony and the serio-comic events that
characterised it.

> The coffin had been brought downstairs and was waiting in
> the hall covered with the black velvet sweeping soft pall,
> white bordered. Boom went the great bell of the Cathedral.
> Church was over, and someone said they ought to have used
> the tenor bell, but they were using the great bell and no
> mistake. Boom went the bell again. The coffin went out
> immediately and the pall bearers filed out in pairs after it,
> taking their places and each holding his pall tassel on either
> side. Father and I followed as Chief mourners in crape
> scarves and hatbands. All the rest in silk. The bearers had
> been selected not at all with reference to their fitness for the
> task, but with reference to the friendship entertained for them
> by the servants of the house. One of the bearers on the right
> side was very short, so short that he could not support the
> coffin level. The coffin seemed very heavy. As the procession
> moved across College Green to the Cloister arch, the men
> staggered under the weight and the coffin lurched and tilted to
> one side over the short bearer. One very fat man had
> constituted himself chiefest mourner of all and walked next to
> the coffin before my father and myself. The bearers, blinded
> by the sweeping pall, could not see where they were going and
> nearly missed the Cloister arch, but at length we got safe into
> the dark narrow passage and into the Cloisters. The great bell
> boomed high overhead and the deep thrilling vibration hung
> trembling in the air long after the stroke of the bell.
>   So the clergy and the choir came to meet us at the door,
> then turned and moved up the Cathedral nave chanting in
> solemn procession, 'I am the Resurrection and the Life, saith
> the Lord'. But meanwhile there was a dreadful struggle at the

steps leading up from the Cloisters to the door. The bearers
were quite unequal to the task and the coffin seemed
crushingly heavy. There was a stamping and a scuffling, a
mass of struggling men swaying to and fro, pushing and
writhing and wrestling while the coffin sank and rose and sank
again. Once or twice I thought the whole mass of men must
have been down together with the coffin atop of them and
someone killed or maimed at least. But now came the time of
the fat chief mourner. Seizing his opportunity he rushed into
the strife by an opening large and the rescued coffin rose. At
last by a wild effort and a tremendous heave the ponderous
coffin was borne up the steps and through the door into the
Cathedral where the choristers, quite unconscious of the
scene and the fearful struggle going on behind, were singing
up the nave like a company of angels . . .   (Vol. 1. 271–2)

Even after the funeral the brilliance of the writing is sustained
in the reading of the will, the uncanny night at the Star during
which a madwoman en route to an asylum escaped her warder,
and the brief encounter with the tactless barber.

We went back to the Star to pick up our luggage and there we
parted, my Father and Mother going to the Shrub Hill and I to
the Foregate St. Station . . . Then I had my hair cut and I told
the man to cut my beard square. 'Now,' he said, 'this is very
inconsistent. Your features are round and you want your
beard cut square'. 'Still', I said, 'I prefer it'.

(Vol. 1. 275)

As Plomer says in his introduction to Volume One of the Diary, 'If
this account was a chapter in a novel on the same level, that novel
would be a masterpiece'.

The bequest was a godsend to Robert Kilvert (although it was
probably nearer £5,000 than the £7,000 that Kilvert mentions);
but there are no signs that Kilvert himself ever benefited from it.

However when his father died in 1882, his share, as Maria Kilvert had laid down in her will, went to his children or their heirs; and a sixth went to Elizabeth Ann Kilvert, the diarist's widow, a poor consolation for the loss of her husband three years before.

Maria Kilvert was buried, as she had desired, with her parents in the Cloister Garth at Worcester. Some of her engravings have found their way into the vestry of Clyro Church; and her house, virtually unaltered, is now the home of the Dean of Worcester.

Chapter Ten

Return to Wiltshire

Living in Clyro was the central experience of Kilvert's life. Here he found himself living among a happy, imaginative and un-malicious people. He loved his parishioners and was loved by them. Nevertheless he decided, in 1872 to resign his curacy and return to help his father in Langley Burrell. It is difficult to know precisely what prompted him to leave a parish in which he had been so happy. His own comments are guarded and a note of uncharacteristic obstinacy comes into his voice when he speaks of his decision. It may be that he was influenced by the intention of Mr Venables to resign his living and retire to Llysdinam. Perhaps he felt that he could not face the prospect of working under a new régime. He does not seem even willing to be considered as a possible successor to Mr Venables, speaking obscurely about not being able to afford the repairs to the vicarage which he thought necessary.

Perhaps too he was influenced by his father's increasing deafness, but this again cannot have been too decisive an influence, because after only a few years as his father's curate he accepted the living of St Harmon. It may be that the deciding factor was the refusal of Mr Thomas to consider him as an acceptable suitor to Daisy. We do not know for sure why Mr Thomas persisted in his opposition to Kilvert. There is a suggestion that if he had had better expectations he might not have been so brusquely rebuffed; but there are other aspects to the affair. Was Mr Thomas an over-possessive father or did he mistrust Kilvert for some other undivulged reason? Whatever the explanation, Kilvert's last years at Clyro were clouded by his treatment at the hands of Mr Thomas, and it may be that he came to the decision that if he was not to be allowed to marry Daisy, it would be better for him to leave.

Once he had made up his mind to leave Clyro he was adamant. Not even a generous offer from Mr Venables to increase his stipend from £100 to £160 a year could induce him to change his mind. In March 1872 he sent his resignation to Bishop Thirlwall, and on Sept 2nd 1872 he left Clyro for ever, as he said. The most exciting chapter in his life was closed.

In contrast to the Welsh borderland around Hay, the landscape around Langley Burrell is prosperous but undramatic, intensively farmed, a patchwork of fields, crossed by slow-moving streams. It is rich in country houses, ranging from the modest manor houses at Kington Langley where Kilvert's forefathers lived, through the wealthier establishments of the Clutterbucks (Hardenhuish House), the Longs (Draycot House – now demolished), the Awdrys (Notton House), the Meredith Browns (Nonsuch), to the lordly mansions of Lacock Abbey and Bowood. But though this part of Wiltshire was and still is far more prosperous than Radnorshire, there is nothing here to match those great stretches of hill and moorland that Kilvert loved so passionately, no tracts of open land where the wanderer can feel truly free, no flashing waters to take the place of those of the sylvan Wye. The only hills are the Wiltshire Downs, but, whereas half an hour's walk brought Kilvert from his lodgings to the top of Clyro Hill, a dozen miles and more separate the downs from Langley Burrell. It is a land of farms and picturesque villages, and its unchanged churches and abbeys and farms are evidence of centuries of untroubled settlement. Most of its small towns are bigger than Hay or Builth Wells, but a little beyond them lie the

even greater cities and towns that to a Radnorshire man of the
1870's would have loomed as large as metropolises – Bath and
Bristol and Swindon, all linked to London by Brunel's great
railway, not a modest single-track affair like the Hereford – Hay –
and Brecon line, but a major railway link between two of the
greatest cities in England, double-track and broad-gauge, with
scores of passengers and goods trains traversing it day and night.

If Radnorshire is Wordsworthian, Langley Burrell is Tenny-
sonian. But Kilvert is by no means insensitive to its own peculiar
charms, and, contrary to what one might expect, many of his finest
descriptive passages deal with the pastoral landscape of Wiltshire.

As I went through the yards (of the Manor Farm) where the
cows stood and lay about waiting to be milked I thought I had
never watched a more fair pastoral scene, the milkmen
moving to and fro from the dairy with their pails, the young
rooks cawing in the ancient elms, the laughter rippling and
twinkling up the tall poplar spires and the quiet meadows
studded with elms . . .   (Vol. 3. 29)

A dog barked from a distant house, then came the sound of
clapping of gates from the Common Farm, men's voices
talking and girls laughing on the village road, the cows were
snuffing and blowing through the dark in the Rectory
meadows, a soft rush of wings came through the air and a
rustle in a tree, and a screech owl screamed from the elms, the
three tall black poplars rustled softly through the dark like the
flowing of water, the mail cart came rattling down the road and
Steenbrook Hill from Langley Fitzurse and the church clock
at Draycot struck ten, two miles away.   (Vol 3. 52)

Between ten and eleven o'clock tonight I walked alone up and
down the drive under the clear starry sky, waiting for the
moon to rise behind an oak in the eastern sky and to throw the
shadows of the silver weeping birches across the lawn. The

night was cool and fresh and a slight mist began to rise and whiten over the meadows. Then the eastern sky brightened and behind the oak the moon rose over Bencroft Ridge like a great fire. As she cleared the tops of the trees a soft golden beam stole across the turf from between the two birches, discovering and tipping here and there a bunch of white flowers in the beds and soon the shadows of the tree stems lay across the drive and the foliage of the birches was mapped upon the lawn.   (Vol. 3. 57–8)

There is a beauty in the trees peculiar to winter, when their fair delicate slender tracery unveiled by leaves and showing clearly against the sky rises bending with a lofty arch or sweeps gracefully drooping. The crossing and interlacing of the limbs, the smaller boughs and tender twigs make an exquisitely fine network which has something of the severe beauty of sculpture, while the tree in summer in its full pride and splendour and colour of foliage represents the loveliness of painting . . . Opposite our South terrace windows towers a glorious ash, ivy-muffled to its throat, while its boughs sweeping gracefully fall in drooping showers all about it like a woman's hair softly flowing, or the arched cascade of water falling from the jet of a fountain.   (Vol. 3. 120–1)

This evening Teddy left us to return to London. A sharp frost, the stars brilliant and the roads glassed with ice. I went with him to the white gate where we parted and I turned off across the dark icy fields towards the village to try to read Hannah Williams to sleep . . . The light shone through the night from the girl's sick chamber window, the night was still, an owl hooted out of the South, and the mighty hunter Orion with his glittering sword silently over strode the earth.

(Vol. 3. 126)

These passages all occur in the first two hundred pages of the third volume of the diary; and many more of equal power and beauty could be added to them.

It would be wrong to say that Kilvert was unhappy in Wiltshire. It was his native land and the countryside around Chippenham was indissolubly linked with a happy boyhood. If there was no Mrs Dew and no George Stovin Venables to talk with him about Wordsworth, Mr Daniell of Kington Langley was something of an authority on George Herbert and there was Bemerton itself to visit. He was within easy reach of his friends at Oxford where Mayhew could introduce him to stimulating acquaintances. His father's friend the Rev Henry Moule, himself a man of rare talents, could show him Dorchester and introduce him to William Barnes, the great Dorset poet; and his friend the Rev A. H. Morres of Britford was well-informed on church architecture. There were many pleasures and compensations for Kilvert in Langley Burrell. Yet one feels that a certain rapture has faded from his life; and he is aware of certain social tensions that did not exist in Clyro.

The Social Scene

There was near Langley Burrell one estate far larger and richer than anything in Radnorshire; and perhaps the great estate of Bowood and its owner, the Marquis of Lansdowne may be taken to represent the pinnacle of the Chippenham social pyramid. The Marquis, however, remains to Kilvert a shadowy figure, well beyond the social range of a poor curate. Kilvert walks in the grounds, and the family of his friend Andrew Pope, the Money Kyrles, are entertained there, but Kilvert never sets foot in the great house.

Sir John Awdry of Notton House was a more approachable figure, and Kilvert went to several parties there. Perhaps he was all the more acceptable at Notton House because many of the Awdry's were in Holy Orders, and at least three of them – Charles

(Christian) Awdry, Vicar of Seagry, Charles (Pagan) Awdry, Rector of Draycot St James, and Edward Awdry, Vicar of Kington St Michael, were close friends of the Kilverts.

Besides Sir John there were, living in the neighbourhood, Lord and Lady Cowley*, Lady Dangan, Lady Royston and Lady Feodora Wellesley, all of Draycot House; but in the smaller world of Langley Burrell the identity of the most important and influential man was in no doubt.

One of the Langley Burrell schoolchildren, being asked 'Who made the world?' replied, 'Mr Ashe'.

Robert Martin Ashe owned most of the property in the parish; he and his family lived in the manor house, Langley House; most of the villagers were his employees; and he was the patron of the living.

He emerges from the Diary as an unsympathetic figure, dictatorial, intolerant, doctrinaire. He is said to have demolished many cottages that stood too close to Langley House, and certainly made sure that Robert Kilvert and his family were not too close to him by demolishing the old Rectory that stood near the church (and therefore the Manor House) and establishing them in a new Rectory a quarter of a mile away. He tried to dictate to the Rector, seeking to control the kind of service to be held in the church. He criticised Francis Kilvert for holding mixed lectures in the evenings. He took it upon himself to dismiss the leading choir singer. He opposed the introduction into the church of any heating apparatus, and a harmonium to take the place of the leading singer (both of which had been accepted long ago at Clyro); and he hectored the village schoolmistress, condemning the children to work in conditions that remind one of those the Brontë children had to endure at Cowan Bridge.

But the picture presented by Kilvert may be a biassed one. (Lucy Ashe was once heard to say that she thought that Kilvert had been very hard on her father, and this, coming from a daughter

*Lord Cowley was English Ambassador in Paris from 1851 – 1867.

FK-H

who did not always see eye to eye with him, is worth considering.)*
It is no great wonder that the relations between the Kilverts and
the Ashes were at times strained. Mr and Mrs Robert Kilvert were
the poor relations of the Squire, and in addition the Rector was in a
sense his protégé – and, worse still, his successor. It is easy to
overlook the fact that for many years the Squire had helped his
father, who was both Squire and Parson, to run the parish. It is
probably safe to say that most of the clerical duties were
performed by the son. Again, though he overrode the schoolmistress, he was literally right when he said that the school was
his. The Ashes owned the school, which contained not only a large
schoolroom but also living accommodation for the schoolmaster
or mistress, and the building remained in their hands till only
recently. Before 1870 they may even have paid the salary of the
teacher. In addition, although Squire Ashe demolished some
cottages he was known to be a provider of excellent estate houses;
and it cannot be said that he was unremittingly hostile to the
Kilverts. It was he, after all, who had brought Robert Kilvert from
the poorly-endowed parish of Hardenhuish, and although there is
no record of his having visited the Rector he entertained the family
fairly frequently in Langley House.

   A corrective to Kilvert's uncomplimentary portrait of Mr
Ashe is supplied by *The Wiltshire Independent* for 19 March

---

*Was Kilvert – or his editor – unfair to Squire Ashe? Mr Ashe, according to the
testimony of one of his grandsons, was of Puritan stock, and retained to the end of
his life a certain Calvinism of outlook (he did not approve, for instance of his
daughter's taking part in mixed dancing or even mixed tennis); but he never forfeited
the affection of his family; and contemporary newspaper reports and obituary
notices suggest that there were other more estimable sides to his character than the
Diary reveals. He was a generous landlord. He was genuinely interested in Art, and
was a liberal patron of local exhibitions. He was even more deeply interested in
Literature, and had attended Coleridge's lectures at Highgate, an experience which
must have intrigued Kilvert who enjoyed so much G. S. Venables's reminiscences
of Wordsworth. Can it be that out of desire to make a more effective contrast
between Kilvert's good nature and the Squire's puritanism Plomer excluded
passages that brought out the less repressive sides to Mr Ashe's nature?

1863 in its report of the celebration at Langley Burrell of the marriage of Edward, Prince of Wales.

The village of Langley Burrell held a prominent place in the loyal demonstrations of Tuesday last, and the memorable 10th of March was celebrated with the greatest enthusiasm. By the kind liberality of the Rev R. M. Ashe, and the contributions of the principle *(sic)* inhabitants of the place, a sufficient sum was raised to give a good dinner to every person in the parish. For this purpose a large tent was erected, capable of holding between two and three hundred persons. It was beautifully and tastefully decorated with flags and evergreens, and lighted up in the evening with coloured lamps. At an early hour on Tuesday morning the church bells took the lead of the adjoining parishes, in giving out a merry peal, announcing the universal holiday. At 12 o'clock the schoolchildren assembled at the schoolhouse where Mrs Ashe presented each child with a rosette, a threepenny bun, an orange, gingerbread nuts and a sixpence. At half-past two, all the inhabitants of the parish assembled in front of Mr Ashe's house, where each person was presented with a favour. A procession was then formed, the band leading the way; then followed two carts with two fine young oak trees, 20 feet in height; these were succeeded by four labourers carrying spades gaily decorated with ribbons; then came Mr and Mrs Ashe and the Misses Ashe, also carrying spades; after which all the parishioners followed, two and two, making a goodly procession, till the spot was reached which had been selected for the ceremony of planting the trees . . . At four o'clock a most abundant dinner was spread in the tent, consisting of roast beef, plum pudding, bread, cheese and beer. The provisions were excellent of their kind and excellently cooked, for no pains or trouble were spared on the occasion. The young ladies of the parish volunteered their services as waitresses, and we need scarcely say that their

duties, which were admirably performed, gave great satisfaction. After dinner Mr Ashe made an excellent and
appropriate speech, and then the following toasts were given
and most enthusiastically received and cheered, *The Queen,
The Prince and Princess, Mr and Mrs Ashe, The Rector, The
Farmers and Church-wardens of Langley, the Labourers of
Langley* etc. The evening was enlivened by a good display of
fireworks, the conclusion of which was the signal for
dispersion. *God Save the Queen* was again sung with much
feeling, and after some hearty cheers the party separated in
perfect good order. The festivities of the evening did not
however end here, for Mr Ashe, with his accustomed
liberality and kindness, had provided an entertainment for
those who had, on this and many previous days, spent so
much time and labour in making such excellent arrangements
for the enjoyment of their poorer neighbours. A most
substantial and elegant supper was spread at Langley House,
to which all the farmers, with their wives and families,
amounting to more than 40 in number, were invited. After
supper the health of the Prince and Princess with other toasts
was drunk in champagne, and the party separated, very
grateful to their kind landlord and entertainer for the
thoroughly liberal and hospitable manner in which they had
been received.

This report shows Mr Ashe at his best; but from time to time
both Rector and Curate found his manner provocative; and the
difference between his high-handedness and the tolerance of
Squire Baskerville of Clyro made the diarist fume with indignation. On Wednesday 15 July 1874 (Vol. 3. 52) he confesses that
he has been wishing he 'could go away to some other place where
people were not so unreasonable and hard to please'.

Perhaps Squire Ashe's behaviour was not merely personal,
for in a way Langley Burrell was a less liberal place than Clyro.
Lord Cowley of Draycot makes a brief appearance in the Diary,

but, in spite of his long career as a diplomat (he was for some time the English Ambassador to the court of Louis Napoleon) on that occasion he strikes one as a pettish and silly man; and the Longs who held Draycot before him had produced a notoriously foolish heiress who seems to have been looked upon as fair prey for the worst elements of the Chippenham community. They rioted at her coming-of-age celebrations, and their behaviour was in strong contrast to the courteous ways of the Radnorshire and Hereford-shire poor who put up ceremonial arches for both Henry Dew and Francis Kilvert when they returned with their brides.

The intolerance and ungenerosity of the upper classes trouble Kilvert and stir in him the beginnings of an indignation and a censoriousness that he never felt in Wales. For the first time he begins to be troubled by the inequalities of the society in which he lives.

> As I walked before breakfast across the Common between the 'Lady's Gates' I met Herriman the porter returning through the lovely morning from his night work at the station, and I could not help thinking of the difference between my lot and his, and how much more enjoyment I have in my life than he has in his. How differently we both spent last night, but how much better he spent it than I did. He was doing extra duty that a fellow porter may enjoy a holiday, while I – Surely there will be a compensation made for these things hereafter if not here.   (Vol. 2. 374)

He records too a comment the like of which he never heard in Clyro

> John Couzens foretells a revolution in English society. 'I know it's coming', he said, 'as sure as this prong is in my hand'.   (Vol. 2. 374)

He himself is on one occasion brought to the verge of positive protest.

Miss Mewburn went to the Agricultural Meeting at the Town Hall at Chippenham yesterday and came away furious at the patronising manner in which the labourers were preached at and the way in which the poor old people were kept standing during the whole meeting, while *their betters*(?) were comfortably seated in cushioned chairs. She wished she could have lifted up her voice and borne witness against the proceedings. And I very heartily sympathise with her feelings.   (Vol. 2. 287–8)

But if the upper classes are guilty of intolerance and folly, the poor are also not without their faults.

This evening I had to reprove the boys of the night school for their bad conduct and language last Tuesday.
                                                        (Vol. 3. 140)

This evening I gave the seventeenth lecture and spoke about the plagues of Egypt. Owing to bad behaviour at the lower end of the room I changed the position of the benches and my table and chair and sat half way down the room to keep the boys in order, and before I began my lecture I spoke very seriously and sternly about the bad conduct which had been going on and told the people why I had made the change. The new arrangement answered admirably and enabled me to keep the boys in order, but they were angry because they could not carry on their usual games.
                                                        (Vol. 3. 239)

We get the impression that this unrest was not confined to the boys.

Went to Peckingell. Found Austin a little better. He and his wife told me things about the parish which drew aside the veil from my eyes and showed me in what an atmosphere and abyss of wickedness we are living in and how little many

people are to be trusted whom we thought respectable and
good.   (Vol. 2. 444)

Nor was it restricted to Langley Burrell. Mr Daniell, the
incumbent of Kington Langley, is as disappointed in his parishioners.

These revelations make Kilvert unusually intolerant and
censorious. He loses his temper and beats the family pony and dog
with unusual severity. He is indignant against the striking South
Wales miners, and in a letter to Marion Vaughan which I have
been allowed to read but not to publish he speaks with
uncharacteristic violence about them (he even suggests that
coolies be imported from China to take their places) and
recommends that the captain of the Spanish steamer *Murillo* who
ran down the English *Northfleet* (see Vol. 2. 316–7) should be
hanged at his own yard arm.

There had been bad behaviour, sin and violence in Clyro, but
the abiding impression left upon Kilvert and upon us is of
remarkable social harmony. In Wiltshire, however, it seems as if
an old order is beginning to disintegrate; and perhaps the coming
disintegration can best be exemplified by reference to what
happened in Mr Ashe's own family.

Robert Martin Ashe's only son and heir died young, but he
had in addition three daughters, Lucy, Emily (commonly known
as Siddie), and Thersie. Of these it was Lucy who reacted most
strongly against the principles and beliefs of her father. Strongly
prompted by those misgivings which Kilvert voiced so timidly, she
left Langley Burrell about the turn of the century, and went to see
for herself the conditions of the poor in the East End of London.
She intended a brief visit, but stayed there for more than forty
years.

Leonard Styles, a Southwark Councillor, has left a moving
account of her. He said that shortly after she came to Southwark
she was so deeply stirred by what she saw that she said, 'I throw in
my lot with yours. I stay among you'.

She joined our early band of Socialist workers and worked eighteen hours a day unpaid. There was no holding such an enthusiast. She became alderman, freeman, first chairman of our maternity and child-welfare committee. She cared for ex-servicemen, for tuberculosis sufferers, became everybody's adviser.

Somewhat shabbily dressed, and always wearing the satchel that earned her the name of 'the Lady with the Satchel', she was a fount of free advice, charity – everything that could save homes, get pensions, and right the 10,000 wrongs that existed in those days.

It was the Blitz that drove her from Southwark. It was popularly believed that she had died in the raids, and a block of new flats built after the war was named after her. But Leonard Styles and others knew that ill-health had driven her back to Langley Burrell, where she lived for the rest of her life. In her will, ironically, the daughter of the almost feudal Squire of Langley Burrell left £150 to the Southwark Labour Party.

Affairs of the Heart

Perhaps the most important and significant events of the years Kilvert spent at Langley Burrell after his return from Clyro were the two love affairs in which he found himself involved – with Katharine Heanley (whom he generally refers to as Kathleen Mavourneen), and Ettie Meredith Brown; and since these two affairs overlap in some degree, they are here taken together.

Kilvert first met his Kathleen Mavourneen when he went to Findon near Worthing to attend, as groomsman, the wedding of Adelaide Cholmeley, the granddaughter of his father's eldest brother, Francis Kilvert of Claverton Lodge. Katharine was the bridesmaid assigned to him, and impulsively as always, he fell in love with her on the spot, and, greatly to the amusement of some of the boys who knew of his weakness, began to give her the sentimental nickname that appears not only in the diary but in a poem that he wrote about the wedding

The Wedding at Findon, August 11th 1874

The Bride

Dear child, may thy path be a pathway of flowers
    As those cherubs sweet-smiling strew blooms on the way,
And though life be a April of Sunshine and Showers,
    May the storms pass as lightly as they drifted today,

And after each storm may swift sunshine returning
    Light heaven and earth with its radiance again,
As we saw from the hillside on this happy morning
    The landscape more brilliant after the rain –

The prayers from our full house this morn that ascended
    Shall draw their blest answers in happiness down
Upon thee around whom angels viewless descended
    And placed on thy pure brow love's radiant crown.

The Priest

How majestic his reverend beard was descending
    As sweeping in silver it flowed on his breast,
How stately he rose when the banquet was ending
    And silence was held for the Patriarch Priest.

He looked round the table from brother to brother,
    And bright in his keen eye there trembled a tear,
As in accents subdued he spake yet of another
    A spirit beloved who was lovingly near.

The Bridesmaids

Sweet Findon, adieu! – but of ne'er from my spirit
    Shall this day's sunny memories fading depart,
A remembrance that far distant days shall inherit,
    An amaranth flower cherished close to my heart –

Sweet Kathleen Mavourneen, the flower of the lowland,
  Abloom with the breath of the easterly sea,
The pride of Kesteven, the glory of Holland,
  How dear the remembrance I cherish of thee.

Ye bright sister blossoms through wind and rough weather,
  Mid snows of December and roses of June,
May your heart's tendrils ever twine fonder together,
  Sweet Kathleen Mavourneen and Eileen Aroon.

Ye graces the train of the bridal adorning,
  Your names fondly twining inwoven shall be.
Here's a toast to the beauty of Annie Mavourneen,
  And Jessie Acuthla and Ella Ma Chree.

(The bride was Adelaide or Addie Cholmeley, and the groom
Charles Heanley. The priest was the Rev R. Cholmeley, the uncle
of the bride. Kathleen Mavourneen was Katharine Heanley; Eileen
Aroon, Ellen Heanley; Annie Mavourneen, probably Annie
Heanley; Jessie Acuthla, Jessie Russell; and Ella Ma Chree,
Eleonora Cholmeley, the bride's sister.)
    Katharine was actually a distant relation of Kilvert's, for she
was also cousin to the bride. She was the daughter of Marshall
Heanley, a farmer of some substance and standing at Croft near
Skegness, a lonely and remote part of Lincolnshire, perhaps too
remote for Katharine's enquiring and earnest mind. Kilvert
mentions 'how deeply she regretted the enforced apparent idleness
of her life.' Mrs E. Farmery, who has patiently uncovered the
details of Katharine's brief life, says that Katharine's cousin,
Charlotte Heanley, wrote a story called *Bytoft Grange*, one of four
that make up a book called *The Toll of the Marshes* (1929). The
author confided to one of Mrs Farmery's informants that many
aspects of her story were based on life at Croft Grange, the home of
Marshall Heanley, and that Katharine was the model for her
heroine, Janet.

In the story Janet falls in love with her local vicar, and suffers a severe disappointment when he marries someone else. Her will to live is undermined and she dies young. In actuality, Katharine seems to have had an affection for the Rev Evelyn John Monson, the Vicar of Croft, but she survived her disappointment when he married someone else, and was sufficiently attracted to Kilvert to make him and Adelaide believe that she cared for him. In October 1874 he spent a day with her at Bristol, at the home of Adelaide Heanley's mother, sightseeing and talking about Tennyson and Chatterton.

From then on they kept in touch, mainly through Adelaide Cholmeley; and although there is a suggestion that Mrs Heanley did not care for her daughter's writing to a single man, Katharine may not have given in completely, and communication between her and Kilvert (largely through Adelaide Cholmeley) was kept up till midsummer 1875.

But in September 1875 a new figure enters Kilvert's life. His references to Katharine had been growing cooler and cooler. They had a great deal in common – mainly literary and religious interests, but though he mentions on one occasion 'her capital letters, so hearty and affectionate, like herself', the only specimen he quotes does not make exciting reading and sounds excessively pious to modern ears. Was he beginning to find Katharine and her Mutual Improvement Society too intense and humourless for him? And though local people spoke of her as being considered very beautiful in her twenties, and a local connoisseur of beauty called 'The Rose of the Marsh', Kilvert's comments on her appearance in a photograph he received of her are a little reserved.

I thought the face a little stern at first, but when I had looked at it a little time, I saw the kindly loving light come into the eyes and the firm sweet mouth began to smile.

(Vol. 3. 217)

But Ettie was a different story and new note enters his prose as soon as he begins to speak of her.

Etty Meredith Brown is one of the most striking-looking and handsomest girls I have seen for a long time. She was admirably dressed in light grey with a closely fitting crimson body which set off her exquisite figure and suited to perfection her dark hair and eyes and her dark Spanish brunette complexion with its rich glow of health which gave her cheeks the dusky bloom and flush of a ripe pomegranate. But the greatest triumph was her hat, broad and picturesque, carelessly twined with flowers and set jauntily on one side of her pretty dark head, while round her shapely slender throat she wore a rich gold chain necklace with broad gold links; and from beneath the shadow of the picturesque hat the beautiful dark face and the dark wild fine eyes looked with a true gypsy beauty.   (Vol. 3. 229)

This rhapsodic passage was written less than a month after receiving Katharine's photograph.

Ettie or Etty (Kilvert uses both spellings and her full Christian name was Henrietta Maria) was the daughter of a rather enigmatic landowner, the Rev Meredith Brown, who had been the Vicar of Chittoe, near Trowbridge, from 1846 to 1855. It is not known for certain why he resigned his living, but it seems as if he experienced some kind of revulsion against the Church of England, for in the closing sections of his will he expresses the strange desire that the words 'The Reverend' should not be applied to him, but that the word 'Esquire' should be used. He was clearly a man of some substance. One of his houses, Nonsuch, which Kilvert implies was Etty's home though for the greater part of the seventies it was apparently let, is a handsome Cotswold stone manor house, architecturally and socially a cut above Croft Grange where Katharine Heanley's father lived; and June Badeni, in her *Wiltshire Forefathers* implies that the family also owned Hullavington House, which was used as a hunting lodge, and Stanton Park. When Kilvert first meets Ettie the Meredith Browns are living either at Nonsuch or Hullavington, but less than a year later we find them 'breaking up their establishment' and moving first to London for the season, and then to their other house, the Pines, Bournemouth*. When Kilvert goes back to see Nonsuch it is to visit the tenant, Mr Gwatkin, another friend of the Kilverts.

Ettie was the most striking of all the young women with whom Kilvert fell in love. A photograph which turned up some time ago in Norway, in an album in the possession of one of her descendants, General Rolstad, reveals her as the handsome girl of Kilvert's description, with a determined profile and a fine head and shoulders. The affair between her and Kilvert seems to have developed rapidly. He is not drawn to her till early September 1875, but early in the following year we find him writing about 'the happy days of last summer before our trouble came and our separation'. (Vol. 2. 244).

We shall unfortunately never know the details of Kilvert's ill-fated courtship of Ettie, because that part of the Diary that covers the period from 9 Sept 1875 to 1 March 1876 was removed, apparently by Mrs Kilvert, shortly after the death of her husband; but, piecing together what evidence we have it looks as if objections were raised against Kilvert as soon as it became clear that he and Ettie were fond of each other. At that time the Meredith Browns were living at Bournemouth, but Kilvert had clearly been in the habit of meeting Ettie there, and in secret. He speaks of the 'wild sad trysts in the snow and under the pine trees, among the sandhills of the East Cliffe and in Boscombe Chine'. (Vol. 3. 244).

He saw her for the last time on 7 December 1875, but over the winter they must have kept up a clandestine correspondence which was discovered early in April 1876 for it was on 20 April 1876 that Kilvert received a letter from Ettie's mother forbidding him to have any further communication 'by letter or poetry' with her daughter.

*He also owned a house in Westbourne Terrace, Bournemouth.

Why was it that the humiliations Kilvert had suffered at the hand of Mr Thomas were repeated by the Meredith Browns? Kilvert was still of course a poorly paid curate, and for anyone who needed a reminder of the miseries of the life of a poor curate Anthony Trollope had painted a salutary picture in his portrayal of the miseries that had to be endured by Mr Crawley and his wife in *'The Last Chronicles of Barset'*. It is possible too that Mr Meredith Brown was by this time deeply prejudiced against the church and churchmen, but the late Col Awdry once mentioned to me in a private conversation that the Meredith Browns had not cared for Kilvert's known association with other girls, and of this something more may be said later.

Whatever the explanation, Kilvert seems to have accepted his dismissal at the hands of the Meredith Browns as uncomplainingly as he had accepted the decision of Mr Thomas. However, if it was his lack of prospects that Ettie's parents objected to, that barrier might easily have been removed, for only four days after receiving the letter from Mrs Meredith Brown, he was offered the living of St Harmon; but although some time later he accepts the living he does not seem to have mentioned that to Ettie or her parents.

On Sunday 14 May he delivered twice (on the same day) a highly personal and probably very indiscreet sermon on his parting from Ettie. The contents (the fullest indication in the Diary of the kind of sermon Kilvert preached) can be found on pp. 298–9 of Volume 3. Another lengthy entry for 19 June is full of passionate longing for Ettie.

> In a sweet daydream I seemed to see the white frocks of three girls sitting on the grass . . . and among them shone like stars the one pair of dark eyes that were once all the world to me.

The day after this passionate entry he met Katharine Heanley again. His reference to her is cool (unlike the ecstatic passage the next day on the beauty of Gertrude Headley, the daughter of the

Rector of Hardenhuish). It comes as a surprise therefore to learn that less than a year later he was again at Croft, presumably visiting Katharine. Mrs E. Farmery has discovered a note in the Croft School log referring to a visit he and the vicar made to the school on May 8 1877. About the same time he gave Katharine a poem, a paraphrase of the 23rd Psalm, which she forwarded to the editor of *Sunday at Home,* who published it. By this time Kilvert had been Vicar of St Harmon for some time, and any objections that might have been held against him on the score of poverty and poor prospects would by that time have been invalid. However, according to Mrs Farmery, by the beginning of 1879 the affair between him and Katharine was at an end. A note by Dr K. Heanley stated that Katharine was engaged to Kilvert but she broke it off. Certainly Kilvert's last reference to her (19 Dec. 1878) is almost off-hand, totally without that warmth that colours almost every mention of Ettie.

By this time another woman had entered Kilvert's life. It is generally understood that some time after Kilvert had received that dismissive letter from Mrs Meredith Brown, his friend Mayhew invited him to join a party planning to visit Paris. Mayhew, who was a good friend, hoped that the holiday might help him to get over his disappointment over Ettie. In all probability the visit took place in the summer of 1876. Among the party was Miss Elizabeth Rowland, of Holly Bank, Wootton near Woodstock; but we shall never know the full story of the relationship between Miss Rowland and Kilvert, because at this point we come up against another break in the Diary. Presumably the missing entries (June 1876 to Dec. 1877) were removed by Miss Rowland when she became Mrs Kilvert. She was a modest and retiring person, and seems to have made sure that all the diary entries referring to herself were suppressed; but it may be that the missing pages also contained indiscreet entries relating to Katharine.

The rest of Katharine's story is a sad one; and perhaps it will be in place to tell it here although her life extended for some years beyond that of the diarist. Mrs Farmery has revealed that she recovered sufficiently from the termination of her affair with Kilvert to take up a new career as a nurse. But fate continued to deal out to her intolerable blows. Shortly after Kilvert's last diary entry, Adelaide, the bride of the Findon wedding, died of scarlet fever. By 1882, three years after the death of Kilvert, Katharine's mother had suffered a stroke and was paralyzed. Her father began to suffer from delusions and in a fit of depression hanged himself. It was Katharine herself who found him dead by his own hand. Again she recovered and took up duty as Matron of the Boston Cottage hospital. But in 1890 she had to undergo a serious operation. In the following year she had influenza, and in September of the same year she too was found dead. At the inquest she was cleared of the charge of suicide, but the circumstances in which she died were very unusual, and the possibility that she took her own life cannot wholly be dismissed.

Poor Kathleen Mavourneen – for her was reserved the saddest death of all the girls whom Kilvert loved.

In the meanwhile Kilvert had left Langley Burrell and gone to take up his first living – at St Harmon.

Clyro c. 1870. On the right the inn, once the Swan, now the Baskerville Arms. On the left Ashbrook House, Kilvert's lodgings.

Clyro Church as it is now

The Rev. R. L. Venables, Vicar of Clyro.

Mrs Venables, the Vicar's second wife.

Clyro. Nineteenth century village scene.

Clyro Court, home of Squire Baskerville.

Cottages in Clyro.

Hay in the nineteenth century

Rev. R. L. Bevan, Vicar of Hay.

Hay Station as it was in Kilvert's time.

Wye Valley near Clyro.

H A M

Carte

de

Danse

Clifford

Priory

April 5th.

1872.

Dances.	Engagements.
1. Quadrille	1 Alice Bevan
2. Valse	2
3. Lancers	3 Lizzie Bevan
4. Galop	4
5. Quadrille	5 Miss F. Thomas
6. Valse	6
7. Galop	7
8. Lancers	8 Miss Wyatt
9. Valse	9
10. Quadrille	10 Fanny Bevan
11. Galop	11
12. Lancers	12 Miss J. Dew
13. Valse	13
14. Quadrille	14 Miss Dew
15. Galop	15
16. Lancers	16 Mary Oliver
17. Valse	17
18. Sir Roger de Coverley	18 Miss E. Alley

Kilvert's dance card for Clifford Priory Ball.
(original belongs to Jonathan Cape Ltd.)

Tuesday. 19. July. 1870

Left Chippenham 11.35. by the down
mail with a tourist ticket for Truro.
The carriage full. hot to Bristol
which relieved us of some passengers.
From Weston Junction we caught a
glimpse of Weston & the dim sea.
Then the tall white Burnham lighthouse
among the pine trees. Windmills whirling.
I looked out for the white sails of
boats passing up & down the Parret
& from Bridgewater & Burnham. but
there were none to be seen. Perhaps
the tide was out. Sometimes these
white sails may be seen sliding
along above the flat green meadows
& the river being invisible. They
look as if the boats were sailing
on land.
The best things worth looking at were
the long blue waving ranges of the
Mendips & Quantocks. Like a ridge of
the line. And at Taunton the

A page of Kilvert's Diary (Durham University Library)

Home of the Solitary.

Tulliemaar, the home of the Hockins where Kilvert stayed on his holiday in Cornwall.

Langley Burrell School.

Ettie Meredith Brown in 1875.

School Feast near Bredwardin. 1869.

Mrs Francis Kilvert (née Rowland)

Bredwardine Vicarage, Kilvert's first and only home.
(Copyright. Guardian)

Chapter Eleven

St Harmon

St Harmon, or St Harmon's, as it is more commonly called, is a lonely parish about four miles north of Rhayader. It could be reached by the Mid Wales Railway from Llechryd or Builth Road Junction near Builth, and there was a halt only a few hundred yards from the church; but, compared with Clyro and Langley Burrell, it was remote, scattered and indifferently provided for.

The church too was neglected. Kilvert's disappointment when he first saw it has already been noted, but he was very much a man of his time as far as churches were concerned, and anything that smacked of the classical (and therefore pagan) style of the eighteenth century was anathema to him. (It is interesting that the architecture of Hardenhuish Church which the twentieth century finds charming and elegant is never commented on by him). According to Mr Jonathan Pugh, in an article in the *Transactions of the Radnorshire Society*, St Harmon had many quaint and interesting features – a fine ceiling, a double decker pulpit and box pews, each with the name of a local farm painted on its door. When the church was built many of the farmers bought a seat, that is, they gave to the building-fund a sum sufficient to cover the cost of a pew. When the donor died or moved the pew became the property of his successor. This practice was also followed at Disserth, where the names of the pew-holders can still be seen painted or carved on the pew doors. But to Kilvert it was a church

FK—I

belonging to the 'dark ages of fifty years ago' (presumably the pre-Pugin years) and he disliked it.

The year that Kilvert spent at St Harmon is one of the lost years of his life. That part of the Diary which deals with his ministry there (there is no reason to assume that he discontinued his diary for a year) is missing. William Plomer, who had access to the full diary, remarked in his introduction to the third volume which came out in 1940, on the gap between June 1876 and December 1877. All we know about Kilvert's life at St Harmon we must piece together from two sources other than the few prospective and retrospective notes to be found in the Diary itself. These entries refer to the two visits he paid to the parish before deciding to accept the living; and a return visit on 26 April 1878, when he travelled from Bredwardine to officiate at the marriage of two of his old parishioners.

The first other source is the diary left by Mr Hastings Smith, eldest son of Kilvert's sister, Thersie, who married the Rev W. R. Smith, Rector of Monnington. He visited the Rhayader and St Harmon district, several years before the publication of the Diary, to collect what information he could about his uncle, and his notes were passed on by his sister, Essex Smith, later Mrs Essex Hope, to the Kilvert Society. They can be found in *Looking Backwards* published by the Kilvert Society in 1969. In his notes he tells how an old man recalled Kilvert.

> Yes, I do mind Mr Kilbert... He lived at the Old Bank House just across the street... Mr Kilbert never lived at St Harmon's. Lived at Rhayader, he did, and went up to his parish by train on weekdays. Sundays he walked up or was druv. Most always he walked. Bad weather or snowy roads, I have druv Mr Kilbert myself to St Harmon's of a Sunday. And I mind driving a young lady with him. No he wasn't a married gentleman. Ah, a real nice gentleman was Mr Kilbert. Quiet gentleman. Great black beard. Like a foreign gentleman, as my father used to say. No we don't see such gentlemen

nowadays. Not such beards. 'E was a great walker, sir. Many a pair of boots my father soled for Mr Kilbert...

In all probability the young woman with Kilvert was Miss Elizabeth Rowland whom he was eventually to marry; but there is always the possibility that it was Katharine Heanley, with whom, although he had only recently been compelled to cease communication with Ettie Meredith Brown, he was still on friendly terms.

One of the objects of Hastings Smith's search was the missing section of the Diary, but he failed to find it, and his comments lend support to the family belief that all the St Harmon entries were destroyed by Kilvert's widow after his death.

The Kilvert Society has published a second document relating to Kilvert's incumbency at St Harmon. It was sent to Mr Wright, the first president of the Society by Mr Jonathan Pugh of Berth, St Harmon's, the same Mr Pugh who contributed the description of the old church to the Radnorshire Society.

It should be remembered that Kilvert was probably known to less than half of the inhabitants of the parish, for the majority of the parishioners in 1876–7 were Non-conformists. It seems that Kilvert was less intolerant in religious matters than some pages in his diary suggest. He was certainly friendly with some of the St Harmon Free Churchmen.

For example my parents and grand-parents were prominent Methodists and Kilvert was very friendly with them. He called at Berth many times during the winter of 1876–7, visiting my grandmother during her last illness. He read the Committal at her funeral in January 1877. I gather from his diary that Kilvert was intimate with another prominent Non-conformist of the parish, for his entry for 26 April 1878 reads 'I went on to Cymyrychen and had a glass of wine with Mr Edward Meredith, the young squire'. This 'young squire' was a very prominent Presbyterian. I remember listening to a conversation between this gentleman and my father in the village of Pantydwr on Polling Day of the 1910 General Election. The Disestablishment controversy was raging then, and among other things they discussed the Vicars of St Harmon that they had known, and my father mentioned Kilvert thus – 'But Mr Kilvert was different, he was a friendly likeable man' – a statement with which the 'squire' warmly agreed. This seems to prove that St Harmon's Free Churchmen had a good opinion of Kilvert.

There are several mysteries surrounding Kilvert's stay at St Harmon. It is not known for sure, for instance, why he did not occupy the vicarage. Maybe the tenant who already occupied it was unwilling to vacate it; but one cannot imagine that Kilvert was happy with an arrangement that compelled him to live four miles from his parish and to travel to his services by train or carriage.

The second mystery relates to Kilvert's knowledge of the Welsh language. St Harmon was known as a largely Welsh-speaking parish; and there is a document (which may not be wholly reliable) that states that two sermons were preached every Sunday at St Harmon in Welsh.

We know that Kilvert was interested in the Welsh language; but he was only too well aware of the embarrassment that could be caused by a preacher with an imperfect command of the language (see his note on the callow curate of Llangorse who made such a fool of himself in the pulpit) and there are no solid indications in the Diary that Kilvert had anything more than an academic interest in Welsh. Perhaps the note in the National Library document was out of date.

The third puzzle relates to his sudden decision to leave St Harmon after a ministry of less than a year. He himself tells us that no one took his place, and he must have known that he was leaving the parish without a pastor. Perhaps in this case the deciding factor was the young lady whom the old man in Hastings Smith's memoir remembered.

It is sometimes assumed that Kilvert's marriage was a hastily arranged affair, but Mrs Essex Hope, his niece, was of the opinion that he had met Miss Rowland during the holiday in Paris which had been arranged by some of his friends to help him to recover from his disappointment at losing Ettie. The visit to Paris is generally thought to have taken place some time after Kilvert received Ettie's last letter (April 1876); and the second gap in the Diary begins after the entry for 27 June of that year. One of Mrs Kilvert's nieces, writing to the first President of the Kilvert Society, said she could remember her aunt saying that she meant to give the Diary to Kilvert's younger nephew, Percy, but that she intended first of all to remove all the parts that referred to herself. It is to be presumed then that the first reference to Elizabeth Rowland occurs almost immediately after the diary ends on 27 June 1876 (the earlier gap has already been accounted for) and that there was a period of at least three years between the first meeting between her and Kilvert and their marriage on 20 August 1879.

Perhaps Kilvert left St Harmon because he felt that it was asking too much of his intended wife to bring her to so remote a parish where there was not even a proper home for her. The Rowland family was by no means without standing, and had its own coat of arms. Mr Rowland lived in a modern and spacious house a mile or so out of Wootton-by-Woodstock. It may well be that Kilvert felt that he could not fix the date of his marriage until he had something better than his lodgings in Rhayader to offer his well-born wife. When in 1877 he was offered the living at Bredwardine and the comfortable and picturesque vicarage that went with it, he must have felt that it would be folly to turn down the offer.

Chapter Twelve

Bredwardine

In Sept 1877 the Rev J. Houseman, Vicar of Bredwardine, and Rector of Brobury, died, probably of a heart attack (the Diary says 'apoplexy'); and Kilvert was offered the living, probably through the good offices of Miss Julia Louisa Newton (referred to in the Diary, after the fashion of the time, as Miss Newton). Miss Newton, who lived with her sister Catherine in The Cottage (now known as Bredwardine Hall) was the daughter of the Rev J. D. H. Newton, in whose gift the living was. On his death the right to present passed to his trustees, of whom Miss Newton was almost certainly one. It was intended that her nephew, Arthur Newton, would eventually be preferred to the living; and until he came of age Mr Houseman held it; but for some reason or other (did he die or simply decline to enter into Holy Orders?) he never came into the living; and it went to Kilvert. Miss Newton had known Kilvert when he was at Clyro. On 30 August 1872 he went to a picnic in her garden and from there with her to another picnic in Moccas Park, the home of Sir George Cornewall (see Vol. 2. 252–3).

Miss Newton was apparently fond of Kilvert. She allowed him the use of her carriage on many occasions to go to Moorfields or Kinnersley stations. She did the same favours to his sisters. She took him in her brougham to the Re-dedication Service at Mansel Gamage. She entertained him at parties (presumably rather sober ones) at The Cottage (he and his sister spent his last Christmas

Day there); and it was she who arranged for the erection of the floral arches that greeted him on his return from his honeymoon. In return he did her little good turns, such as bringing home from Gower a big bottle of sea-water for her aquarium. It is probable that Miss Newton felt more than friendship for her vicar, although she was nearly thirty years his senior. Who was it that arranged both she and her sister – Julia in 1886, Catherine in 1896 – should be buried on either side of him, to the exclusion of poor Mrs Kilvert, who had to be accommodated in a grave in the new churchyard on the other side of the road?

Bredwardine in the 1870's was a scattered, not heavily populated village, although the number of inhabitants was four times what it is now. The nucleus was formed by the Red Lion, the Cottage, the Church, the school and the vicarage. Most of the villagers lived in a curiously detached community known as Crafta Webb, in a huddle of cottages (now almost entirely vanished) that straggled up the hill behind the Red Lion. It was a big enough community to have its own grocer and shoemaker, and it was in one of the houses there that Kilvert gave his 'cottage lectures'. Kilvert says little about the church at Bredwardine, but it is more interesting and attractive than the heavily-restored church at Clyro; and his second church at Brobury, which has now been converted into a dwelling, was a humble picturesquely-sited mediaeval church. Kilvert assessed the two livings at £412 gross, £375 net (the *Hereford Times* gave lower figures), and with the Rectory of Brobury went 20 acres of glebe land which Kilvert leased out. He later supplemented his income by taking, for private tuition, at £80 a year, Sam Cowper Coles, son of the widowed Mrs Cowper Coles whose husband went down in the *Captain*. For the first time in his life Kilvert had a home of his own. The romantic and beautifully sited vicarage had been built in 1805 on the site of an older building, and was even roomier in his day than it is now. Since Kilvert's death the servants' quarters have been pulled down. He kept no less than four servants

(probably in addition to Mrs Price, his housekeeper) and he was
now in a position to furnish his home fairly lavishly. Most of his
new furniture came from Shoolbred's, a very fashionable shop in
Tottenham Court Road, though some items were bought in Bath.

Unfortunately we have no record of Kilvert's first impressions of Bredwardine, for the pages relating to his early days
there have been removed from the Diary. He does not seem to
have been as unreservedly happy as at Clyro. He was warned by
Mrs William Newton that 'it had become a difficult parish to
manage and one that would require much care and judgment and
tact'. It was true that many undesirables had come to live in the
village to qualify for benefits under the famous Jarvis Charity of
which Kilvert was one of the Trustees; that there was a certain
amount of drunkenness and disorderliness, and dissatisfaction
with the administration of the Charity; and that the children were
as backward and ill-informed as at Clyro; but he had friends near
at hand – his old friends at Hay, his new ones at Moccas, and his
sister and brother-in-law within walking distance at Monnington.
He was now able to look forward to married life, and he seems to
have settled down to fulfil his pastoral duties gladly and
conscientiously, visisting regularly, teaching in the village school
and giving his cottage lectures. He renews his ties with old friends,
the Bevans and the Popes (now living at Blakemere), and he sees
more of Sir George Cornewall and his curate, Mr Bishop. There
are no girls in his new parish such as Gypsy Lizzie and Florence
Hill to bewitch him, but the place of Hannah Whitney, with whom
he had loved to talk at Clyro, was taken by an even more
remarkable old woman, Priscilla Price, who cared, with exemplary devotion and understanding, for her handicapped stepdaughter – Kilvert's accounts of his visits to them are among the
most poignant in the Diary – and who entranced him with her
memories of George the Fourth and his unfortunate Queen, of the
famous Coronation in 1830 and of the first steam-boat seen on the
Thames, and her anecdotes about the old man at the Weston (a

cottage on the outskirts of Bredwardine) who claimed to have seen the oxen kneeling and weeping on Old Christmas Day at Staunton-on-Wye.

But perhaps the most dominant theme of this last section of the Diary is Kilvert's failing health. When we first meet him in 1870 he is a high spirited, vigorous and apparently healthy young man;* but by 1878 he had aged greatly and his constitution seems undermined. Early in 1878 we find him suffering from a cold, a troublesome cough and a sore throat which persists into February. Then in March when he is on holiday at Langley Burrell he falls ill with congestion of the lungs and is away from his parish from 4 to 23 March. He recovers with the better weather in April but later in the month is troubled with neuralgia and cannot sleep for pain.

Some time before this he had begun to have a presentiment that he would not live long, a feeling that he expressed in an ominous entry for 9 March 1878

> I went out for a little while on the terrace this morning and walked up and down on the sunny side of the house. After how many illnesses such as this have I taken my first convalescent walk on the sunny terrace and always at this time of year when the honeysuckle leaves were shooting green and the apricot blossoms were dawning and the daffodils in blow. But some day will come the last illness from which there will be no convalescence...
>
> (Vol. 3. 379)

This presentiment he also seems to have voiced in a poem found in his blotter after his death, and published by the Kilvert

---

*A recently discovered photograph of the guests at the wedding of Dora Kilvert and James Pitcairn at Langley Burrell shows what a fine figure of a man Kilvert was. Unfortunately the photograph is not available for general reproduction but it can be seen in Kenneth Clew's *Kilvert's Langley Burrell*, a parish guide available from Mr J. Payne, Old Brewery House, Langley Burrell, Chippenham, Wilts.

Society in *Kilvert and the Wordsworth Circle*. The poem is as
follows

> Who but knows the Royal Walk that broadens to the Chieftains
>   Hall,
> Reddened fir stems, breadth of green sward, where the barred
>   shadows fall.
> Down the solemn avenue, the green ride stately, passeth on
> To the gray and ancient Court and Owen's grave at Monnington,
>
> Thro' the fair stems, looking southward, stands a house with
>   garden fair,
> Lawn and orchards, where the birch weeps clouded by her
>   dusky hair,
> And the rising wind that passes, sighing on from tree to tree,
> Makes a solemn murmur like the roaring of the distant sea.
>
> Here within this Temple stately let us muse and walk awhile
> Up the range of columns vast that guard this grand Cathedral
>   aisle,
> Till amid the woodland gleaming there below us deep and far,
> We may see Moccas meads and winds of Wye from Brobury
>   Scar,
> And beyond the river reaches pleasant uplands, sloping green
> Firry clumps and nestled homesteads mark the hills of
>   Bredwardine.
>
> Low beneath that ivied tower, and deep within that cedar shade-
> By the rippling of the stream a nightingale his nest has made;
> And the people stand and listen to the voice so sweet and clear,
> As he sits within the sunset, singing by the broad water,
> Singing to the wandering river of the way which he has come;
> Singing of the love still faithful in his dear Avonian home,
> Singing, as the wind breathes softly from the West sweet
>   mem'ries still,
> Of the green vale of Saint Harmon and the slopes of Clyro Hill.

Let him sing a little while in peace, his songs will soon be o'er,
And the singer spread his wings with joy to find a happier shore,
When the nest is found forsaken, some will smile, and some
    will sigh
For the voice which now no longer mingles with the murmuring
    Wye.

                                        27 May 1879. Eos Gwy.

A fascinating analysis of this poem was made some time ago by Miss Lois Lang-Sims in a letter to the Kilvert Society.

'The poem is one of great interest, as providing us with the only *(sic)* indication we have that Kilvert had a strong premonition of his own death. This seems strange and pathetic, considering that he was by this time engaged to be married (or at least on the verge of becoming so), and that his death, when it came, appears to have been sudden and unexpected. The Editor of the publication in which the poem appears says that no doubt Kilvert meant the title *Nydd Eos* to be the Welsh for *Nest of the Nightingale*, although it ought to have been *Nyth yr Eos*; and William Plomer says that it contains references to the grave of Owen Glendower, to a weeping birch and to a nightingale.

We should first note that the poem is signed Eos Gwy (the Nightingale of the Wye). This gently romantic pseudonym was frequently used by Kilvert in signing his poems, as may be seen from the *Collected Verse*. So the poem is not really about a nightingale; it is about Kilvert himself.

The poem has a date later than that on which the Diary ends. By this time Kilvert must have known his future wife, probably he was already engaged . . . The fourth verse of the poem introduces the nightingale (Kilvert) who has made his nest in what, if we read the poem with attention, is clearly the village of Bredwardine.

The people stand and listen to the voice so sweet and clear. 'Stand and listen' suggests a sermon; however we need not suppose that Kilvert is praising his own voice. He was a very fine prose writer but not a good poet, and his metaphors are often mixed. The nightingale sings 'of the way which he has come' The last three lines of the verse, detailing that way ('from his dear Avonian home' via Clyro and St Harmon to Bredwardine) so obviously refer to Kilvert that we can no longer be in doubt. How moving then are the last four lines, written by a young man who had only four months to live, but could not have known this by any rational inference. Had a doctor warned him that he had some serious condition he would surely not have become engaged and married so soon.

There is some evidence in the Diary that Kilvert was what we loosely call 'psychic'. His senses were abnormally acute. He was occasionally overwhelmed by psychic invasions. Evidently he suffered from a severe form of migraine, a common accompaniment of psychic sensitivity. Whatever the explanation, there can be no doubt that he had a momentary premonition of his own death.'

A year before he had written the poem he had been offered the Chaplaincy at Cannes, and was advised by his doctor Mr Giles of Staunton to accept the offer.

> I asked him if I ought to go to Cannes on account of my health. He said, 'Go, by all means. It is the very place. It may prolong your life by some years'.   (Vol. 3. 398)

However, he declined the offer. Instead, late in July he went on holiday with his sister Thersie and her family to Aberystwyth, and in October to see his friends the Westhorps at Ilston in Gower. But by November he is having trouble (again) with his eyes, and is suffering from an unpleasant attack of what he calls 'emerods'. In December he has a sore throat. Later in the month he has a severe nose bleed, followed by a second on Christmas Eve; and on 7 Jan 1879 he is indoors with a severe headache. From here onwards the entries in the Diary grow more perfunctory, briefer and less enthusiastic. Then, as suddenly as the journal had begun, it ends. The last entry is on 13 March 1879.*

We cannot, of course, be sure that it did end there. By now Kilvert was preparing for his marriage later in the year, and it may be that the later sections of the Diary contained many references to his future wife that she preferred to destroy.

We hear no more of Kilvert till we listen to him replying to his well-wishers on his wedding-day. For the rest of his brief life we have to rely on the evidence of outsiders.

---

*In a recently discovered letter to Mrs Venables written just after Kilvert's death, Frances, his sister, mentions his feeling that he would not live long, and implies that a disappointment in love brought on a breakdown from which he never wholly recovered. 'It is terrible to think of the sad cause of (the breaking up of his health). I hope she will never know what she did (humanly speaking).' It was, in the opinion of Frances, from this point that he lost his will to live. The 'she' of the letter could have been Katharine Heanley, who is known to have jilted him, but was more probably Mrs Meredith Brown. I am indebted to Lady Delia Dillwyn-Venables-Llewelyn for the privilege of reading this letter, which came to me via the Archdeacon of Brecon and the Rev. D. N. Lockwood.

Chapter Thirteen
The Last Five Weeks

On 20 August 1879 Francis Kilvert and Elizabeth Anne Rowland were married at Wootton-by-Woodstock, not far from Blenheim Palace.

Miss Rowland was the daughter of John Rowland Esq of Hollybank, Wootton, a substantial house about a mile from the main village. Mr Rowland had first taken up a course of medical studies at St Thomas's and Guy's Hospital, London, but had given them up to become a landowner in Oxfordshire, having probably inherited some property there. He had seven children, four daughters and three sons. At least one son went into the Church, becoming the Vicar of Puriton, Bridgwater, Somerset. Kilvert and Miss Rowland had known each other for three years, having met during the tour of Paris mentioned in an earlier chapter.

The known photograph of Elizabeth Rowland suggests that she was rather plain-featured and less personable than Daisy or Ettie; but what we know of her leads us to believe that she was a modest unassuming young woman, tall, with a genial expression, charitable and unselfish, fond of gardening, animals and birds. She ran a Sunday Bible school for the older girls of Wootton, and constantly visited the sick and poor. She seems to have been a ready-made choice for a conscientious clergyman.

Unfortunately we know little about the wedding. The newspaper report is disappointingly brief, far less detailed than, for example, the account of the wedding of Kilvert's sister, Dora. Miss M. A. Rowland, Elizabeth's niece, said that the day of the wedding was wet, and the rain spoilt the arches of evergreen that had been put up by the people of the village. After the wedding the pair set off on their honeymoon which was to be spent on a tour of York, Durham and Edinburgh.

They returned from their honeymoon on 1 September, and first went to Wootton to see Mrs Kilvert's parents. They stayed there for a few days, but by Sunday 7 September they were at Langley Burrell. According to the local newspaper, the *Chippenham News* of 27 September 1879, Kilvert conducted a service there for his father. He took another, a Missionary Service, during the week following, probably on Wednesday, 10 September. They did not reach Bredwardine till Saturday 13 September. The following account of their reception there is taken from the *Hereford Times* (20 September 1879)

RETURN OF THE REV R. F. KILVERT AND MRS KILVERT TO BREDWARDINE

The inhabitants of Bredwardine and Brobury on Saturday last welcomed to their home their Vicar and his wife. Though rain fell all day, and drenched those who were not encased in material weatherproof, it did not seem to quench the warmth with which the poorer people of Bredwardine brought flowers, made nosegays, decorated poles, and hung upon them inscriptions of "WELCOME HOME". This was the work which they were all either engaged in, or looking on at, criticising, or approving. And all this work of hearty love was being carried out because they had been informed that they might expect their pastor – The Rev R. F. Kilvert, home that evening after his marriage which, we are informed, took place on 20th August, at Wootton, Woodstock; a place of

some historical interest, as being the place where Fair
Rosamond is said to have been poisoned by Queen Eleanor.

The first archway was erected at "Church Turn", the
entrance of the drive from the high road to the church, and
was a mass of flowers and evergreens – very well disposed,
with a motto, "Welcome Home", the painting being the work
of a local genius, and the decoration that of Miss Annie Lewis
of Clappits Cottage. The second was at the entrance to the
Vicarage, and was erected under the instruction of the Misses
Newton, of The Cottage. The words "Welcome Home" were
enclosed on either side with the initials of the happy pair, all
being well wrought in ornamental letters, and the whole
structure decorated with bannerets. Over the entrance to the
Vicarage were various artistic designs and mottos, the whole
being made to look as attractive and festive as possible. But
conspicuous amongst the many and various demonstrations
of hearty welcome in the parish of Brobury were two
triumphal arches of elegant design, bearing appropriate
mottos for the occasion. The first stood opposite the
residence of Mr Williams of Brobury Court and bespoke
much taste, pains, and care; the second near the residence of
Mr James Powell, coal agent etc, which was quite a model of
good taste, the construction being solely due to the exertions
and industry of Miss J. Powell.

Under the giant limbs of a very fine cedar, extended over
the gravelled entrance to the Vicarage, tables covered with
snow-white cloths, were spread for a tea, with which the
school children were first regaled, then the old women, and
lastly sober-minded men, such as chose to partake of it. The
tables were tended by the Rev W. R. and Mrs Smith of
Monnington; the Rev Rhys Bishop of Moccas; the Rev and
Mrs A. Pope of Blakemere; Miss Palmer of Eardisley; Miss
Stokes of the Old Court; the Misses Davies, The Weston;
Miss A. Davies; Miss Sarah and Miss Eliza Abberley; Mr

and Miss Bates; Mr Algernon Bates; Miss Wilmot; Mrs
Price; Miss Jones, Crafty Webb; Mrs B. Hammond and Miss
F. Smith. Everything was done to make their guests happy.
The Misses Newton came down in their carriage and
remained during the evening.

A committee of farmers (with Mr Stokes of the Old Court
as secretary) had collected certain moneys, with which they
had purchased half a dozen silver dessert forks and half a
dozen dessert spoons with a caddy spoon. These gentlemen
were Mr F. Evans, The Weston; Mr Davies, Fine Street; Mr
Jones, Cross-End; Mr Griffiths, The Pentre; and Mr Jenkins.

Mr George Price, the coachman to the Misses Newton
of The Cottage, had set to work among the cottagers, and soon
got enough money to purchase a very handsome and massive
pair of solid silver gravy spoons.

About five o'clock a band of labourers crossed the
picturesque old bridge at Bredwardine and went towards
Brobury, where they shortly met the carriage containing the
happy pair, who were received with the waving of banners
and hearty shouts. After re-crossing the river to the
Bredwardine side, the horses were taken from the carriage,
ropes attached thereto, and amidst hearty cheering the happy
pair were safely drawn to the Vicarage door.

Mr Frank Evans, of The Weston, the churchwarden,
came forward (with the presentation from the tenant farmers
and others) and read the following address, which had been
printed in gold, within a floriated border:– TO THE REV R.
F. KILVERT MA, VICAR OF BREDWARDINE, ON
HIS MARRIAGE. Reverend Sir – It is with heartfelt
pleasure and gratitude that we, tenant farmers, occupiers, and
others of the Parish of Bredwardine, assemble on this
occasion to offer you our sincere congratulations on the
auspicious event of your marriage. As the pastor of this
important parish, we have had ample means for judging your

personal worth and Christian character, and rejoice to have
this opportunity of testifying to our appreciation of and
admiration of the same by asking you to accept from us a
small token of our esteem, which we are sure you will value,
not for its intrinsic value, which is small, but as an outcome of
generous wishes on our part for your future happiness and
that of your amiable partner, throughout life. In making to
you and Mrs Kilvert this small presentation of domestic
articles – the use of which will no doubt frequently recall to
you this important and pleasurable epoch along the road of
life – allow us to express a hope that God will bless you and
yours with a prolonged and useful existence, health, and
happiness, and crown your Christian labours with their well
deserved reward. September 13th 1879.

The Rev Gentleman said:— Mr Evans, dear friends and
neighbours; believe me this most kind reception given to me
and my dear wife on our return home has taken me by the
greatest surprise, for I really did not expect anything of the
kind. Much less did I expect such a mark of respect from the
dear little children, who have so kindly flocked around us; and
which I assure you I feel most deeply. Dear friends and
neighbours, you have not only congratulated me on my return
home, but also my dear wife, who is a stranger to you, but who
feels the compliment as deeply as I do, and who, although you
do not know her yet, you will in time learn to love as much as
you have today shown you do me. Believe me, words fail to
express half the gratification I feel at receiving this very
handsome present at your hands. Mr Evans has spoken of the
testimonial as but a slight mark of your esteem, but I assure
you I think its intrinsic value very considerable, and I do
value these articles most highly as a token of your regard for
me. I do hope that I have the real affection of my parishioners,
and that the kind way in which you have come forward today
to welcome me and my dear wife will draw us nearer together

in heart and mind then ever (cheers). It has ever been, believe me, the aspiration of my heart that we may live in confidence, and love one another as members of one great Christian family, and I sincerely trust (as I said before) that this kind of reception will draw us nearer together and cement our hearts in Christian unity. (Applause). Although the rain has made the weather most unfavourable for out-of-door enjoyments, I hope you will regard this as a bright and happy day, when you welcomed your clergyman after his marriage (applause). Once more accept my thanks for your great kindness today and ever since I have been here, and I assure you I have learned to love you more and more since I came here. I wish I could entertain you all better than I am able to on this occasion, but I hope you will be as comfortable as possible under the circumstances. I thank you again for your beautiful presents, which I shall value as some of the greatest treasures I possess. (Applause.)

Mr Bates then stepped forward (with a pair of heavy silver tablespoons in a morocco case), and read the following address from the cottagers, also printed in gold and bordered:–

To the Rev R. F. Kilvert, MA, Vicar of Bredwardine on his marriage. Rev Sir, – We your Parishioners, being Cottagers and others of Bredwardine are delighted to have this occasion of acknowledging the kind and Christian interest you have since your residence in this parish, ever manifested for our social and spiritual welfare, and pray God that your recent union to the amiable lady of your choice may increase your happiness an hundredfold. As a slight token of the esteem and respect which we have always held you and which we sincerely hope may never be interrupted, but year by year be strengthened and matured – we beg of you and Mrs Kilvert to accept this small presentation of silver from us, both as a memento of the love we bear you and yours, and of the

auspicious event which has brought us together.
September 13th, 1879.

After a pause, the Rev Gentleman replied:– My dear friends,
I am more than deeply touched and moved by your kind
reception, love and affection towards me. Much as I am taken
by surprise by the last beautiful gift from my friends who
occupy good positions in life, this touches me more deeply
still, because I know it is given from slender incomes and
pockets not very deep. This beautiful gift has, I believe, been
prompted by a love which I feel I very little deserve (No, No).
But if God spares me I will try to deserve your affection and
show you how deeply grateful I am for these kind efforts
today (applause). I hope, notwithstanding that the rain –
coming down as it does – has made it unpleasant, that you
have still sunshine in your hearts, and that you will try to
make yourselves as happy as you possibly can. To you I also
say that I am sorry that I cannot entertain so large a company
any better than I have done, but hope you will be content with
what I can do. I hope you may all live long, and that the longer
we live the more closely we may be drawn together in the
bonds of Christian love. God bless you all, I can say no more.
(Applause.)

Some individual presentations were subsequently
made – one a silver pickle spoon in a morocco case, from Mrs
Matthews and family; a preserve spoon in a morocco case
from Mrs Preen, Rectory Farm; several articles of handsome
cut glass, including water jug and tumblers, from the school
children; similar articles from Mr and Mrs Broome-Giles of
Staunton-on-Wye, a pair of antique terra-cotta vases, a
bookstand and a Dresden card plate, from Miss Westhorpe,
etc. etc. – not included in the "wedding presents" which were
very numerous.

Then there was an unpretentious note handed in which

ran thus:– 'The servants of the Cottage, Bredwardine, beg the
Rev R.F. Kilvert to accept this small present as a token of
respect for him on the occasion of his marriage. They all join
in one wish – that he may be blessed with every happiness
this world can afford – signed H. Parry; J. Jones; T. Price;
G. Price; and T. Pearce'. It was a Harlequin set of dessert china.

Unfortunately, although Kilvert had returned from his
honeymoon in high spirits ('he was so pleased and ready to
describe all he saw, especially in Holyrood'), the day after his
arrival at Bredwardine he complained of feeling unwell. His
father, who must have come from Langley Burrell with his son and
daughter-in-law, took the morning service at Bredwardine, and
Andrew Pope, now Vicar of Blakemere, took the evening service
at Brobury. We have unfortunately no record of Kilvert's
condition during the following week, but it seems that he took none
of the services on 21 September. No one however seems to have
been seriously concerned about his condition until, either late in
the afternoon of Monday or early on Tuesday, (the newspaper
reports are contradictory) his illness took a serious turn, and on
Tuesday, 23 September he died. It is generally assumed that the
appendicitis with which he had been struck turned to peritonitis,
for which in the 1870's there was no known cure. On Saturday 27
September he was buried in the grave he had chosen for himself
some time before. His death occurred less than five weeks after his
wedding and exactly a fortnight after his return from his
honeymoon. The local newspapers carried two accounts of his
death and funeral (*Hereford Times* and *Hereford Journal*). Only
the *Hereford Times* account is given here.

FROM THE "HEREFORD TIMES"
of 4th OCTOBER 1879 (Page 6, Column 2)

A more lamentable occurrence it has not fallen to our lot
for some time to chronicle than the death of Rev R. F. Kilvert,
which took place on Tuesday, the 23rd of September, after a

very short illness, and not five weeks after his wedding day. It was only on the 20th September that the *Hereford Times* contained an interesting report of the return home of Mr Kilvert and of the joyous welcome given to, and the numerous presents received by them, the inhabitants from the highest to the lowest all striving to show their affection and esteem. The news of his illness and decease coming so quickly afterwards struck with surprise and sharp sorrow many residents not only in the neighbourhood of Bredwardine, where he was so beloved, but throughout the county. Deep sympathy is but natural under such sad circumstances. Truly "one touch of nature makes the whole world kin".

The reverend gentleman graduated at Wadham College, Oxford, and eventually became curate at Clyro, under the Rev R. Lister Venables, (the respected chairman of Radnorshire quarter sessions) and was so for a time with his father in Wiltshire. The Bishop of St David's afterwards presented him with the living of St Harmon's, Nr Rhayader, and in 1877 he succeeded in the livings of Bredwardine and Brobury, the Rev Mr Houseman, who died on a visit in Northamptonshire in a somewhat similar and distressing manner to that of his successor, after six year's pastorate. The Vicarage of Bredwardine is united with the Rectory of Brobury, and Mr Kilvert entered into his duties with great earnestness. He conducted two services at Bredwardine church, and one at Brobury church, every Sabbath, and sermons, the composition of which showed him to be a scholar of no mean ability, had the merit of touching and impressing the hearts of his hearers. Being the son of a clergyman, too, his duties came to him naturally. In a quiet gentlemanly way, he did his work thoroughly, and won the love of his parishioners. It was well-known throughout the county that he was doing a great and good work in the parishes of which he was a pastor. The poor have lost an

unostentatious friend, a comforter, and a benefactor, and
some of the most genuine sorrow was manifested by them
when his death became known. On the 20th August, the Rev
gentleman was married at Wootton, Woodstock, Oxfordshire,
to a daughter of Mr J. Rowland, of that place. He returned
with her to Bredwardine on 13th September, and although
rain fell all day and drenched those who were not encased in
material waterproof, the inhabitants of Bredwardine and
Brobury heartily engaged in erecting beautiful arches,
decorated poles, and handsome mottos with the initials of the
happy pair and inscriptions expressing a welcome that it
seems to make more appalling by the rude contrast of this
untimely and sorrowful event. But it will serve to show what a
good man has been, as it were, snatched away when life was
most useful. The words of the burial service, "He cometh up
and is cut down like a flower", never fell on the ear more
forcibly. But to refer to the rejoicings on the 13th, which must
be so fresh in the minds of our readers as to be scarcely
necessary to recall. The presents by the farmers, the
cottagers, the servants of different houses, the school-
labourers, taking the places of the horses, and drawing home
the carriage of the happy pair who were met with waving
banners and hearty shouts, and the reading of addresses and
the affectionate replies.

On the next day (Sunday) he conducted divine service at
both churches and was in his usual health; but in the evening
he complained of being unwell, and was obliged to desist from
his duty. His father officiated at Bredwardine church on the
next Sunday, and the Rev Andrew Pope officiated at
Brobury, and the patient remarked to the latter that he
thought he should be able to get about in a few days. On
Tuesday morning his illness took a dangerous turn, and
Mr P. B. Giles, surgeon, of Staunton-on-Wye, who had been in
attendance on him, considered it necessary to telegraph for

Dr Debenham, of Presteigne, who arrived as soon as possible, but the patient was dying, and twenty minutes after the doctor's arrival he died. The event caused consternation throughout the neighbourhood, and nearly all work was brought to a standstill.

The funeral, a simple unostentatious one, in accordance with the wishes of the deceased, took place on Saturday last. The weather was exceedingly gloomy and depressing, enough to intensify the melancholy that filled the hearts of the mourners, for hardly a breath of air stirred, and the sun strove unsuccessfully to break through the sombre, misty clouds, from which showers occasionally descended, the sunlight appearing to be reflected glaringly above the clouds, and the lovely wooded scenery of the Wye looked wet and dull. As the vicarage is only about sixty yards from Bredwardine church, the sad proceedings did not occupy a very long time. Eight bearers, parishioners, carried the coffin which was covered with a dark velvet pall and the mourners who followed were:– Mrs R. F. Kilvert, and her father Mr J. Rowland; deceased four sisters – Mrs W. R. Smith, Monnington; Mrs. Wyndowe, London; Miss F. Kilvert and Mrs Pitcairn, London (who had formerly resided at Bredwardine Vicarage); Rev R. Kilvert, Rector of Langley Burrell, Wiltshire (father of deceased), Mr E. N. Kilvert (brother); and the Rev W. R. Smith of Monnington. The funeral party also included Mr F. Evans, Weston; and Mr T. Stokes, Old Court (churchwardens); Mr Bates, Bredwardine; and other farmers; six Foresters, members of Moccas "Court" (of which deceased was an honorary member) wearing their scarves; and a large number of cottagers and schoolchildren. The cortege slowly passed under the giant limbs of a fine old cedar tree, near where a fortnight before the Vicar had watched with pleasure the children and the old people regaled with tea, and it was met in the church gate by the deceased's venerable friend, the Rev R. L. Venables, who read very touchingly the first part of the Burial Service of the Church. In the sacred edifice the procession was met by the Rev Sir G. H. Cornewall, Bt, of Moccas (lord of the manor), the Rev Henry Dew, Rector of Whitney; Rev C. S. Palmer, Vicar of Eardisley; Rev F. Andrews, Rector of Kinnersley; etc. The psalms and the Lesson having been read – there was no singing – the cortege moved to the grave which is situated on the north side of the church, next to the road. Some beautiful wreaths were placed on the coffin by the mourners, and the school children afterwards put a number of wreaths and other floral emblems into the grave. The coffin was of oak, with white metal furniture, the inscription being – "Robert Francis Kilvert, died Sept. 23rd 1879, aged 38", Mr A. C. Edwards, High Town, Hereford, was the undertaker.

Kilvert's father does not seem to have recovered completely from the shock of his son's death. He must have resigned his living immediately afterwards, for on 10 Dec 1879, the Rev J. J. Daniell, who had been at one time Vicar of Kington Langley, was presented to the living of Langley Burrell in his place.

For Mrs Kilvert there was no alternative but to return to Wootton, but before she left she wrote the following letter to the children of Bredwardine School. It was copied from the school log-book by Miss Lang-Sims, and it was prefaced by these few lines.

The Teachers and School Children of the School received the following letter from Mrs Kilvert before she left the parish and all without exception desired that it should be transcribed into the Log Book.

The Vicarage, Bredwardine
Oct 27th 1879

My Dear Children,

Mrs Bates has told me of your kind and loving subscription for giving a present to your late Vicar Mr

Kilvert. I want to thank you and anyone else who may have joined in it *very very* heartily. It would have given my beloved husband the greatest of pleasure to have a remembrance from you. He would have valued it so much as a proof of your love to him. The kind and hearty welcome from you and all in the parish at out homecoming touched us both very much. I shall carry away with me very kind thoughts of the people in Herefordshire. Your beautiful present I shall always look upon as one of my treasures. It will often remind me of you all, and the kindness and consideration shown to me during these weeks of overwhelming and inexpressible sorrow. Again thanking you all *very very* much.

Believe me always
Your affectionate friend
Elizabeth Kilvert

Mrs Kilvert survived her husband for over 30 years. She died at Redlands, Hartfield Road, Eastbourne in 1911, and her body was brought to Bredwardine to be buried, unfortunately at a distance from her husband.

Some time after Kilvert's death the following poem appeared in the *Hereford Times.*

The Reverend R. F. Kilvert, obit., September 23rd 1879

In Memoriam

The Marriage feast was spread. With his fair young wife,
The joyous Bridegroom sat, while each young heart
Look'd forward to a long and happy life,
To which true love should fragrant bloom impart.

The Marriage feast was spread in Courts above.
'Let him I love be with Me where I am!'
The Saviour said. He pass'd from human love
To share the Marriage Supper of the Lamb!

October 1st, 1879   SYMPATHY
The author of the poem has not been identified.

Chapter Fourteen

Unpublished Diary entries

The Surviving Notebooks – The Plomer Notebook

This notebook, given to William Plomer by Mrs Essex Hope, and
now in the care of the Keeper of Rare Books in the Durham
University Library (Plomer was given an Honorary Doctorate by
Durham) deals with Kilvert's holiday in Cornwall in the summer
of 1870. It is a surprisingly stout little book, and can hardly be
described (as it has been) as an exercise book. Inside the box
which contains it is pasted the following note in Plomer's hand.

> MS. notebook of the Diary of the Revd Francis Kilvert for
> 1870 (19 July – 6 Aug) describing his visit to the Hockins in
> Cornwall. This was presented to W.P. on 16 Sept 1958 by
> Mrs Essex Hope (née Smith), Kilvert's niece. She said she
> had destroyed all but three of the original notebooks. This one
> was given to me. Another was given some time ago to Jeremy
> Sandford, living in Herefordshire. I don't know what
> happened to the third.
>
> W.P. 17.9.58

On the inside of the cover Kilvert had written

> Journal No. 4.
> 1870
> from July 19th to August 6th
> Cornwall

The notebook, which was made up originally of approximately 180 pages (all ruled) is bound with a fairly stiff embossed cover which gives the appearance of a hymn-book rather than an exercise book. For some reason the last three sheets of the book have been cut out, but it seems unlikely that anything was ever written on them. The numbering of the used pages (done presumably by Kilvert) ends at 179. Except (possibly) for one or two words all the entries are in Kilvert's hand, which is regular, fairly small, but not always legible.

One surprising feature of the notebook is that the entries are not continuous. Several parts of pages, and, on occasions, whole pages are left blank. The explanation of these gaps may be the unusual circumstances in which this journal was written. Kilvert was on holiday and a guest. He may have felt that to spend too much time on a private activity was discourteous (there are no signs that his hosts knew what he was doing). He may have hoped that later, when he was back in his own rooms in Ashbrook he might be able to fill in the blank spaces he had left. The general impression is that Kilvert had to write in shorter spasms than usual. Even then the journal is a very full one. In the space of three weeks he filled nearly 180 pages, writing on an average about two hundred words a page.

There are signs that at some stage he went over what he had written. Where he was unsure of the name of a person or a place he left a blank space. *Lander*, for instance, the famous African traveller, has been entered in pencil some time after the original entry had been made. On another occasion the name *Port Curnow* has been inserted. Perhaps when he talked over the day's doings

with Mr and Mrs Hockin he was reminded of names he had not
caught clearly, and entered them later; but although the journal is a
holiday journal, it is still a very private document. There is, for
instance, a warmth in his reference to Mrs Hockin (of whom he
clearly grew very fond) which both she and her husband might
have found embarrassing.

Apart from these slight alterations and additions there are no
signs of major revisions. One has the impression that this is a fair
copy. Apart from what the published diary reveals it throws little
light on his methods of composition; and of its literary value more
will be said later.

The Sandford Notebook

This notebook, which was sold by Jeremy Sandford on 24 July
1979 by Sotheby's, and went ultimately to the National Library of
Wales, is in size and format similar to the Plomer notebook,
approximately seven by four inches with a patterned imitation
leather binding. It is titled, in Kilvert's own hand again, Notebook
no. 2, 27 April to 10 June. Unlike the Plomer notebook all the
pages are filled; like it, it looks like a fair copy. Like the Durham
notebook it is rather carelessly marked with vertical lines in red
crayon or pencil in the margins, probably Plomer's indications to
his typist what passages he had chosen from the volume to be
published

This notebook is far more interesting than the Cornwall
notebook. It is not a holiday journal, but deals almost wholly with
Clyro (except for a period from 16 - 28 May when he went to
Langley Burrell to see his sister Emily who had just returned from
India). It was clearly written under the spell of that flush of
excitement Kilvert felt when he first began to write about Clyro.
The daily entries are long and detailed, and must have presented
Plomer with an acute editorial problem. There are several entries
which he might with profit have included, eg, this sharp vignette

I took (from Mrs Jones) the key of the Oaks door padlock tied
to an empty cotton reel and went down to see Mrs Williams.
In the silent deserted rooms downstairs, cold and cheerless
and full of peat reek and peat dust, though the mawn fire had
gone out, a fine yellow tabby cat lay asleep upon the red
covered seat of a chair. She opened her eyes sleepily and
stretched out her head to be scratched.

Wed. 28 April 1870

There is an interesting account of Kilvert's walk with his friend
Morrell to that fascinating waterfall, Craig-pwll-du, which
supplements the other account of his visit there in the company of
the molecatcher (no one is quite sure where Mrs Essex Hope who
published this in her *Occult Review* article found this account).
But the outstanding passage which Plomer failed to include in his
selections is the famous Dawn-chorus passage. In the long entry
for 7 May Kilvert tells how he stayed up with Richard Williams,
Jim Rogers and William Morgan to look after Mr Venables's mare
Gypsy, which had been taken ill.

It was not cold but a fresh morning, cloudless and there was a
broad suspicion of light in the east. I listened for some time.
Then I heard a cuckoo near Peter's Pool, and another near
Cilblythe. They had only just begun singing. It was just cock-
crowing and the cocks joined in. The cuckoos began to call
thicker and faster, and now and then might be heard from the
woods the hooting of the owls. Presently the cocks ceased for
a while. Then the owls gradually stopped altogether, and the
cuckoos had it all their own way. At 3.15 the birds woke and
burst into song, full chorus almost simultaneously. I never
heard birds singing like that before. I did not know they could
sing so. No one who has not heard the first marvellous rush of
song when the birds awake and begin to sing on a fine warm
May morning can have any conception what it is like or how
birds can sing. No idea can be formed from the singing of

birds in the daytime of what they can do in the early spring morning. It was wonderful, ravishing, passing anything that I could have imagined. Round Cae Mawr and in the great pear orchard behind the school the whole air was in a chorus of song, and the air shook thick with rapture and melody. The air was so full of sound that there was scarcely room for another bird to fit a note in. From every tree and bush the music poured and swelled and every bird was singing his loudest and sweetest. The morning air was crowded with singing and the matins lauds and praise went up altogether like a cloud of melodious incense. Morning hymns sung in full choir. Truly the time of the singing of birds is come. So it was very curious to see and hear the night shading into morning and the birds of dark and light recognising the limits of their domain. The cocks at midnight. Then the cocks becoming silent. The owls keeping up the cry of the night like watchmen. The cocks again at dawn crowing. The cocks ceasing again. The owls gradually becoming silent and giving way to the cuckoos who took up the watch, relieved guard and introduced the morning when their cuckooing had awakened the singing birds. For the cuckoos seemed to be tolling the chapel bell and calling all the other birds to their orisons. The owls mourned for the departing night. The cuckoos and the singing birds rejoiced in the morning. Thus God never leaves Himself without witness and some bird always keeps vigil and praises Him.

7 May 1870

Perhaps the explanation of Plomer's omission of this striking passage is this:– it forms part of a long narrative dealing with the illness and subsequent death of the mare Gypsy. The account is by no means without interest. In fact it throws a great deal of light on the state of veterinary surgery in the 1870's. Neither the local vet nor the expert brought in from Hereford seems to have any clear idea of what the illness is from which the mare is suffering, or how

to treat it. Even Kilvert is appalled by the lack of agreement
between them, and the callous treatment to which Gypsy is
subjected; but William Plomer once told me that he had felt that
the narrative was too long to include in its entirety, and to include
only a part would have been confusing. So the fine Dawn-chorus
passage had to go.

This comment leads on naturally to an examination of
Plomer's editorship of the Diary. He was clearly faced with a
difficult problem. There was no possibility (in 1938) of publishing
the Diary in its entirety. It was a risk that no publishing house at
that time could have taken. If it was to appear in print, it would
have to be, in the first place, in the form of selections; and the fate
of subsequent volumes depended on the public reactions to the
first.

On the whole Plomer did an excellent job. It may be that
certain aspects of the journal that continue to mystify readers
(such as the relationship between the Kilverts and the Ashes, the
position of Mr Thomas in Llanigon etc) might have been made
clear by a more judicious selection; and there is one instance
of editorial tact that makes one wonder if Plomer did not on
occasions improve on Kilvert. Towards the end of the fine passage
on Whitehall (3 May 1870) these sentences occur

> Now all is changed, song and dance still, mirth fled away.
> Only the wind sighing through the broken roof and crazy
> doors, the quick feet, busy hands, saucy eyes, strong limbs all
> mouldered into dust, the laughing voices silent. There was a
> deathlike silence about the place, except that I fancied once I
> heard a small voice singing, and a bee was humming away
> among the ivy green, the only bit of life about the place.

In the MS what Kilvert wrote was

> I fancied I heard a small voice singing (perhaps it was a
> fairy) . . .

Plomer undoubtedly improved the passage by removing the twee words in brackets, and one cannot help wondering on how many other occasions he improved on Kilvert. My conjecture is that he did not frequently tamper with Kilvert's prose. His integrity was too great for that. He was guilty of a sad error in destroying the typescript of the full Diary, but I cannot believe that he was guilty of falsifying many passages.

Further Unpublished Extracts

When William Plomer was preparing his selections from the Diary, he gave to Mrs S. Mumford of Sugwas Court, near Hereford, a copy of some entries which he did not propose to include and which related to the Dew and Bevan families. A few years ago Mrs Mumford very kindly allowed the Kilvert Society to publish, in cyclostyled form, these extracts. Apart from a few odd sentences and phrases they are all new material, in the main factual and brief, but occasionally expanding into passages that are worth preserving. One example is this picture of Whitney at blossom time.

> The pear blossom at Whitney is perfectly magnificent. The orchards, gardens and fields are in a blaze with it. The park and orchards at the Court are studded with large pear trees so white with thick blossom that scarce a bit of green can peep out. Two fine pear orchards there are on the bank above the Rectory, which may be seen four or five miles like an island of white bloom against the dark woods. Another white island of pear blossom there was also in an orchard by the river. All the cottage gardens, too, were brilliant with bloom of pear. Whitney certainly is a beautiful place.

A few days later, Kilvert, who was never afraid to laugh at himself, was the innocent cause of merriment in Hay Church.

I went to Hay this morning and took the Union duty, a full service in church with the offertory and a churching afterwards. Cyrus Morgan played the organ to the tune of "See the conquering hero comes" in honour of Mr Pritchard's return from the wedding with his lovely bride, once Nelly Broad. Just as the organ struck up I appeared in full canonicals marching down the chancel from the vestry to the reading-desk. "See the conquering hero comes" thundered the organ, and Mary Bevan nearly expired with inextinguishable laughter.

And later still, towards the end of his stay in Clyro, comes this account of a high-spirited outing to Merbach Hill.

Luncheon at Whitney Rectory and then we started for Merbach Hill. Emily, Jenny, Armine and Helen got into the old Clyro Vicarage single seated brougham, while Walter and I sat on the box, and Willy Bevan rose upon the roof waving a tricolor flag, and blasting upon a brass horn. With the coachman we were "eight precious souls and all agog to dash through thick and thin". Edward rode the pony Balaam, put it up at Miss Domville's at Winforton Court and was to have joined us at Andrew's farm where we alighted and walked across the meadows to the Clock Mill ferry on the Wye, but he unluckily missed us. It is a beautiful reach of the Wye at the Clock Mill Ferry. The broad river comes shimmering down round the bend from Castleton Hill, sparkling and glittering in the sunshine, with millions of dancing diamonds and glides on between the woods lower down the reach still and glassy as a lake.

The ferryman came across from the Clock Mill with the ferry boat and took us all over at once. A little way up the Bredwardine road past the Castlefield Inn we turned aside to the right across some meadows to the foot of Merbach Hill and began the ascent. The sun was burning hot and the hillside steep. Walter led the way and was at the top first in 15 minutes. There was a glorious view from the cairn on the summit, seven fair counties or more, Radnor, Brecon, Hereford, Monmouth, Worcester, Shropshire, Carmarthen, perhaps Cardigan and Gloucester, certainly the Malverns. The girls were delighted for they said they could see what they never saw before from this hill top, Hereford city with the church steeples, and the tower of the old cathedral – but Armine faltered coming up the steep brash and Helen had a sad headache from the fierce glare of the sun. The girls made tea in a meadow with some hot water and tea things borrowed from a small farm house (we had brought up our own materials in a basket) while I went down the green lane to visit Arthur's Stone. After tea we returned to the top of the hill and Willy waved the tricolour flag and we all waved our handkerchiefs and shawls in hopes that they might be seen from the Rectory. Then we all came pelting down the hill, laughing and shouting, Walter first and Willy and I with Edward – the long-lost Edward – who had at last turned up and joined us at the cairn. We went in to the Castle Field Inn hoping to get some good sherry, but found only some decent beer. We found the carriage waiting for us at the field gate into the road by Andrew's farm and went back in the same order in which we had come. Willy Bevan sitting on the roof waving the tricolour flag, blasting away on the brass horn like a dying cow, the villagers all rushing to their doors to see the show pass, the boys solemnly and reverently saluting the flag.

Fragments of Diary found at Langley House

Among the papers of the late Major Scott-Ashe, Mr Arthur Scott-Ashe found three sheets containing copies of passages from the Diary. The period covered is from May to August 1875, and the

passages are written in a hand that looks like that of Dora Kilvert,
the diarist's sister. They do not add very much to our knowledge of
Kilvert but they do confirm his love of children and his genuine
sense of loss when Emily's family leaves the Rectory at Langley
Burrell to go to Clifton; and they contain a few striking sentences
on the scenery between Langley Burrell and Kington St Michael,
as well as a picture of Kilvert conscientiously playing the role of
spiritual pastor.

The entries are reproduced with the kind permission of Mr
Arthur Scott-Ashe, the grandson of Squire Ashe of the Diary.

31 May 1875
This is our children's last day in the old home.

1 June
There was a great scramble of packing and cording boxes this
morning. Mrs John Knight lent Emmie a cart and horse, and
her son John came across to help load the luggage. Emmie
and Charlotte Hatherell with the three children who were in
high spirits, went down to Bristol by the 2.6 train and took up
their quarters at their comfortable house at 16 Sion Place,
Clifton.

June 2
The old house is very quiet this evening. No children's
footsteps on the stairs, no children's voices about the
passages – the silent empty nurseries, the little untended
gardens, two or three old toys forgotten and left behind with
an old lesson book, seem to ask for the children and wonder
where they are.

6th June
As I went down the garden path today I saw some forget-me-
nots in the children's little gardens – The children's eyes
seemed to look at me through the blue beautiful flowers, and I
almost heard their voices saying 'Forget me not'. It almost

overcame me. 'No, dear children, I will never forget you'.

Wed. 9th June 1875
This morning I drove my mother after tea through the
beautiful sunny lanes and village greens to Foxham Farm to
call on dear old Mrs Pegler. The house is a pretty picturesque
farm house nestling in fruit trees, and climbing clustering
roses on the edge of the green behind Foxham Church. The
geese were grazing and the children playing on the green, and
the sun slanted tenderly over the rich country between the
elms with brilliant gleams and long shadows. We found Mrs
Pegler at home. She is a fine handsome old lady with a
singularly pleasant open countenance.

Foxham seems to be in a sad state ecclesiastically and
parochially, and miserably neglected by Bremhill and the
clergy there. The Holy Communion has only been administered in Foxham Church *five times in two years*. Mrs
Pegler told us that the curate, Mr Rivett Carnac, who goes
about in a cassock, was attacked one day by their gander,
which tore a grievous hole in his 'petticoats'. He said he
should tell his friends what a ferocious house guardian Mrs
Pegler kept. 'Perhaps, sir', suggested the old woman slyly,
'Perhaps, sir, the gander was excited by some peculiarity in
the dress'.

18th June
I went down to Sydney's wood to see Tom Cole, who was
better and down stairs. Talking of Steart's Lane, he said it
went to London. The continuation broke here and there but it
could be traced all the way. It was recognisable at Swindon,
where it is called 'The Old Lane to London'. Cattle could be
driven from Wiltshire and Gloucestershire to London in old
days without paying toll.

Sunday 15th August
After our own services I walked over in the beautiful evening

to Kington St Michael to help Edward Awdry. The sun was still hot, but lowering fast and sending long shadows across the brilliant green of the meadows. As I went down into the alternate shade and sunshine of the Happy Valley, the cooing of the wood-pigeons floated quietly down from the dark woods of the Marsh, and a sweet peace of Sabbath stillness brooded over the Vale. Down the road from Kington to the Plough it was warm and sultry, and there was no sound but the 'drowsy tinklings' of the sheep from the Lodge Farm. The little mournful piping of a bullfinch and the occasional sudden sweet song of a robin. 'The Twelve Apostles' (the twelve oaks, one crooked and broken for Judas Iscariot) stood upon their hill, then 'The Four Evangelists' (the four elms on the Top Hill) came into sight. Around lay the rich undulating country, the emerald meadows in their setting of golden cornfields, and below nestled the King's town, the house of my forefathers with the gray Church Tower embosomed amongst its limes, and the long village street climbing the gentle slope beyond. I found the good vicar hot and lonely, walking disconsolately in his garden, and wishing someone would come and help him with his duty. Seeing me, he started and came forward joyfully, 'You're the very man I wanted to see', he exclaimed, 'I want you to preach for me'. He read prayers and I preached to a most attentive congregation.

24th July 1875
In our garden this evening I found the two nice girls Elizabeth and Mary Knight who had come by invitation to gather blackcurrants for their home wine-making. They were in their black and white striped dresses and had their sleeves rolled up, and their hands were stained with the blackcurrant juice. Presently they wanted another basket and I went to fetch them one.

When I came back with it, Mary suddenly said, 'Mr Frank, I want you to do something for me'. 'Well, what is it?' 'To speak to Mother about coming to the Sacrament, I think she would come if you would ask her.' 'I will gladly ask her if you will give me an opportunity of seeing her alone, to have a little talk. I think she will speak more freely to me when no one else is by.'

The girls agreed, and spoke very nicely and sensibly about it. 'Now', I said, 'will you let me ask you to do something for me?' 'Yes', they said, 'What is that?' 'To come to the Holy Communion with your Mother. I have long wished it and hoped you would.' 'I have often thought of it', said Mary. 'I think it is a thing people ought to do. I told Mother I would come when she did.' 'People say', said Elizabeth, 'That you oughtn't to come to the Sacrament till you are good. But I don't think that's right. I think if we stay for that we shall never come at all. It was meant, I believe, to help us to be good'. 'Certainly', I said, 'and remember that after the Last Supper Peter denied his Master, and all the disciples forsook Him and fled. We shall never be quite without sin in this life, but if we use the means of grace and help which God has given us, we shall sin more and more seldom'. We had a good deal more talk of the same kind, and the girls spoke nicely and heartily. When they had finished picking their currants the sun had set, and the glory had died off the tops of the highest elms. The little brook at the bottom of the garden tinkled on quietly and chimed in with our voices.

The girls had gathered their baskets full and I walked up with them to the farm through our orchard, carrying the heaviest basket for them. I parted with them at their gate with a hearty clasp of the hand. I hope that some good may have been done, and that something may come of our evening talk in the garden.

Aug 4th

I bought in Bath today a copy each of 'Thoughts and Prayers for Young Communicants' for Rosamund, Elizabeth and Mary Knight and took them to the Farm. Rosamund was at home with her Mother. When I was coming away, Mrs Knight said to my great joy, with a softened look on her face, putting her hand in mine, 'You must please to teach and instruct me all you can'. Surely this humble child-like spirit that asks for instruction and desires to enter into the Kingdom of Heaven shall never be cast out.

Chapter Fifteen
The Other Missing Manuscript

We know from several entries in his diary that Francis Kilvert was deeply interested in the language and customs of his parishioners in Radnorshire, Herefordshire and Wiltshire. He comments frequently on local words and usage.

> Jinny (of Clyro) says 'unhackle' for undress, and 'squeeze your ears against your head and say nothing' means to be discreetly silent and cautiously reticent.　　(Vol. 1. 36)

> When people rose early (in Clyro) it was a saying that they were 'beating for day', because it was supposed that they went out and knocked on the earth for day to come.
>
> 　　　　　　　　　　　　　　　　　　(Vol. 1. 250)

On one occasion Kilvert sent a list of unusual Radnorshire words to his friend Anthony Lawson Mayhew. Mayhew forwarded the list to *Notes and Queries,* and it appeared there (10 August, 1878) and was subsequently (inaccurately) reprinted in the *Hereford Journal* (17 August, 1878). The list includes such words as gorkerel (a cormorant), pembolade (a tadpole), gambo (a cart of simple construction), etc. Kilvert was clearly fascinated by odd words and occasionally uses what he thinks are Old English words for the months – Wind Monat, Barn Monat, Sproutkele, Trimilki etc.

But Kilvert was as interested in local customs and traditions as in local language; and in this connection Mr Le Quesne has turned up an interesting entry in Mr Venables's diary.

> 20 Nov. Kilvert dined. He talked of writing something about this locality – including the traditions etc. which he has picked up.

This was more than a vague aspiration, for Kilvert went on to assemble a great deal of interesting information on Radnorshire folklore, and spoke about his collection to a Mr Poole whom he met at Bredwardine.

> Friday 30 August 1872
> Miss Newton's house and garden were looking entirely lovely in the bright summer morning. We found staying a Mr and Mrs Poole with two nice boys and a sweet lovely little girl . . . Mr and Mrs Poole asked me to call on them in London. He is a keeper in the British Museum. During the day I had some conversation with him about my collection of folklore and he said he would like to see my papers and show them to a friend of his and advised me to publish them in the *Archaeologian*.
> (Vol. 2. 252–3)

On 21 February the following year he mentions the collection again.

> In the morning I went to the British Museum. Called on Mr Poole the keeper. He gave me some hope that the Society of Antiquaries would publish my MSS in the *Archaelogian*. He looked at the MSS and thought the matter interesting and valuable.   (Vol. 2. 328)

The notes however were never published. There is no further reference to them in the diary, and no mention of them in the files of *Archaeologia* (Kilvert got the name of the periodical wrong). But it is more than likely that, although Kilvert may never have

submitted his notes to *Archaeologia*, he kept them by him. In
September 1921 his niece, then Miss Essex Smith, later Mrs Essex
Hope published in *The Occult Review* an article on *Radnorshire
Legends and Superstitions* which she described as 'compiled from
MS left by the late Rev R. F. Kilvert'. By MS she may of course
have been referring to the diary which at that time was in the
possession of her brother and was presumably available to her.
Many of the traditions she mentions appear in the published diary
(e.g. the ordeal of the key and bible, the kneeling of oxen on old
Christmas Eve, the sowing of hempseed, the offering of money on
the grave shovel to the officiating parson, the burning of the bushes
at the New Year etc). But Essex Smith gives different versions of
these customs from those appearing in the published diary. In the
diary it is a Mrs Jones who uses the key and bible test; in the
article it is an old woman from Llanships. The article gives the
words of the song sung by the girls sowing hempseed. No words
appear in the diary. In the diary the burning of the bushes gets only
a brief notice.

There are many other customs which appear in the article but
to which there is no reference at all in the diary. It is possible of
course that reference to them may have been omitted when the
diaries were edited, but at least one passage does not read like a
diary entry, being clearly written some time after the event. This is
the account of the famous Mari Lwyd ritual which Kilvert
witnessed at Clyro.

This ritual was also known as 'The Feast of the Ass' and was
said to be a jumble of three events in Scripture history, each
connected with an ass – the journey of Balaam, the Flight into
Egypt, and the Triumphal Entry into Jerusalem. This is Kilvert's
account.

It was between the Christmases, and at eight o'clock I was
sitting with some other people around the fire, when we heard
tramping outside, and a loud knocking on the door, which was
locked. There was the sound of a flute a moment later, and a

man began singing – I could not distinguish the words – then a few minutes later another man, inside the room, went to the door and sang what was apparently an answer to the song without. Then the door was thrown open, and in walked about a dozen people, headed by a most extraordinary apparition, an animal covered with a flowing sheet, and surmounted by a horse's skull to which a bridle was attached. This apparition, I saw a moment later, was really a man covered with a sheet; his head was bowed down and a skull had been fastened on to it. The people sang, collected some money and then went off . . .

Just before his death I asked William Plomer, one of the few ever to have seen the whole of Kilvert's diary, if this was one of the passages he had decided not to include, but he assured me that he had never come across that extraordinary passage in the pages of the manuscript diary. If he had done so he certainly would have included it.

It seems then that Kilvert left behind him not only a diary, but his collection of folklore notes. Mrs Essex Smith admitted to Mr Charles Harvey that they had been in her possession but said that they had been 'unfortunately destroyed'. She justified her destruction of the diary notebooks on the grounds that they were essentially private or family documents, and now that the Plomer selections were in print, it was in the family interest to suppress the rest. She may have been right, but it is difficult to see what justification she had for destroying the folklore notes. From what she reveals of them in her own article they were scholarly, objective and not at all likely to divulge family secrets. They would not have thrown new light on Kilvert. They would have been an invaluable record of Radnorshire folklore.

However all is not lost, and the light that is thrown on Radnorshire folklore by Kilvert and one of his friends, Edith Burham Thomas, is examined in a later chapter.

Chapter Sixteen

Kilvert as a Poet

Kilvert seems to have been writing poetry long before he began his journal. One poem, *Easter Sunday Evening (In Mill Lane, Clyro)* is dated 1865. There is no reason to believe that, having begun to compose verses in the mid-sixties, he discontinued the habit. We can safely assume that he was a versifier for most of his adult life – at least from his coming to Clyro. *Hill Flowers* is dated 1876, and *Minnie Vaughan* and *Paradise, Clyro*, 1878. He sent several poems to the *Hereford Times* (1876. 1877, 1878) and one to the *Aberystwyth Observer*. He had his poem *Honest Work* privately printed for distribution among his friends and parishioners. Later he did the same for *The Welcome Home*. In 1874 he joined the Harrow Weald Poetical Society, and remained a member for many years. In 1878 there was printed in Shrewsbury a volume of verse by members of the Society called *Selections from Our Poetical Portfolio*. It contains a list of 20 members and among them are Kilvert and his brother Edward. Then, some time later, largely through the good offices of Katharine Heanley, Kilvert's poetical paraphrase of the 23rd Psalm was published in *Sunday at Home*.

Kilvert was quite serious about his poetry. There are many references in the Diary to his planning or composing poems. He had a great ambition to write songs in the style of Robert Burns, to

be set to music and sung at village concerts; and he showed his
poems to Katharine Heanley and Ettie Meredith Brown. He made
a special collection of his verses for Ettie and had it bound for her
as an Easter offering in 1876. By 11 March 1878 he thought he
had written enough to contemplate publishing; and, against the
advice of his father, he submitted a selection to J. C. Longman, a
college friend of Mr Middleton Evans, with whom Kilvert had
stayed at Llwynbarried, asking him on what terms he would publish
a small book of poems for him. Mr Longman was not encouraging.

> 15 March 1878
> This morning a letter came from Mr Longman, very
> courteous but not encouraging the idea of my publishing a
> volume of poems.

After his death, however, his wife (or possibly his friend, Mayhew)
arranged for a selection of his poems to be published by E. C.
Alden, Oxford. Whoever took upon himself or herself the
responsibility for the publication, prefaced the selection with the
following note.

> This little volume would most probably never have seen
> the light in its present form but for a desire expressed by the
> author, shortly before his death, to make at some future time a
> selection from his poems for publication. Removed, as he
> was, after an illness of only a few days, it was found that no
> pieces had been specially set apart by him for that purpose
> and those which now appear had not received such correc-
> tion as further and more mature thought might have suggested
> to him.
>
> If any record is looked for regarding the author himself, it
> will be found in the hearts of those who valued and loved him,
> rather than in an elaborate obituary.
>
> For the information of strangers who may open these
> pages it may be enough to say that his life, both before and

throughout his ministry, was passed in quiet and retired country places where "he could see God's blessings spring out of his mother earth and eat his bread in peace and privacy". Thus his musings were continually amidst the objects of nature in which he had an intense delight.

After taking orders and serving as curate of his father's parish in Wiltshire for a short time, he spent seven or eight happy years as curate of Clyro in Radnorshire: then, for a short time, he was vicar of St Harmon's in the same county until finally he became vicar of Bredwardine near Hereford. In each of these places he was happy in making friends among all classes, especially among the poor, very many of whom repaid his earnest ministrations with affection and love.

But that which marked his ministerial course more than anything else was his devoted daily attendance at the schools of his several parishes. He possessed a happy faculty and felt an unceasing delight in teaching young children. There was something in his manner of speaking to them which had an attraction almost magnetic. It was so wherever he went. He was most tender in his ministrations to them in sickness and nothing touched him so deeply as officiating at the funeral of a little child.

Thus exercising his ministry with acceptance and effect during fourteen or fifteen years, he was, within five weeks of his marriage, suddenly called away from his deeply sorrowing and still fondly regretful friends; lost to them for a while "until the day dawn and the shadows flee away".

Kilvert compiled his journal largely for himself (although like most diarists he probably secretly wished that ultimately he might find a wider audience); but his poetry was meant for publication, and the fact that he was writing to be read by his contemporaries made him pay more attention to the conventions of his time. Compared with the best of his prose, *Musings in Verse* has little

literary merit, and is little better than many a long-forgotten
Victorian collection. If we had no more than these poems to go on
we would be tempted to think of Kilvert as a very ordinary mid-
19th century versifier, a typical man of his time, a moraliser with
the conventional admiration for the virtues of honest work, pious
thoughts, the propriety of observing one's station in life, pure
maidens, innocent children, the rural scene, domestic bliss etc.
Most of this is album verse with its pallid copies of Spenser,
Wordsworth and Tennyson, its well-worn themes, its poetic
clichés, its constant moralising. The poems are rarely
anthologised and are largely unknown outside the circle of Kilvert
Society readers.

Yet, beneath the layers of sentimentality, almost concealed
by the conventional language, are real experiences. In the *Hill
Home* and *Hill Flowers* (both punning titles) we can recognise the
family to which the beautiful Florence Hill belonged, and Kilvert's
delight in visiting them. (Like Hardy he had the habit of treating
the same subject in prose and verse.) The Aberystwyth poems
recall happy holidays he spent there in 1877 and 1878 (the diary
account of these was omitted by Plomer.) *The Rocks of Aberedw*
is one more allusion to that memorable day in 1865 when
something unforgettable, but alas never clearly recorded,
happened to Kilvert, a mysterious event that seems to have filled
him with mingled feelings of joy and guilt. *The Welcome Home* is
the metrical version of his diary account of the funeral of Little
Davie. *The Shepherd's Farwell* may refer either to the people of
Clyro or St Harmon, both of whom Kilvert felt he had abandoned.
Fading Away may have been inspired by the death of Emmeline
Vaughan or Lily Crichton; *Lost* by the death of Captain Cowper
Coles; *Unsuspected Love* by his affair with Ettie (not Daisy to
whom he never confessed his partiality); and as recorded in
Chapter 12 Miss Lang-Sims has brilliantly unravelled the
autobiographical elements of what may have been his last poem,
Nydd Eos, the poem found in his blotter after his death.

The world will rank Kilvert as no more than a mediocre poet; but as William Plomer said, though it is 'easy to point out the limitations of Kilvert's poeticising . . . those who best understand and appreciate his character may find it reflected in his verse, interestingly and sometimes touchingly'.

Chapter Seventeen
The Fate of the Diary

Kilvert may have shown his wife his diary before his death; when he was in love with Daisy Thomas, he once wrote that he hoped they might one day be able to read together what he had written. Whether or not Mrs Kilvert had seen her husband's journal before his fatal illness, she must have gone through at least part of it after his death. Her niece, the late Miss M. A. Rowland said her aunt told her that she meant to remove from the diary all the passages that referred to herself. In fact she seems to have removed two lengthy sequences, the first covering the period from 9 September 1875 to 1 March 1876, the second from 27 June 1876 to 31 December 1877. This was the first act of censorship, and apparently it consisted of removing not only single sentences or pages, but whole notebooks. Kilvert, in full flow, could fill a notebook in a fortnight, as he did when he went to see the Hockins in Cornwall, but normally one lasted him something short of two months. It may be assumed then that Mrs Kilvert destroyed as many as ten notebooks, though this may be an over-estimate.

Mrs Kilvert's motives for removing the first sequence are not altogether easy to understand. This part of the diary probably dealt with Kilvert's ill-fated love affair with Ettie Meredith Brown. He himself admits to certain indiscretions in his relations with Ettie, and perhaps Mrs Kilvert thought that the record might prove a source of embarrassment if ever it came to the notice of Ettie's husband, Mr Wright. We can be fairly sure that her motive was not jealousy. From what we know of her she was a gentle and tolerant person. It is noticeable that she did not remove the Daisy Thomas passages – perhaps because Daisy had remained unmarried.

The second part of the diary which she removed was almost certainly that part that contained a number of references to herself. It is generally thought, on the testimony of Miss M. A. Rowland (see Looking Backwards. Kilvert Society. p. 23) that Kilvert and his wife first met in Paris, where they were both members of a party organised by Anthony Lawson Mayhew, whom Kilvert had first met at Wadham, and whose acquaintance he had kept up. In all probability she was the young woman who visited him when he was Vicar of St Harmon. That part of the diary that dealt with Kilvert's year at St Harmon must have contained many references to her, so many that she decided to remove the entire section.

There remains, however, one little mystery. In the pages of the journal that deal with the period between his appearing at Bredwardine and the last entry, there is not a single mention of Kilvert's fiancée. The record is apparently a continuous one (Plomer usually made a point of indicating where pages had been cut out.) It could easily be that after an initial period of affectionate friendship, Kilvert and Elizabeth Rowland drifted apart. Kilvert had a knack of forgetting even those who were dearest to him. Once his love affair with Daisy was over, although he often thought of her, he never approached her father again, even after he had ceased to be an impecunious curate; and his ardour for Kathleen Heanley seems to abate rapidly. Perhaps it was after a period of indecision that he and Miss Rowland suddenly made up their minds to marry, and this decision may have been recorded after 13 March 1879, the date of the last published entry. It is possible that the diary did not end where it seems to, but that part of it that dealt with the final stages of Kilvert's courtship was also removed by his widow.

Whatever happened, by the time Mrs Kilvert died in 1911, the number of notebooks had been reduced to 22. Before she died she had, according to Miss M. A. Rowland, her niece, intimated that she wished the diary to go to her nephew Percy (Perceval Smith) the younger son of Thersie, Kilvert's sister, although Perceval himself, in a letter to be quoted below, said that the notebooks went first to Dora, (Mrs Pitcairn and Kilvert's younger sister). Thersie had an older son, Hastings. Hastings had had at one time access to the diaries, because it was he who visited Rhayader and St Harmon in an attempt to recover the lost notebooks – an act that suggests he had not been in his aunt's confidence. Eventually it was Perceval Smith who submitted the diary for publication and authorised the abridgment made by William Plomer. The following account, apparently the copy of a letter to Macmillan of New York was found among the Plomer papers in Durham University Library.

After my uncle's death in '79 the Diaries (MSS) remained in the possession of his widow. She, at her death, left them to the Diarist's sister (the Dora of the Diaries) with instructions that at the latter's death they were all to be burned. She, however, having a great affection for the diaries (she used to read from one or other of them regularly at bedtime to the end of her life) was very unwilling that they should so be destroyed, and in this she was joined by her two surviving sisters, who held that the Diarist's widow had no right to decree their destruction. At the same time, she wished that the MS book should never fall into careless or unknowing hands, and that, if there should be any danger of this, it were better that they should be burned. With this stipulation she left them all to my two sisters (viz Florence and Essex Smith), who, after holding them for a while, sent them about 17 years ago all to me at King Stag. For a long time after they had come into my possession I felt that their merit was too great to be allowed to pass into oblivion without some attempt to save them. I knew that when our generation of the family had passed there would be no one who would care anything about the MS of the Diary – that they would be met with the scantiest of interest, and would without doubt be destroyed. Thus it was that I selected two of the MS books and sent them up to Messrs Jonathan Cape, who at once wrote in reply most favourably about them, only wishing to know if I could assure them that the interest was sustained throughout and not confined to the two I had sent them. I was able of course to satisfy them about this, and thereupon I sent up the first eight volumes of MS to be edited and published as Vol. 1 of the Diary . . . I am glad you wrote to me for the facts for my sisters and myself are the only ones still living who could have given them to you.

It is ironical that Kilvert, who was one of the most open and least devious of men, should come to be connected with so many mysteries. Already there is discrepancy between Miss M. A. Rowland's and Perceval Smith's account of Mrs Kilvert's intentions; but the mystery that surrounds the subsequent history of the diary is just as hard to unravel.

When Perceval Smith sent the Diary to Jonathan Cape it consisted of the 22 surviving notebooks, of varying size and shape, but presumably more or less like those now in Durham University Library and the National Library of Wales. Plomer had a typescript of the whole MS prepared and used this from which to make his selections.

The decision to publish selections only from the Diary was virtually forced upon him. To undertake, in the year of Munich, the publication of the whole diary (which would have run to at least nine largish volumes) was almost an economic impossibility, particularly since the public response to the journal was unpredictable. Plomer made a sensible decision, and the warm reception given to his selections by critics, reviewers and readers was ample justification for his editorial policy.

From the moment when he first read the Diary, Plomer had always at the back of his mind the vague hope that what had been done for Woodforde and what was being done for Pepys might in the end (probably with the assistance of some university press) be achieved for Kilvert, and that sooner or later the whole unabridged Diary might appear in print; but some time after the publication of the third volume there occurred two events that at once thwarted his plan and crippled further serious Kilvert studies. The first related to the typescript of the full diary which Plomer had prepared and which he mentions in one of his introductions. It seems unlikely that one or two carbon copies of the typescript were not prepared, but by a series of accidents or acts of negligence all the typed copies of the full diary were lost. Plomer was never totally explicit about what had happened, but he once intimated that during the war he grew concerned about the mass of papers he was accumulating (he always had a preference for living in small flats and unpretentious suburban bungalows and was always short of storage space); and when the Kilvert typescript was destroyed or vanished, he did not greatly trouble because he knew the original notebooks were still in existence.

By this time, however, the notebooks had passed from Perceval Smith to his sister, Essex Smith, later Mrs Essex Hope.

Essex Smith had inherited the literary flair that most of the Kilverts possessed. During the twenties she had published several moderately successful novels, had contributed to periodicals and written at least two talks for the BBC. Mr Charles Harvey, who knew her in her later years, was impressed by her charm and intelligence, but Plomer found her a reserved and unpredictable woman with whom he could never feel at ease. He felt that she was never wholly candid with him, that she did not wholly trust him, and was certainly prepared to defy any advice he might give her. Without consulting him she set about the destruction of the precious notebooks she had inherited.

Plomer recorded what she had done in a letter to the Secretary of the Kilvert Society dated 21 July 1958.

'I paid a visit to Mrs Hope, who speaks very warmly of you. She said she had a confession to make and told me that she has in fact done away with most of the Diary. She said this was in accordance with the wishes of Kilvert's sister Dora (who formerly owned it) that it should eventually be destroyed because she (Dora) thought that it was at least to some extent a private document. Mrs Hope told me that both she and her late brother had felt it was all right to publish what had been published, and that I had extracted all that was best in it and most suitable for publication. We now know that it will never be possible to have the whole of the diary printed, or even to see it. I did not scold Mrs Hope . . .'

Plomer's letter is surprisingly mild, but he was a very diplomatic man. His real feelings came out later when he said to the Secretary of the Kilvert Society that 'he could have strangled her with his own hands.'

An interesting commentary on these events is to be found in an article written by Brian Jones for the *Guardian* (2 February 1977) on the publication of the new three-volume illustrated edition of the Diary.

The only surviving participant in this literary drama is Mr Jeremy Sandford. He had written a radio play based on Kilvert's life. Mrs Hope heard it and invited him to visit her in Worthing, saying she hoped to make the visit worthwhile. She invited him a second time. On that occasion, quite unexpectedly, she went to a bureau and took out from it one of the original notebooks. She said that he could have it, that she had given two to Plomer; the rest she had destroyed.

Sandford recalls that he was at once engulfed in mixed emotions, both moved with surprised gratitude and shocked at her disclosure. He asked what had caused her to destroy the notebooks. Mrs Hope answered that there were sides of Kilvert that she would not wish the general public to know. 'He had not always been a happy man', and the three notebooks that remained were those he would have wished to see survive. Mr Sandford feels that in acting as sole judge for posterity, Mrs Hope, by that time an elderly and lonely woman, was probably applying her own code of Christian and moral standards that was inevitably at odds with the honest and revelatory passages in Kilvert already published.

A further motive . . . is that Mrs Hope, herself a between-the-wars novelist of modest achievement, acted partly in resentment against the contrast with her uncle's belated fame. Her actions over Kilvert were equivocal. She restored his grave, used in her own writing some of his unpublished material on local folk-lore, but destroyed it, and gave some help to the Kilvert Society. Yet she destroyed his greatest memorial. It is even possible that, ambiguous to the end, she did not destroy the notebooks but said she had done so to put an end to further inquiry. But if she kept them hidden or deposited safely, they have stayed so for the years since her death in 1964.

So has the third notebook she claimed to have given away. Contrary to what she told Mr Sandford, only one went to Plomer. One theory is that the third was given to someone in the Birmingham area. But the best known Kilvert researcher there, Mr Charles Harvey, assured me he was given no manuscripts even though she had passed on to him numerous paintings by Kilvert's sister, Thermuthis. He never met Mrs Hope but corresponded with her frequently. He too found her always guarded about the fate of the notebooks; he remembers her saying that they were 'no longer available'.

With Plomer she was even more casual. When he asked who had been given the third notebook, she said 'she had forgotten'.

Mrs Essex Hope was guilty of serious insincerity in her treatment of Kilvert's papers. Her claim that she was acting in accordance with the wishes of Dora, Kilvert's sister, is plainly contradicted by Perceval Smith's letter in which he represents Dora as being unwilling to see the notebooks destroyed, and resenting Mrs Kilvert's initial acts of censorship. Besides we have enough evidence now to prove that Mrs Hope destroyed not only the diary notebooks, but the valuable collection of folklore notes that Kilvert had made, and which could in no sense be considered a private document.

It is difficult to make a reasonable estimate of what we have lost by the destruction of the unpublished sections of the Diary. Plomer always contended that the passages he omitted were in no way memorable; and this was literally true as far as he was concerned, because, when asked what sort of things the rejected passages had dealt with, he replied that he had totally forgotten – a strange off-hand admission which he justified by saying that the nature of his work as a publisher's reader meant that he could not dwell too much on tasks he had completed. New editorial undertakings drove the old completely out of his mind.

Fortunately the two surviving notebooks are now in good hands, the Plomer notebook in the Library of Durham University and the Sandford notebook in the National Library of Wales, who bought it from him in 1979.

Chapter Eighteen

The Value of the Diary

Kate O'Brien, in her little book, *English Diaries and Journals* (Collins, London 1943) makes some interesting but debateable points on the diary as a literary form.

> A good diary is not necessarily literature; for of its nature it must be free from most of the disciplines and tests of a work of art. Vision, imagination, passion, fancy, invention, scholarship, detachment, and the steely restraints and consciously selected embellishments of form and design – none of these has a vital place in diary writing.

Miss O'Brien overstates her case. For a good diarist passion, detachment and even imagination are by no means indispensable; in fact the absence of these qualities will often make a diary humdrum and jejune. But there is some substance in her general contention, for diaries, like collections of letters and even biographies, tend to be a hybrid form, existing on the fringe of pure literature, and often more valued for their historical and sociological interest than for their literary value.

To many readers the chief merit of Kilvert's Diary lies here, in the unique picture it presents of rural parish life in the 1870's; and before an assessment of the purely literary value of the Diary is attempted, it may be wise to clear the ground with a preliminary study of the Diary as Social Documentary; and to evaluate this

aspect of its appeal the study has been rather arbitrarily divided
into five sections which by no means cover the whole ground but
may serve as starting points for some fuller survey at a later date.
The headings are Work and Leisure, Transport and Travel,
Health and Sickness, the Church, and Folklore.

The Diary as Social Documentary

Work and Leisure

Work
Although Clyro was an unusually harmonious community, there
was a clear division between the gentry and the lower classes. The
gentlefolk who made up Kilvert's social circle – the Morrells, the
Haigh Allens, Baskervilles, Crichtons, Hamers and Hodgsons –
seem to have possessed endless leisure. Whatever work had to be
done in their establishments was done by their servants. Squire
Baskerville kept eight, and Haigh Allen of Clifford Priory probably
as many, Morrell seven, Mr Venables six, Hamers of Boatside six,
and Hodgson of Lower Cabalva another six. A total of nearly forty
servants was employed in six gentlemen's houses, and many more
in the larger farms. Miss Bynon of Pentwyn kept a servant and so
did Mrs Chaloner, Kilvert's landlady. Most of the men in the
parish worked as carpenters, gardeners, farm workers, millers,
grooms, blacksmiths, masons, wheelwrights, gamekeepers, carters
and tailors – and there was one mole-catcher, though his was a
decaying trade. A few women worked as dressmakers.

Midway between the gentlemen and the labourers came the
professional classes – the doctors, veterinary surgeons, the men in
the armed services, and the clergymen. The latter occupied an
anomalous position. Most of them were accepted into the ranks of
the gentlefolk; but many had public duties which took up a great
deal of their time. Mr Venables was a J.P. and conscientiously
attended Assizes, Quarter and Petty Sessions and other committee

meetings. Mr Bevan of Hay busied himself with the Literary Institute, and superintended the fortunes of the famous Hay School; and if the life of the other curates in the area resembled that of Kilvert, they had to keep up a fairly arduous round of pastoral visits. None of the curates or vicars, however, seems to have been over-burdened with work, and Kilvert always had time for a walk or a picnic or croquet or archery party whenever one was mooted.

At Bredwardine and Langley Burrell the social pattern is very much the same. Sir George Cornewall of Moccas was a conscientious public servant, a J.P. and a representative for Herefordshire in musical circles. Kilvert had his own particular duties as a member of the Trustees for the famous Jarvis Charity, but he still had a reasonable amount of leisure. At Langley Burrell of course the scene is dominated by Squire Ashe, an employer on a large scale. There were nine servants in Langley House; and most of the men entered on the 1871 census as farm labourers must have been his. The Census gives the usual quota of labourers, wheelwrights, carpenters, brewers, bakers, grooms, plumbers etc; but a new employer has appeared on the scene – the new Great Western Railway, with its porters, switchmen, cokemen, ticket-collectors, telegraph clerks and foremen. There is even a Refreshment-room Manager, probably employed in Chippenham.

Here too we hear more frequently of a special career open to aspiring gentlemen – India. It is surprising how many of Kilvert's relatives and friends found a profitable career in the Indian sub-continent. One of his brothers-in-law, Lt. Col. Samuel Jardine Wyndowe, was surgeon general in Madras, and took his wife Emily, Kilvert's sister there. One of their children, Annie Frances Essex Wyndowe ('The Monk') was to repeat in some measure her mother's career, for her husband, Col. Walter Ernest Philips, rose to be commanding officer of the 28th Punjab Regiment. Mountague Cholmeley, who married Adelaide Mary Kilvert, daughter to Francis Kilvert of Claverton Lodge and mother of Adelaide or

Addy whose wedding to Charles Heanley Kilvert attended at Findon, had been a captain in the Madras Native Infantry. The Rev Edward Kilvert, the diarist's uncle, served for a time in India as a chaplain. Colonel and Mrs Law of Christian Malford went out to work on the west coast of India. Selby, a Langley Burrell friend, caught pleurisy on the way home from service there and died a few days later. George Warlow, another Langley Burrell friend and probably the son of Mr Warlow the Chippenham auctioneer, also found a career in India; and in his last reference to Ettie Meredith Brown Kilvert mentions that she is going there with her husband, Mr Wright.

But it was not only the middle class men who found a living in India. One day, at the house of Eliza Farmer in Langley Burrell, Kilvert met James Gough, the son of an old soldier who had been in the Indian Mutiny, and learnt from him his story.

> He had gone out to India when he was two years old and had been there ever since at school in an orphanage at Dinapore till he joined the band of the 19th, his father's old regiment, as drummer boy, and came to England a year ago. His father did not know him, nor did he know his father. When he landed he thought England a 'poor place', very cold and always raining. He liked the Hindus better than the Mussulmans. The Mussulmans were savage and murderous and would kill English soldiers if they found them alone or in small parties. Cholera played havoc with the 19th . . . Sometimes when bathing in the Ganges he had seen bundles of straw floating down the river and lifting the straw had found under it a Hindu corpse. The Hindus do not bury their dead but send them adrift down the sacred river having first set fire to their hair and covered them with straw.

(Vol. 2. 321–2)

Kilvert must have listened with an even more horrified fascination to the reminiscences of old Mr Gough who had volunteered to go to India at the time of the Mutiny.

He landed at Calcutta and his regiment marched through
Cawnpore 48 hours after the Massacre. He said the scene
was horrible, so horrible, shocking and disgusting that it could
not be explained or described. Women's breasts had been
chopped and sliced off and were still lying about with their
other parts which had been cut out . . . Numbers of the poor
women had jumped down the great well to avoid the horrors
which were being perpetrated on the bodies of women all over
the place. The soldiers were furious, almost ungovernable, as
they marched through Cawnpore and saw those shameful
sights. If they had caught the rebels then no mercy would have
been shown to those who showed none. The scene of
shameful horror was indescribable. Gough saw 500 mutineers
executed at once, the rank and file shot by musketry, the ring-
leaders blown from guns. One stout fellow stepped lightly up
to his gun as unconcernedly said Gough, 'as you or I would go
into service'. 'I have killed the English,' said the ruffian, 'and
I don't care for death.' . . .

(Vol. 2. 310–11)

Disease, as well as mutiny, took its toll. Lechmere Thomas, a
member of Daisy's family, who had been married to Mira de
Winton for no more than eighteen months, died of cholera in
Colombo.
    Parallel with service in India went service in the Navy in
which Roderick Dew, brother of the Rev Henry Dew of Whitney
found a successful career; but of the dangers of such a service we
are forcibly reminded over and over again. Captain Dudden who
married Georgie Spencer of Chippenham was drowned when his
cable-laying ship, *La Plata*, foundered off Ushant; and on one
occasion when on holiday in the Isle of Wight Kilvert found
himself in the company of three ladies, Mrs Powles, Mrs Boxer
and Mrs Cowper Coles, who had all lost their husbands in the

disaster that overtook the ill-fated *Captain*, a turret ship, which
went down with 500 men in September 1870.

Leisure

The poor of Clyro and Bredwardine had few entertainments
to fill their limited leisure hours. Hay Fair was clearly an occasion
for high spirits, too often, for Kilvert's liking, accompanied by
noise and followed by drunkenness and violence. On one occasion
a circus came to Hay, but it was a very third-rate affair and most
seemed to have been disappointed in it. Itinerant musicians were
not unknown, and once a most improbable figure appeared in the
streets of Clyro – an Italian bagpiper. Most of their diversions
were home-made, and were less entertainments than traditional
rituals, such as the ceremony of the Mari Llwyd which Kilvert
recorded in his Radnorshire notes, and the burning of the bushes
on New Year's Eve. More sophisticated entertainments seemed to
have been staged at the prompting of the local clergymen –
concerts and Penny Readings (see below for a specimen programme), choir suppers, children's parties, lectures and magic
lantern shows, celebrations, particularly in honour of the gentry
and their families (on the first birthday of Mr Venables's daughter,
Minna, there was a fireworks display), volunteer concerts in which
all who could play and sing took an active part, and cottage
lectures. Those who could do so, such as the old mole-catcher who
took Kilvert to Craig-pwll-du, joined in the local hunts whenever
they could. Henry Warnell or Warner was no doubt not the only
poacher in Clyro. Football was played at Whitney, and Kilvert
records two cricket matches, one between Portway and Wyeside
Wanderers and another at Eardisley. In the summer there were
flower shows and bazaars, but the long winter nights must have been
inexpressibly tedious, and the few families that had musicians
among them, such as the Hills of Upper Noyadd (Florence played
the harmonium), the Bengoughs (he could play the flute) and the
Vulliamys (two brothers played the harmonium and the cornet)
must have counted themselves very fortunate.

At Langley Burrell there seems to have been more organised sport. Cricket matches were more frequent and not limited to the gentlemen. Football (not of course the organised game we know today but something closer to the Shrove Tuesday football which is still played in some parts of the country) was more regularly played. Bath was not too far away, and excursion tickets for the Flower Show and probably the Circus were in demand. In the village there were more Penny Readings and concerts (though Squire Ashe disapproved of both); and for those who could get as far afield as Weston there were concerts on the pier, sea trips, popular lectures such as that given by the hypnotist which Kilvert attended, and sea-bathing.

At Hay and Clyro, where a tradition of hospitality and largesse almost mediaeval in scope still survived, the poor were often generously drawn into the festivities of the gentry, and the Hereford newspapers carried in April 1877 the following accounts of the wedding and return from their honeymoon of Edward Lechmere Thomas, (brother to Daisy) and Miss Annina Margaret (Mira) de Winton.

> Nothing could have been more gratifying than the reception the pair met with upon their return from their tour in the North of England and Scotland, they having journeyed as far as Edinburgh . . . At Hay the Foresters, with band and flags, met them on their arrival at the station, and passed up the principal streets of Hay, where smiles and welcome were the order of the day amongst the inhabitants of that stirring and spirited little town. Accompanied by the band, they reached the confines of the parish of Llanigon, where the parishioners, dispensing with animal assistance, drew the happy pair to Llanthomas, with shouts of joy and every token of esteem . . . Games in a field and presents to the poor became the order of the day; and for hours afterwards until the shadows of evening approached, all was innocent hilarity and pleasant greeting . . .

Luncheon being over . . . the Foresters with their band again put themselves in motion, and all walked in procession to a spacious meadow, kindly lent for the occasion by Mr Jones of Penywerlod farm, where a series of athletic and other sports were gone through. (Here the reporter mentions the long jump, a hurdle race, a tug o' war, a long pipe race (what was that?), and diving into a tub for oranges). There was also dancing and the inevitable game of 'Kiss-in-the-Ring', and one of the most interesting events of the afternoon was the graceful distribution of little parcels of tea, snuff and sugar amongst the old people of the parish.

There were similar rejoicings in December 1875 when the Squire of Clyro, Mr Baskerville brought home his wife, Miss Bertha Maria Hopton of Canon Frome Court. Again the pair were met by the villagers who stopped the carriage in Clyro village and took out the horses.

Willing hands were soon applied (to the ropes attached to the carriage) and the procession moved off at a brisk pace to the seat of the bridegroom. On arrival at the entrance the couple alighted amidst a roar of cheers and hearty wishes for their future happiness. Soon afterwards Mr Baskerville came to the entrance and invited all to partake of refreshments, and in a few choice words thanked them all for the kind reception they had given him and his wife and hoped to see all his tenants, their families and friends at a Ball which he intended giving in about six weeks' time... A dinner to all the cottagers and workmen on the estate was given at the Baskerville Arms Inn when upwards of fifty sat down to a sumptuous repast.

Disaster, alas, followed both these marriages. Edward Lechmere Thomas died of cholera in Colombo, where he had a coffee plantation; and Walter Baskerville's son was killed in the First World War.

When we come to consider the gentlefolk, the picture is very different. Though Kilvert was a conscientious parish priest, he still had a great deal of leisure, and time for many of the croquet, archery and fishing parties, picnics, balls, dinners and card and skating parties with which his well-to-do friends filled their lives. Many were able to travel widely. Mary Bevan seems to have been constantly on the move, attending parties and balls and calling on friends, and most of the ladies in the Bevan family spent months at a time in Weymouth. At home there were concerts, dinners, musical evenings, walks and excursions, battledore and shuttlecock and lawn tennis. Kilvert was a frequent visitor to London, and when he was there he visited art galleries and exhibitions, went to concerts and theatres and museums. At home he took no pleasure in shooting parties, and is a spectator rather than a participant at fishing parties. But he walks constantly, collects wild flowers, and finds a great deal of satisfaction in keeping his diary. Journal-keeping must have been one of the most common pleasures of the educated. At least four members of the Kilvert family (Robert Kilvert, Emily, Dora and Francis himself) kept a diary or wrote their memoirs. Mr Venables kept two kinds of diary. Mary Bevan and Mr Daniell of Kington Langley both kept a journal. I wonder how many more kept records which have since been thrown away and lost.

The following extracts from the *Hereford Times* and Kilvert's and Mary Bevan's diaries tell us more about the entertainments available at Clyro.

The Penny Reading at Clyro on 3 February 1871
(*Hereford Times*. 11 February 1871)
Popular Readings. The 4th of these readings was held yesterday (Friday) sen'night (3rd February 1871) in the National School Room, the Rev R. Lister Venables kindly presiding. The Room which will hold 250–300 people was literally crammed. The readings throughout were listened to

with marked attention and were frequently applauded. The
music was very efficient. Mrs Partridge's and Miss Haines's
rendering of the *Barbier de Seville* was everything that could
be desired, and elicited loud applause. The Church choir sang
the several Glees with capital precision; the Carnovale being
strongly encored but the rule of 'No Encores' was strictly
adhered to throughout. We understand that it is intended to
hold one more reading some time in March. We copy the
programme.

Mrs Partridge and Miss Haines	Duet Piano, Barbier de Seville
Mr J. Williams	Reading, Tall Talk
Mr Evans	Song, Jones's Sister
Reverend R. F. Kilvert	Recitation, Reflections by Miss Jean Ingelow
Choir	Glee, Sigh No More, Ladies
Mr Evans	Reading, Jonathan Muggs's Letter
Mr Lacey	Song, That's the Style for Me
Mr L. Williams	Reading, Selection from Childe Harold
Miss Gibbins and Mr Evans	Duet, The Gentle Stranger
Mr O. Meara	Reading, Nothing to Wear
Miss Williams	Song, The Wishing Cap
Choir	Glee, Hail Smiling Morn
Mr Partridge	Song, My Old Friend John
Reverend R. L. Venables	Reading, Selections from Macaulay
Mrs Partridge	Piano Solo, German Air
Mr L. Williams	Reading, The Misadventure at Margate
Mr H. Anthony	Song, Little Daisy
Mr Harris and Party	Trio, Song, The Lordly Gallants
Reverend R. F. Kilvert	Recitation, The Fairy Ride
Choir	Glee, The Carnovale
Mr Liggins	Reading, The Knight's Lady
Mr Williams and Party	Trio, The Travellers' Song
Mr Dallman	Recitation, Sign Boards
Mr Vaughan	Song
Finale	GOD SAVE THE QUEEN

The End

It is interesting to see that both the Vicar and his Curate took part
in this Reading, and that most of the participants were Clyro
parishioners. Mr Evans was almost certainly the schoolmaster,

Miss Gibbins was Frances or Fanny Gibbins, lady's maid to Mrs Venables. Mr Lacey was Charles Lacey, the coachman; Mr and Mrs Partridge were the tenants of Clyro Court Farm; Henry Anthony was either the wheelwright or more probably his son, also Henry; there was a Mr Vaughan, a carpenter, living in Hay Road, Clyro; a Mr Harris at Penycae, the home of Gypsy Lizzie; and the Mr Williams of the programme may have been Mr J. Williams of Great Lloyney. The Choir was the Clyro choir whom Kilvert heard practising on Easter Eve, 1870. Perhaps Mr Dallman, Mr Liggins and Mr O. Meara came from Hay.

Two Versions of the Ball at Clifford Priory
Friday 5 April 1872
I dined at the Vicarage at 6.30 and went with the Venables to the ball at Clifford Priory at 8. We stopped at Hay Castle to pick up Fanny and Willie Bevan. There were 52 people at the party. I danced with the following young ladies in order – Alice Bevan, quadrille – Cousie Bevan, Lancers – Daisy, quadrille – Miss Draper, Lancers – Fanny Bevan, quadrille – Jenny Dew, 16 Lancers – Katie Allen, Sir Roger de Coverley. Besides these I was engaged to Emmie Dew for Lancers, and to May Oliver for a quadrille, but these dances were omitted as the night was wearing. May Oliver was simply lovely, brimming over with excitement and delight and in a flutter of happiness, full of life and beauty. Her feet and hands were keeping time to the music even when she was not dancing . . . Fanny Bevan was enjoying herself intensely. Her face was fairly beaming with happiness and delight . . .

We danced in the drawing room and all sat down together to supper in the dining room. After supper about midnight that endless Cotillon was danced, but there was plenty of dancing afterwards.

Daisy promised to dance the fifth dance – a quadrille – with me and gave me her card and pencil to write her name.

Morrell and Miss Child were vis-a-vis to us, but I am afraid we did them out of their fair share of dancing, for Daisy and I were soon absorbed in conversation and each other – I at all events was absorbed in her – and became quite oblivious of the figure and the whole thing . . .

She was dressed in white almost entirely, with a faint sweet suspicion of blue, a white flower in her bright hair, and a quantity of dainty frilling and puffing almost hiding her fair shoulders. I thought I had never seen her look prettier.

When the quadrille was over – much too soon – she took my arm and we went out into the cool hall. I found her a comfortable chair screened from general observation by a beautiful azalea. She sat down and we began to talk again. But, alas, 'the course of true love never did run smooth'. We had not been talking long when our seclusion was broken in upon and our happiness marred – at least mine was – by hearing her father's voice behind us. As soon as she heard his voice she rose, I thought in a slight and pretty confusion. Then he called to know if she were engaged for the next dance, and I saw she was obliged to go . . .

The Venables went away between one and two o'clock, but as I wanted to see the ball out I remained . . . I was quite prepared to walk home, but at the last moment it appeared there was room in Crichton's omnibus so we went home all together, a merry noisy party. Crichton and his friend Mr Lucas, a Ch. Ch. man, the heir of Sir Harford Brydges, and Colonel Scudamore, Morrell, Willie Bevan and myself. When I got out to knock up the man at the turnpike gate going into Hay, the gate was icy with rime and the night was very cold . . . I got to bed at four-thirty just as dawn was breaking.

Kilvert's Diary (Vol. 2. 172–6)

Last Friday there was a dance at the Priory and Alice and I
went to stay there for it – it went off very well – but there was
no one there I cared to dance with.

Mary Bevan's Diary p. 18.

The New Mobility

For a man who, for the greater part of his life was a curate of
limited means in country parishes, Kilvert enjoyed remarkable
freedom of movement. He was, of course, unusually energetic and
adventurous as a young man, with a Wordsworthian love of
walking. In his early days at Clyro he seems to be constantly on
the move. When he is not visiting his parishioners he is exploring
northward towards Newchurch, Glascwm and Colva, eastward
towards Aberedw and Craig-Pwll-Du, and south over the Black
Mountains to Capel-y-Ffin and Llanthony. He frequently covered
twenty miles a day, mostly over rough country, and was
apparently none the worse for it.

At Langley Burrell, too, he was in the habit of walking long
distances. On one occasion (recalled, not recorded in the Diary)
he walked to Bath and back; on another to Malmesbury and back.
Occasionally, in Clyro, he takes to horseback, or rides in someone's vehicle; but in general he prefers to walk.

His longer journeys were, however, taken by train, and the
line he used most was the newly-opened Hereford Hay and Brecon
Railway. It was only a year old when Kilvert came to Clyro, and
even in 1870, when he begins to record his journeys, the newness
can hardly have worn off; the paint on the engines and the little
wooden stations must still have been fresh, and the fittings new
and untarnished. The new line provided a highly convenient
service up and down the Wye Valley. There were six passenger
up-trains and six down-trains a day, and by the junctions of Three
Cocks and Llechryd it was connected with the Mid-Wales and
Central-Wales systems. By means of these lines Kilvert was able

to explore a great deal of Wales. He used them to get to Haverfordwest when he went with his father on holiday to St David's; to explore the Cader Idris area; to Tenbury to stay with friends at Bockleton; to Gower to see his friends the Westhorps at Ilston; to Chepstow; to Brecon for church conferences; to Aberystwyth for another holiday; to Llanidloes and St Harmon to inspect the living he was offered there; and on beyond the limits of Wales to Liverpool via Shrewsbury and Chester. But the main use he made of the newly-opened line was to make quick visits to his friends up and down the valley, to Llysdinam, for instance, the family home of the Venables, and Whitney to see the Dews. He used the railway as we would use a bus; and it is probably true to say that he had at his disposal a public transport system superior to anything in existence a century later.

The eastern terminus of the Hereford Hay and Brecon line was Hereford, and from there, although it involved a change of stations, the whole of the British Railway system was open to him. Contrary to the opinion of his Clyro parishioners, who in general believed that he could not get to Wiltshire to see his father without crossing the sea, Kilvert could get to Chippenham (via Gloucester and Swindon) in a few hours; and from Chippenham it was an easy ride to Paddington. From Chippenham he also travelled to Bristol, Bath, Taunton, Truro (for a long holiday with his friends the Hockins), Oxford (to see his friend Mayhew), Lyme Regis, Worthing, The Isle of Wight, Weymouth and Canterbury and Skegness.. He must have covered several thousands of miles, even excluding the long journey he took on his honeymoon to Edinburgh via Durham; and his records throw a considerable amount of light on railway travel in the seventies – the cold unheated carriages, the absence, at times, even of lights, when passing through tunnels, accidents and mishaps, the look and feel and smell of trains and stations.

On at least two occasions Kilvert went even further afield. A note in Mr Venables's diary reveals that in 1869 he spent a long holiday in Switzerland, a journey that explains a number of disconnected references in his diary (to his Swiss haversack, his close knowledge of Strasbourg, the musical box he bought in Geneva etc). Then some time after his parting with Ettie and before his going to St Harmon, he paid a second visit to the continent, the trip to Paris, where, according to Miss Rowland's niece, he met the future Mrs Kilvert.

All these journeys were undertaken within the space of little more than ten years – a considerable achievement for a young man who was not in the habit of neglecting his parish duties, and who, for the greater part of this time, was not well-off; but it was here that his gift for friendship stood him in good stead. It was the Hockins who invited him to Truro and Taunton. Mr Gwatkins, who used to live near Claverton Lodge and who came to live in Nonsuch for a while, was his host in Liverpool; Mrs Westhorp with whom he stayed at Ilston was sister of Mrs Venables; at Bath he stayed with his sister Thersie; at Oxford with his friend Mayhew, and Mr Symonds, the father of Mrs Dallin, who had lived at one time at Langley Lodge; in London with a variety of friends; at Faversham with the Hiltons; and at Skegness, presumably with the Heanleys.

One has only to go back to Parson Woodforde and even to Gilbert White to see how limited and parochial the world of the eighteenth century cleric was, and what a liberating effect the coming of the railway had upon the life of an enterprising and curious young nineteenth century curate.

But Kilvert was not the only member of remote Radnorshire for whom the world, not only beyond Clyro and Hay, but beyond London and Paris, became suddenly readily accessible. Mrs Webb of Hardwick had been to Switzerland and gave lectures on her travels; so had Louisa Wyatt whom he met at the famous party at Clifford Priory on 7 July 1870. Edith Thomas, Daisy's sister had been to Gibraltar (probably to see her friends the Collingwoods) and had brought sketches back; Pope went on his honeymoon to

Paris; Squire Baskerville took a holiday in the Engadine; Mary
Bevan in her journal tells us that her father visited Italy; Miss
Cornewall of Moccas knew Cannes and told Kilvert about it when
he was considering the offer of the Chaplaincy there; Tomkyns
Dew went to Italy and brought back some plants for his garden;
even Miss Bynon of Pentwyn had been to Paris and Marseilles;
and (shades of the Vesey Stanhopes) Mr Prickard, who succeeded
Mr Venables at Clyro, spent a whole year in Genoa for the sake of
his wife's health. Perhaps she was suffering from the same malady
that took little Florence Hill from the Upper Noyadd to
Switzerland and recovery.

What Kilvert, in the notes he makes on his journeys,
particularly communicates is the pleasure of railway travel, the
sense of enjoying a new and wholly exhilarating experience.

Left Hay by the 10.16 train. I never had a lovelier journey up
the lovely valley of the Wye. A tender beautiful haze veiled
the distant hills and woods with a gauze of blue and silver and
pearl. It was a dream of intoxicating beauty. I saw all the old
familiar sights, the broad river reach at Boughrood flashing
round the great curve in the sunlight over its hundred
steps and rock ledge, the luxuriant woods which fringe the
gleaming river lit up here and there by the golden flame of a
solitary ash, the castled rock towers and battlements and
bastions of the Rocks of Aberedw . . . the famous rocky
wooded gorge through the depths of which the narrow
mountain stream of the Edw rushed foaming to its Aber to
meet the Wye, the house of Pant Shoni gleaming white
through the apple-laden orchard trees . . .

(Vol. 3. 83–4)

The railway did not only bring a new ease of travel; it made
possible new vistas, a novel and frequently dramatic view of the
landscape. Kilvert on one occasion describes how he was struck
anew with the beauty of Bath seen from the train, a moment of

surprise and delight that has its visual parallel in J. C. Bourne's
lithograph of the same scene. In fact Bourne, one of the finest artists
of the railway age, makes an almost perfect visual counterpart to
Kilvert. For Kilvert the railway is not a despoiler. The impact it
makes on the landscape is slight and more often picturesque than
otherwise – a sudden plume of steam shot up into the air, carriage
lights reflected in the water where his father has come to fish. So it
is with the famous lithographs that Bourne made to illustrate his
books on the Great Western and London and Birmingham
railways. The new railway bridge bestrides the roadway at
Chippenham, but through its arches crowd flocks of sheep and
herds of cattle, labouring men on foot and coaches and waggons.
The picturesque engines and diminutive carriages are inoffensive
and minor intruders in a world of meadows, streams, farms,
grazing cattle and anglers.

The railways that Kilvert knew best were mainly small, and
neither the trackway nor the unpretentious, often wooden, station
buildings seriously scarred the landscape. They were never
thought of by him as a violation, but as agents of a new liberty,
offering unparalleled access to new worlds, open not only to
himself, but, through him, to his parishioners.

And not solely through him, for it is clear that the new
freedom of movement was by no means restricted to the well-to-
do. By the 1870's people of all classes were on the move, and the
opening up of the country to the less-privileged was bringing into
existence a new class of sight-seers whom Kilvert labels 'tourists',
and to whose apparent trespassing on what had hitherto been the
preserves of the gentry he finds difficulty in reconciling himself.
Excursion trains were becoming common, and he used them; but it
is clear that he did not like the company he had to put up with when
he went on one to the Bath Flower Show (this was the occasion on
which the train had to pass through an unlighted Box Tunnel); he
disliked the excursionists who crowded into Beer while he was
there; and twice he exploded into uncharacteristic anger, once

against a 'vulgar crew of tourists (real British)' who jostled him and his friends near Land's End, and once against two visitors to Llanthony whose only offence seems to have been that they kept Kilvert waiting for his dinner. 'Of all noxious animals,' he says, 'the most noxious is a tourist. And of all tourists the most vulgar, ill-bred, offensive and loathsome is the British tourist.'

This is Kilvert at his most unreasonable. He claims to be annoyed by the sight of one tourist using his stick to point out objects of interest to another, but he does not mind when Canon Thomas shows him and his father round the cathedral at St David's, or Mr MacDonald, Claremont, or the servant girl, parts of Yaverland; and on occasions he himself behaves like one of the most irresponsible of tourists, climbing to the top of the walls of Tintern Abbey, and poking his umbrella through a hole in the tomb of the Earl of Richmond to 'stir up the kingly dust'. Kilvert's reaction to the party of ladies who descended on Llanthony when he was there, to the people who spoilt his pleasure at Land's End, and to the 'snobs' of Sketty, looks like the resentment of a middle class traveller against the invasion by less acceptable travellers of beauty spots hitherto looked upon as the special provinces of his own class. Clearly for Kilvert there were tourists and tourists, and the new lower-class travellers were of the less acceptable kind.

Kilvert's attitude here is surprising, because intolerance is not one of his shortcomings; and in general he is an unprejudiced and earnest traveller. He is a kind of natural explorer, at home everywhere. He soon tires of London, it is true, but Bristol excites him, he is not offended by the mines of Cornwall, and the docks and exchanges of Liverpool stimulate him. At one point he even contemplated a trip to see the steelworks of Glamorgan. He is remarkably open-minded (except on the theme of tourists), always curious and appreciative, and eager to share his new experiences with those of his parishioners whom poverty or toil kept at home. This is one of the characteristics that made him a good parish priest. He went out to see the world and brought back news of it to

his parishioners, opening to them whole new territories of
experience the existence of which they had never suspected.

Health and Sickness

In the three parishes with which the Diary chiefly deals, medical
services for the poor, especially in Clyro and Bredwardine, were
very rudimentary. There were at least three doctors in the Hay and
Clyro area – Dr Clouston, who was based on Hay, Dr Giles of
Staunton-on-Wye, and Dr Bennett of Builth (it is not clear
whether the Mr Tyler who is mentioned in Vol. 3. 373 is a doctor
or not). Whatever their qualifications and training, they do not
seem to have been outstandingly competent, or to have effected
many cures. Isabel Davies of Bettws was cured of an abscess on the
breast, but it was to the Infirmary (probably at Hereford) rather
than to any of the local doctors that the credit was given. Mr
Vincent of Langley Burrell was cured of water around the heart by
the extraordinary expedient of getting it to run out of his heels, but
Mrs Vincent never told Kilvert who was responsible for this
bizarre remedy. Dr Clouston relieved Kilvert of the pain caused by
a boil on the thigh; and maybe it was one of the local doctors who
arranged for Florence Hill to go to Switzerland where she
recovered from the tuberculosis that threatened her life. But in the
main the cures proposed by the local practitioners were at their
best rather naîve. Mrs George Davies of Bredwardine, who had
jaundice, was given a decoction of the inner bark of the barberry
tree, which, being the same colour as she was, presumably made
her more yellow than ever; and the father of Maria Jefferies of
Langley Burrell, whose liver was being gradually eaten away by a
great worm, was advised 'to take to smoking and draw the worm
up that way'. The worm did come up, but this was not the end, for
the liver 'enlarged greatly and covered his stomach.' What
happened next we are not told. At its worst, however, the
treatment ordered and carried out was horrifying. It was to the

credit of Mr Tyler of Maloun (wherever that is) that he would not
let Mr Giles treat Mrs Meredith of Brobury, who suffered from a
cancer of the eye, by putting a needle through her nose and
working it backwards and forwards; William Hulbert's experience
with the Chippenham Doctor (Mr Jay) who not only removed
seven teeth and stumps but cut out three tumours from his head as
well, was clearly traumatic (Vol. 3. 191–2); and what must have
been the sufferings of young Meredith of the Tump, Clyro, who
has lock-jaw?

> Went to the Tump to see young Meredith, who has had his
> jaw locked for six months, a legacy of mumps. He has been to
> Hereford Infirmary where they kept him two months, gave
> him chloroform, and wrenched his jaws open gradually by a
> screw lever.
>
> (Vol. 1. 261)

Provincial medicine seems on the whole to have been
unenlightened. None of the doctors mentioned in the Diary except
perhaps Mr Clouston seems to have been as well-informed and
progressive as Mr Gaine, Kilvert's very able dentist of whom Mr
Colin Davies has written (Kilvert Society, Newsletter, June
1974); and none seems to have been as aware as that unprofessional
hygienist, the Rev H. Moule of Fordington, of the links between
epidemics and inadequate water supplies and bad housing. It is
noticeable that Mr Venables took Mrs Venables off to London to
have her babies; and Mr Crichton of Wye Cliff may have done the
same for Mrs Crichton.

In general the qualified doctors attended only on the gentlefolk. They were too expensive for the poor, who had to fall back on
their own folk medicines (ointments made from fern, eel oil and
elder twigs for deafness etc), and on practical help from their
pastors. Both Mr Venables and his curate were very alive to the
needs of the poor. In very bad weather they distributed food,
sheets and blankets. Kilvert on occasions provided brandy out of

his own pocket, and even went so far as to prescribe medicines
(sulphur and hog's lard for young John Williams of Paradise, who
was suspected of having the itch) (Vol. 1. 158); and to make
certain recommendations about the imperfect Clyro water supply.
The Victorian country parson had clearly to be a man of many
parts. Kilvert did not only attend to the spiritual needs of his flock.
He had also to be welfare officer, teacher, current-affairs officer,
and unpaid medical assistant. At Bredwardine the charity made
available by church funds, as it was at Clyro, was supplemented
by the famous Jarvis Charity, invaluable in relieving the real needs
of the poor.

Most of the ailments from which the poor of Clyro,
Bredwardine and Langley Burrell suffered were the legacies of a
life-time of hard toil in the open air, poor food and inadequate
housing conditions – rheumatism, rheumatic fever, apoplexy,
colds, coughs, paralysis, fits and what Kilvert calls 'stoppage',
and the consequences of such accidents as that which happened to
Emma Griffiths of Clyro who was gored by a bull at Bron Dhu, to
Mr Haigh Allen, who, according to Mary Bevan, lost his arm in a
farm accident, and the many who were drowned by falling into the
treacherous mawn pools. But the plight of the mentally ill was the
worst. The well-to-do could be cared for in private institutions
such as Dr Fox's asylum at Brislington near Bristol to which
Kilvert's Aunt Emma was committed; and there were mental
homes for the poor such as the asylum at Devizes (to which poor
Mary Strange was taken), and at Abergavenny. But in general the
poor and mentally ill of Clyro and Bredwardine had no one to care
for them but their own relatives. Sometimes they were fortunate.
The 'idiot' stepdaughter at Bredwardine was lovingly cared for by
that remarkable woman Priscilla Price; and Meredith's sister at
the Homme, Clyro, had friends.

The poor crazy woman with faded face and wild strange eyes
came tottering downstairs leaning on the arm of Mrs Phillips

of the Burnt House . . . stretching out her hand before her as
if she were blind.

(Vol. 2. 27)

But the plight of poor Mrs Watkins of Lower Cwmgannon was
pitiful. She was kept in her room and at first her son did not want
Kilvert to see her, but he changed his mind and asked the curate to
speak to her.

He led the way up the broad oak staircase into a fetid room
darkened. The window was blocked up with stools and chairs
to prevent the poor mad creature from throwing herself out.
There was nothing in the room but her bed and a chair. She
lay with the blanket over her head. When her son turned down
the blanket I was almost frightened. It was a mad skeleton
with such a wild scared animal's face as I never saw before.

(Vol. 2. 24)

For poor unhinged creatures such as these there was only one
release; and the same fate awaited those who could not face the
destitution and disgrace that life had brought upon them. A
barmaid from the Blue Boar in Hay threw herself into the river –
she was, in Kilvert's phrase, 'enceinte'. William Jones, who lived
near Chapel Dingle Cottage, becoming helpless and infirm, and
not being able to bear the idea of not being competent to care for
himself, cut his own throat. Mary Meredith, who was pregnant,
and was refused by her brother the money that might have
persuaded her seducer to marry her, plunged into the Wye and
drowned herself.   (Vol. 2. 47–8)

    The most dreaded and dangerous disease of the age was
undoubtedly tuberculosis. It was this that killed poor little Lily
Crichton (Mary Bevan in her journal confirms this); Mary of
Penllan; Mrs Prosser of the Swan and her sister Mrs Hope of the
Rose and Crown in Hay; Lizzie Powell who lived opposite the
Vicarage; Hannah Gore Price of Whitty's Mill – the third of her

198 THE VALUE OF THE DIARY

family to succumb; John Hatherall of Langley Burrell; possibly Emmeline Vaughan and Madeleine Crichton; and it was this that threatened the life of Florence Hill.

Kilvert's records reveal several remarkable facts. In the main it was the girls and young women who succumbed to it (just as most of the Brontë daughters did). The men were less vulnerable. John Hatherall is the only man to be mentioned by Kilvert as a tubercular victim. Possibly their open air life left them more immune to the disease, while at the same time exposing them to the aches and pains brought about by working too long in the open without adequate protection.

The other point that is worth noting is that tuberculosis is commoner in Radnorshire than in Wiltshire. The explanation is probably several-fold. In the first place the climate of Wiltshire was less harsh than that of Clyro. Kilvert does not experience there the extremes of weather that he had to put up with in Wales. Secondly the standard of living was probably higher in Langley Burrell. There were desperately poor people there, such as poor Summerflower who could not eat till he had sold his watercress; but in general living standards were a cut above those in Clyro and Bredwardine. Housing conditions in Clyro were, at their worst, appalling. There is no parallel in Langley Burrell for the filthy hovels in which old men such as old Mr Price had to live, or Edward Evans' cabin.

> It was so dark . . . that I could not see his face or him all the time I was in the low and crazy loft in the dark, and only heard a feeble voice proceeding out of the darkness . . . A small and filthy child knelt or crouched in the ashes of the hearth before a black grate and cold cinders . . . Almost all the glass was smashed out of the bedroom or rather bed loft window, and there was only a dirty cloth hanging before the ruin of the window to keep the wind away . . .
>
> (Vol. 1. 251)

Credit for the superiority of Langley Burrell to Clyro has probably to be given to the much-maligned Squire Ashe. Mr Millard who lived for many years in Langley Burrell told me that the estate cottages on the Langley estate, probably put up mostly in the last century, are in general well-built, strong and generously designed. Of course the most thoroughly documented medical history in the Diary is that of Kilvert himself, and a close scrutiny of the entries relating to his physical and mental welfare reveals a sad story. In the first volume there are six occasions on which he feels unwell, but on three of these he may be said to be suffering from self-inflicted wounds. He hurt his back falling off a pony, and he had headaches from eating and drinking too much and sitting in an over-heated room. In Vol. 2 there are six more entries, but this time only one of his ailments is of his own provoking. He suffers most frequently from neuralgia and face ache (probably both the same) and from colds and coughs. In Vol. 3 there are no less than fourteen entries, and especially after going to Bredwardine he seems to have suffered with distressing regularity from colds, coughs and sore throats. This may have been the reason why Dr Giles, thinking of him as a potentially tubercular patient, advised him to take the offer of the chaplaincy at Cannes. The bouts of illness grow longer and more serious, and mention has already been made of evidence both from the diary and his poetry that he was beginning to have premonitions of an early death. Within nine years the strong athletic young man who had astonished everyone with his walking prowess has become a sick man, and when his last illness comes upon him the medical world is as helpless as it had been when confronted with the plight of young Lily Crichton, Mrs Dewing and Mrs Prosser of the Swan. Would he have had better fortune if he had gone to Cannes? It is possible that the constant small ailments he suffered at Bredwardine undermined his resistance and left him fatally vulnerable to a serious attack. Kilvert and so many of his friends lived a life closer in many ways to the Elizabethans than to those who live in our century, enjoying a brief and brilliant flowering of vitality followed by an early collapse and a premature death. Perhaps if he had only been born a generation later he might have survived to write as he desired to write and to fulfil the faithful ministry which was so dear to his heart.

Francis Kilvert as a Clergyman
(Rev D. T. W. Price)

The Clerical World
Francis Kilvert lived during what was perhaps the most halcyon period for the country parson in England and Wales. The world revealed by his *Diary* is full of clergymen, many of them of aristocratic or gentle birth, like the Rev R. L. Venables, vicar of Clyro, the Rev Sir George Cornewall, rector of Moccas, the Rev W. J. Thomas, vicar of Llanigon, the Rev W. L. Bevan, vicar of Hay, and Lord Arthur Hervey, bishop of Bath and Wells. There was one clergyman to almost every parish, including such tiny parishes as Bryngwyn, with the Rev John Hughes; Llanbedr Painscastle, with the Rev John Price, 'The Solitary'; and Newchurch, with the Rev David Vaughan. Mr Le Quesne has drawn attention to the Rev David Vaughan as a representative of the Welsh Anglican tradition of a peasant clergy. (*After Kilvert*, p. 96). In the Wye Valley the clergy were of a more exalted class. Clyro had a curate as well as a resident vicar. The population of the parish was 842 in 1871, considerably larger than most neighbouring parishes, and with an area of 7,370 acres Clyro parish is almost twice as large as the next largest contiguous parish. The vicar and curate served the chapel of Bettws Clyro as well as the parish church of St Michael.

This golden age of the country parson, like any other golden age, is less inviting at closer inspection, than when viewed in a sentimental and nostalgic fashion, but in one important sense it was quite unlike our own time – very few clergymen had any serious doubts about their role in life, their work, or indeed their faith. Charles Darwin had published *The Origin of Species* in 1859 and *The Descent of Man* in 1871, but the problems posed by these works did not apparently affect the country clergy in Kilvert's pages. A topic of greater concern to them was one within the Church, namely ritualism, but this was confined to a very small minority of rural parsons in the 1870s, and these were on the whole dismissed as eccentrics by Kilvert.

Churchmanship
In churchmanship Kilvert was very much a moderate Anglican. He disliked the low-church Mr Winthrop who said 'that a man became a clergyman just as he became a gardener by taking up that particular line of life'. Francis had no time at all for high-church priests like the vicar of Monkton Wyld, Dorset, whose service he attended on 6 August 1871: 'The clergyman, Mr Carn, late 14th Light Dragoons and Curate of Horsham, wore a green stole and gabbled the prayers. The singing drawled and droned by a weak surpliced Choir. No Sermon. Imitation Mass, the clergyman going about the chancel, to and fro like a puppet on wires in a play. He was playing at Mass'. Fr Stanley Luff has commented that 'dislike of an imitation Mass implies some respect for a real one'. The eccentric rector (Kilvert calls him vicar) of Llanmadoc, in Gower, Mr Davies, was 'an uncommonly kind good fellow, a truly simple-minded, single-hearted man' but Kilvert's description of him and his church is revealing. He 'looked like a Roman priest, close shaven and shorn, dressed in seedy black, a long coat and broad shovel hat . . . (The church) was beautifully finished and adorned but fitted up in the high ritualistic style'. The diarist's taste of very advanced Anglo-

Catholicism at St Barnabas's Church in Oxford is described at great length. Solemn Evensong was clearly most unfamiliar to Kilvert, and he was not very sure of the names of the various vestments, for the officiant was probably wearing a cope rather than 'a chasuble stiff with gold'. The whole service seemed 'pure Mariolatry' to Kilvert. Even the sermon preached by the very famous Father Stanton, of St Albans, Holborn, disappointed him: 'The matter was not original or interesting, and the manner was theatrical and overdone'. The incense was stifling. As they came out of church, Francis's companion asked him if he had ever seen such a function as that. 'No, I never did and I don't care if I never do again. This was the grand function of the Ascension at St Barnabas, Oxford. The poor humble Roman Church hard by is quite plain, simple and Low Church in its ritual compared with St Barnabas in its festal dress on high days and holidays.'

Kilvert cared little for monasticism, as one might expect. On a number of occasions, notably in April and September 1870, he visited the abbey of Fr Ignatius at Capel-y-Ffin. The monks were unfavourably contrasted with the fair-haired girl he met in the hamlet near the abbey: 'It does seem very odd at this age of the world in the latter part of the 19th century to see monks gravely wearing such dresses and at work in them in broad day. One could not help thinking how much more sensible and really religious was the dress and occupation of the masons and of the hearty healthy girl washing at the Chapel House, living naturally in the world and taking their share of its work, cares and pleasures, than the morbid unnatural life of these monks going back into the errors of the dark ages and shutting themselves up from the world to pray for the world. "Laborare est orare".' Without doubt this was the attitude of the vast majority of clergymen towards the revival of Religious life within the Church of England. When Kilvert met Fr Ignatius, Francis was, probably for the first time in his life, addressed as 'Father'. Ignatius was very conversational, and revealed that he made £1,000 a year through his preaching: 'He gets on much better with the Low Church than with the High Church people he says, best of all with the Dissenters who consider and call him a second Wesley'. Kilvert hoped that one of the novices would never become a monk: 'I hope he is reserved for a better fate'.

Towards the end of his short life Kilvert was offered an Anglican chaplaincy at Cannes – there were four Anglican churches in that town in the later nineteenth century – and this fact surely indicates that in churchmanship he was moderate and sensible. Fr Luff is probably correct in seeing Kilvert as a *sound* Anglican, 'neither High, Low, nor Middle'.

Worship
Kilvert fully accepted the Book of Common Prayer of 1662, with the exception of the Athanasian Creed which he abhorred. He was anxious to preserve a right decency in worship, and he was 'very much annoyed at seeing the black bottle put upon the (altar) Table' at Holy Communion in Langley Burrell. He was greatly attached to the concept of the Established Church, as is shewn by his remarks about a meeting of the (anti-Establishment) Liberation Society held at Chippenham on 11 May 1876. He was a fervent supporter of the monarchy, and was deeply affected by the illness of the Prince of Wales in December 1871. He disliked the Puritans, especially in their 'gloomy, hideous and repulsive' ideas on burial and death.

On Sundays he conducted, or assisted in, the normal services of the Prayer Book, Morning Prayer, Litany, and Sermon in the morning, and Evening Prayer and Sermon in the afternoon, or occasionally in the evening. Holy Communion followed Morning Prayer, usually on the first Sunday of the month and on the great festivals. At Bredwardine and Clyro Holy Communion was regularly celebrated on the first Sunday of the month. At Langley Burrell there are only two references in the *Diary* to Holy Communion outside festivals, on the second and third Sundays of the month. The *Diary* records very few Holy Communion services, however, with, for instance, no mention at all of celebrations at Bettws Clyro and Brobury. Kilvert does note that in Langley Burrell it 'is an ancient custom' to have Holy Communion not on Whitsunday but on Trinity Sunday. Fewer people communicated than we might imagine. In March 1870 Kilvert 'spoke to the people very seriously about coming to the Holy Communion, and the small number of Communicants'. In some parishes the people had very little opportunity to communicate, as at Foxham (Wilts.) where in 1875 it was said that the Sacrament had been administered only five times in two years. On Easter Day 1876 there were 41 communicants at Langley 'the largest number that I or anyone else had ever seen in Langley Church at once'. In 1878 there were 20 Easter communicants at Bredwardine, but on a fine morning in July of the same year there were only five 'guests', as Kilvert charmingly terms communicants. On 6 October 19 people communicated, 'the greatest number I have seen since I have been at Bredwardine'. (He had forgotten Easter Day!)

Additional services were held on weekdays in Advent and Lent. At Clyro in Lent 1870 a service, Litany and Sermon, was conducted on Wednesdays at 11 a.m., and Kilvert preached at a Lent evening service at Biddestone (Wilts.) on a Thursday in 1876 when there was a very thin congregation: 'I thought the game hardly worth the candle and the ten miles walk in the snow'. Advent services at Bredwardine on Friday evenings at 7 p.m. drew 30 and more of the faithful. On Ash Wednesday the Commination service was provided, with a sermon. Mothering Sunday was observed by young people returning home to see their parents, and Good Friday was marked by special services. Kilvert officiated at the Union Workhouse in Hay on Good Friday 1870, and observed that 'Good Friday has now become a holiday and mere day of pleasure'. The Sunday after Ascension Day was called Expectation Sunday. Harvest Festival was rapidly becoming a most popular occasion, with much effort being expended on decorating churches. In 1871 Kilvert attended Harvest Festivals at Cusop, Clyro, Whitney, and Newchurch, and in 1878 he was present at such festivals at Bredwardine, Clifford, and Llowes, and presumably at Brobury too. Kilvert travelled very widely, and visited numerous churches, often taking part in services. At St Saviour on the Cliff, Shanklin, for example, on Sunday 14 June 1874 he read the Gospel at 8 a.m., preached at 11 a.m. and 3.30 p.m., and sat in the congregation at 6.30 p.m.

Preaching

Sometimes Francis preached extempore, on occasions to his own satisfaction, but on at least one afternoon 'the thing was a failure'. He found it difficult to deliver a *short* address extempore: 'Somehow I cannot confine my "extempore" sermons within less than half an hour. Half an hour seems like five minutes when you are talking or preaching'. Normally he read his sermon, even when he was using a sermon for the fourth time, as at Newchurch Harvest Festival in 1871. The sermon, on Ruth and Boaz, had already been preached at Eglwys Oen Duw ('The Church of the Lamb of God'), Llowes, and Whitney, but Kilvert still found it necessary to read it, in spite of the inconveniently low pulpit. He must have stirred the congregation, however, for the collection was the highest known at Newchurch. 'Vaughan said I had drawn water out of stony rocks and had hit the Newchurch farmers as hard as Moses hit the rock'. At Langley in January 1878 it was so dark in church that Kilvert could scarcely see to read his sermon. Favourite sermons were frequently re-used, for Kilvert preached in a remarkable number of churches. The sermons on Mizpah and on the Mountain of Galilee are examples of this.

Liturgy

The *Diary* gives useful glimpses of liturgical practice, although there are surprisingly few references to Sundays in the published edition. We do learn, however, that collections in church were rare, and that in some places people stayed away from church 'on purpose to shirk the collections'. There are several references to the churching of women and to baptisms, and a particularly interesting description of a confirmation at Whitney on 30 March 1870: 'The Bishop of Hereford (Atlay) has a new fashion of confirming only two persons at a time, kneeling at the rails'. It was at this confirmation that the curate of Cusop, Andrew Pope, was confirmed again, 'a most unfortunate thing'. We learn later that the bishop of Hereford was not a born orator and did not excite enthusiasm, one of the many small points that help to enliven the 1870's for the reader. Kilvert conducted many marriages, in numerous churches, at many different times of day, and funerals also, some white-glove, some black-glove. He reveals a growing sense of the need for decency in all worship, a sharp contrast with some of the clergy of the previous generation, like the former vicar of Llanbedr Painscastle who preached a sermon at the funeral of a farmer with whom he had quarrelled, with the text 'Hell from beneath is moved for thee to meet thee at thy coming'. The description of the funeral of little Davie at Bredwardine on Christmas Day 1878 is extremely moving, especially when one recalls that this was Kilvert's last Christmas on earth, although he was only 38 years of age.

The *Diary* reveals very close family ties, and we read of family prayers with hymns and of sermons being read in the family on Sunday evenings. It is not easy to discover whether Kilvert read the daily offices. On 17 August 1874 he read the second lessons for the day in the Greek Testament, but there is no other reference to the private reading of Matins and Evensong. Some churches observed Holy Days. At Chippenham, for example, the Candlemas Service was held at 5.30 p.m. instead of 7 p.m. in 1874 for fear of the mob on election day, and there was a service at Eardisley on Monday 1 May 1876 to keep the feast of St Philip and St James. Kilvert frequently uses saints' days, and many other stranger dates, in his *Diary*.

Clyro was in the diocese of St David's, but the clergy and people of the area were seldom troubled by the bishop, who lived at Abergwili, near Carmarthen. Few of the clergy, let alone the laity, had probably been to St David's itself (no ordinations were held in the Cathedral until about 1898), although Francis and his father went there in October 1871, one of the highlights of the *Diary*. The bishop of St David's, Basil Jones, confirmed at Rhayader in May 1878, arriving at the town during a downpour, when 'the Bishop picked up his legs and ran like a greyhound'. The bishop of St David's is scarcely ever mentioned in the *Diary*, although the bishop of Hereford appears quite frequently in the Wye Valley. Occasionally Kilvert attended archidiaconal and ruri-decanal visitations and conferences, but he preferred to avoid such gatherings whenever possible. One would like to know more of the Wye-side Clerical Association, which held a meeting at Hardwick in January 1878. The world of the *Diary* is full of clergymen, frequently meeting each other and dining together.

What distinctive dress did the clergy wear? It is unlikely that Francis wore a clerical collar. He may have worn a white tie, for clergy did apparently wear some obvious mark of their calling, since Kilvert met clergy frequently and recognised them as such. On the other hand he was asked if he was a preacher when he was lost above Llowes in April 1876. In church he normally wore a white surplice over his ordinary clothes, and seldom, if ever, a cassock. He was very inconvenienced at a wedding in Bathwick in 1874 when the surplices available were far too small (as the clergy of the church were short men) and he was prepared to try to hide his knees by wearing a cassock, but the cassocks were also, naturally, too small. Clergymen who wore cassocks were clearly suspect in Kilvert's eyes, men like Mr Welby at Clyro, Charlie Clarke of Kington Langley, who wore a cassock and a shovel hat, and Mr Rivett-Carnac of Bremhill (Wilts.), who wore 'petticoats'. Older clergy still wore gowns for preaching, and Francis's father began to preach in a surplice during the 1870's, while the vicar of Clyro was still wearing a gown for preaching in 1870. The future lay with the surplice, and it is interesting that in 1878 the re-opening of Mansell Gamage church was attended by 'more than 25 clergy in surplices'. (Mansell Gamage church is now redundant, and has been converted into a private house.) The 1870's was a great decade for restoring churches, and Kilvert records several re-openings besides Mansell Gamage.

From time to time Kilvert attended special services. The consecration of the new bishop of Oxford in January 1870 in Westminster Abbey, the service at the opening of the new baths at Bath in the following month, the funeral of Miss Kilvert at Worcester in December 1870, and Morning Prayer at St Michael's College, Tenbury, in October 1871, are especially notable.

Pastoralia

Most of Kilvert's work was, of course, in visiting, or 'villaging' as he calls it. The accounts of visiting in Clyro are particularly fascinating, and one soon comes to know many of the inhabitants well. There was much poverty and disease in the parish, and the stench in the hovels could be almost unbearable. On one occasion Kilvert was afraid to sit down because of the lice; or 'bocs' as Clyro folk called them. Sometimes the curate met with abuse, as from Ben Lloyd in August 1870, and a considerable number of the parishioners were insane. Kilvert was very zealous in taking Holy Communion to the sick, and he was 'very happy and thankful' when Hannah Whitney received the sacrament for the first time at the age of 90.

Kilvert regularly taught in village day-schools, and in July 1871 he was going to school three times a day to prepare the children for the dreaded inspection. All went very well on the day of the inspection, which was carried out by Shadrach Pryce, the Government Inspector for Breconshire, and himself an Anglican clergyman. When he was at Bredwardine Kilvert took a boarding private pupil, in the best tradition of the family. Sunday School took up much of his time. one little girl in Clyro, when asked what happened on Psalm Sunday, replied 'Jesus Christ went up to heaven on an ass'. Kilvert commented that 'this was the promising result of a long struggle to teach her something about the Festivals of the Church'. One of the Langley Burrell school children was asked 'Who made the World?', and replied 'Mr Ashe'.

The image of the shepherd came readily to Kilvert's mind when he heard of the neglected state of Clyro in 1873: 'My sheep wander through the mountains'. He used many opportunities to help his flock – Bible classes, communicants' guilds, penny readings, and lectures. Some of these lectures covered many subjects, as at Langley Burrell on 15 January 1873 when Kilvert spoke on 'Noah's vineyard and drunkenness, the Tower of Babel, Babylon and the confusion of tongues, the Tongue Tower, the death of the Emperor Napoleon III and the Great Coram Street Murder'. The penny readings at Clyro were very popular – 167 attended on 27 November 1871 and nearly 250 on 23 January 1872. Kilvert obviously devoted much time and energy in preparing for these events.

The Church was very powerful in society in the rural areas in which Kilvert worked. At Clyro, for instance, the birthday of the vicar's daughter was an occasion for a whole day's holiday. There were many gatherings of clerical families, and social life was very considerable. The clergy and gentry must have known each other very well indeed. Francis preferred to preach to the poor people when he could speak 'much better and more freely'. He was undoubtedly extremely popular with all classes of society; one senses a very real regret felt by the people of Clyro when he left them in 1872.

Ecumenical Thoughts
On the whole the clergymen in the *Diary* are all Anglicans. Kilvert obviously enjoyed meeting Mr Wilson, the Moravian minister of

Tytherton (Wilts.), but he seldom mentions the clergy of other denominations. Ecumenicism was not fashionable, and we must not judge Kilvert by the standards of a century later. Fr Luff has written that Kilvert's 'sympathy for things Catholic amounts to a nostalgia'. In March 1871 he sat in Clyro churchyard and mused on how congenial he found the Catholic phrase ('unorthodox but beautiful and soothing words of prayer') 'Requiescat in pace'. In September 1875 he was deeply moved by his experience of praying in the Roman Catholic Church at Bath: 'I knelt in the Church and prayed for charity, unity, and brotherly love, and the union of Christendom. Surely a Protestant may pray in a Catholic Church and be none the worse'. He spent 'a quiet solemn half hour' in the same church in January 1878 while waiting for the train after shopping in Bath.

He felt less well disposed towards nonconformists, possibly because they were more in evidence in Clyro and Langley Burrell. He found the chapel at Rhos Goch 'very ugly, high, and boxy-looking'. A woman called Sheen told him about the services: 'On Sunday evenings she said, the Chapel is crowded often and sometimes 200 people are present. I could hardly have believed the room would hold so many. Probably it will not'. A parishioner told him about the two chapels at Painscastle: 'Stones were frequently thrown into the Chapels among the congregation during service, and once a dog was hurled in. There was a great laugh when the dog was seen flying in'. We see considerable prejudice against dissenters in the *Diary*: 'Some barbarian – a dissenter no doubt – probably a Baptist, has cut down the beautiful silver birches on the Little Mountain near Cefn y Fedwas'. Religious strife could on occasions be strong, and, for example, in Clyro in March 1872 in the election for a Guardian for the parish Church and Chapel competed on denominational lines; feeling ran very high. Kilvert records the influence of nonconformist ministers on elections in South Wales: 'Talk of being priest-ridden, 'tis nothing to being ridden by political dissenting preachers'. In the meeting

house at Kington St Michael a ranting preacher once stated that
'the Methodists bring the lost sheep down off the mountains, the
Baptists wash them, and the Church of England shears them'. In
such a world it is not surprising that Kilvert sympathized greatly
with the Cornish curate at Gwythian who, in a delicious phrase,
complained a great deal about the people 'and their ineradicable
tendency to dissent'. Kilvert was, however, far less intolerant than
most Anglican clergymen, and when a nonconformist from
Painscastle declared that he expected the curate to be angry with
him for having read the Bible every Sunday to Mrs Williams,
Kilvert 'begged him not to believe any such nonsense and said that
so far from my being cross with him he had my warmest thanks'.
Kilvert added 'These are the misconceptions that are spread
abroad about the clergy'.

Theology
Kilvert's knowledge of theology was limited – after all he had
received no special training in the subject – but he was able to
argue at dinner on the character of Joel. Much theology just failed
to interest him; when Richard Meredith of Hay asked him about
the Nicolaitans and what Hymenoeus and Philetus meant by the
Resurrection being already past Kilvert wrote 'I am ashamed to say
that I knew as little as he did, and cared to know less, but I
promised to try to find out for him'. He became very excited,
however, about the teaching of the British Israelites, which he
hoped might be true. His morality was very conventional.

Of Times Past
The *Diary* is also useful for some of the stories which Kilvert
heard about clerical life in the early nineteenth century. One
recalls the remarkable extempore sermons preached by Mr
Thomas, the old vicar of Disserth, on sinners and on 'Mr Noe', and
the pugilistic vicar of Llanbedr Painscastle, Mr Williams, who was
beaten in a fight at Clyro and who preached on the following

Sunday with two black eyes, a broken head and swollen nose, and great black and blue bruises, giving an account of the fight, and representing himself as victorious. Kilvert tells of the parish in Wiltshire which never had Holy Communion because, in the words of the clerk, it had 'no tackling'. The vicar of Fordington, near Dorchester, described to Kilvert in April 1874 the state of the parish nearly fifty years earlier. The communicants expected to be paid by the vicar for taking the sacrament, and in a nearby church the old parson did not use water in baptism – 'He spat into his hand'. William Barnes, the poet rector of Winterbourne Came, whom Kilvert met at the same time in 1874, was a survival from an earlier age, with his 'dark grey loose gown girt round the waist with a black cord and tassel, black knee breeches, black silk stockings and gold buckled shoes. He had long silvery hair to his shoulders and a long white beard'. A survivor almost from the Celtic age was the Rev John Price, vicar of Llanbedr Painscastle, a hermit eccentric, whom Kilvert met on 3 July 1872.

Francis Kilvert was a true son of the Church of England, and in his faith and life certainly a child of his time. That is why his *Diary* is worth its weight in gold.

Postscript
This paper originated in a talk given at the Kilvert Conference in January 1975. An earlier version of this paper, with full footnote references to all citations from the *Diary*, may be found in *A Kilvert Symposium* (Kilvert Society, Hereford, 1975), pp. 9–20.

The Folk-Lore of Radnorshire

From the notes made by Kilvert which are referred to in an earlier chapter, from his diary, and from other notes left behind by one of his friends, Edith Burham Thomas, Daisy Thomas's sister, we can judge how rich and diverse was the folk-culture of Radnorshire. Mention has already been made of the short list of Radnorshire words that Mayhew sent on his friend's behalf to *Notes and Queries*; what is equally interesting is the number of local words with which he spices his prose, using them, in general, unselfconsciously, as if they were part and parcel of his everyday vocabulary. Among such words are

askal, asgal	(a newt)
glat	(a gap in a hedge)
mawn	(peat)
cratch	(eat heartily, like a horse)
skillet	(small brass or copper saucepan)
Kiss-at-the-garden gate	(woodruff or pansy)
wittan	(mountain ash)
stoen	(of stone)
soul bell	(funeral bell)
stock	(peck)
pun	(beat or pound)
hardy-straw	(shrew)
bocs	(lice)
steen	(earthenware pot)
jennetings	(kind of apples)

The originality, colour and diversity of local Radnorshire speech is equally evident in the list of local sayings drawn from Edith Thomas's surviving notebook (which Mrs Parker of Woolpit, Suffolk, very kindly let me examine), and the article she published, late in her life, in *Folk Lore* (December 1913). The following is a selection from her notes.

They that do wear a hole in the middle of their shoe, they'll never want bread.
He who takes what isn't his'n, when he's cotched is sent to prison.
Plant and prune, the increase of the moon.
It's the early crow as eats the late 'un's breakfast.
He has too many irons in the fire, and some of them will burn.

Where there are three children, two to fight and one to part
them, that's nice.
Work and I won't quarrel if I'm well.
Many fish can go down the stream but it takes a strong one to
come back.
A lie will travel round the world while truth is putting his
boots on.
I must speak well of the bridge as do carry me over.
Whatever is young learnt is never old forgot.

Among the local superstitions which Mrs Essex Hope took from
Kilvert's notes, and which are mentioned in the Diary, are these
strange beliefs:–

To see the first snail of the year crawling on the hard road and
not on the grass was to be warned of a hard season ahead.
A man who hid iron before his death would return in spirit to
look for it.
Branches of wittan (mountain ash) and birch placed over the
door of a house keep witches away.
You could find the name of a thief by putting a key on the
bible and letting it turn, or by boiling or baking a live toad
in a ball of clay (the toad would scratch the name of the thief
on the clay).
Cattle knelt in the byre on Old Christmas Day.
Unmarried girls who sowed hempseed at Hallowe'en could
learn the name of their husband-to-be by whoever came after
and raked the seed.
Whoever found the bean or grain of wheat in the special
Llanhallant (All Hallows) loaf would be lucky in marriage.
It was unlucky to lie in bed on an Easter morning, or to go
visiting before noon on New Year's Day.
If you didn't wear something new on Easter Day the crows
would spoil all you had on.

You could lay a ghost by turning the corpse's face down in the coffin.

If you counted the spots on a ladybird's back you could tell how many years it would be before you were married.

If you ran nine times round Clyro church on Llanhallant Eve and listened in the porch, you would hear a spirit call out the names of those who were to die before the year was out.

Kilvert and Miss Thomas also mention the curious and beautiful rituals and ceremonies that gave variety and colour to the Radnorshire year. There is nothing in the Diary or in Edith's notes to equal the vivid account of the Mari Llwyd ceremony which has already been quoted (and which Mrs Essex Hope mistranslates – Mari Llwyd means 'Grey Mare'), but Kilvert speaks of the practice of burning the bushes on Twelfth Night and New Year's morning. 'From the Chapel Farm at Bettws I have seen the valley of the Wye alight and twinkling with fires, 'burning the bush' at almost every point.' The fires that were lighted on Twelfth Night were usually twelve in number, probably for the Twelve Apostles; and one of the most moving passages in the Diary is the account of the beautiful custom (which he tried to introduce into Wiltshire) of flowering the graves on Easter Eve. (Vol. 1. p. 89–95). December 21 was Parsnip Day, and the mothers of Llanigon always gave their boys parsnips on that day; and between the two Michaelmases (old and new) the poor of Clyro went round the farms and were given not only free milk, but, on occasions, refreshments too. In all the ceremonies of the year the Church played its part, and at Easter and Harvest Festival the whole community would co-operate to deck the churchyards and churches.

Miss Thomas tells of a curious cure for toothache.

Mr Phillips, wheelwright of Brookside, Llanigon, claimed to have cured Alice Lewis's toothache by giving her the following charm to wear round her neck. "As Peter stood at

the gate of Jerusalem, Jesus saith unto him, 'What aileth
thee?'. He said, 'My teeth do ache.' Jesus said, 'Whosoever
carrieth these lines about them or beareth them in memory,
shall never have the toothache any more, in the name of the
Father, and of the Son, and of the Holy Ghost, Amen! and
Amen!' So be it according to thy faith."

Both tell numerous stories of kings and princes, robber
chieftains and battles, ogres, fairies and folk heroes such as Jack o'
Kent and the braggart Burroughs (the most pestilential practical
joker that ever Radnorshire knew) tales of the Black Mountains,
signs and portents of disaster.

Particularly charming little stories were invented to explain
the form and colouring of common flowers, and many of these
were recorded by Miss Thomas.

The origin of the Moss Rose. The Angel of Flowers once fell
asleep under the rose tree, and enjoyed his sleep so much that
when he awoke he asked what he could do for her as she was
already so beautiful; he said that the moss veil was the only
thing he could think of. So that is how the moss rose has its
moss covering.
Corn Bluebottle. It was called the Devil-in-the-Bush. You
could see his body surrounded with the scales of the serpent,
brimstone torches, and his brazen face in the middle.

Edith Thomas was clearly a very talented young woman.
Kilvert frequently speaks with admiration of her sketches, and
mentions especially her paintings of local flowers and fungi. (Vol.
2. 38). It may have been her keen interest in all things local that
stimulated him to make his collection of notes on Radnor customs;
but it is more likely to have been the other way round. Edith was
not yet twenty when he began to make his notes. But it is a very
pleasant thought to imagine the two friends getting together to
compare notes on the numerous occasions on which the diarist
was at Llanthomas.

Chapter Nineteen
The Diary as Autobiography

There is one more consideration to be disposed of. To the readers of most diaries, side by side with the interest of the record as a chronicle of life in a particular age goes its fascination as the revelation of the nature and personality of the diarist. We value the diary of Samuel Pepys not merely as an invaluable picture of the late seventeenth century, but as a portrait of a man of unusual vitality and complexity, an incorrigible, amusing and infinitely diverting civil servant of whose company we never tire. Similarly we are moved to admiration of the gravity and integrity of Evelyn, enlivened by the wit and vivacity of Fanny Burney, steadied by the incredible composure of Woodforde, and intrigued by the unconventional and incredible affections of Munby. In the same way a great deal of the pleasure and interest of Kilvert's Diary lies in the scrutiny of his warm affectionate but ultimately enigmatic personality.

At first sight Kilvert seems one of the most ingenuous of men, trusting, open, almost transparent; but he was probably a more complex person than he is generally assumed to be, and certainly more complex than he himself suspected. It is not surprising therefore to find that though most of his readers are captivated by his affectionate and candid nature, and some even credit him with near-saintliness, there are others who are concerned about certain eccentricities or quirks of personality which they consider

especially reprehensible in a man in Holy Orders. An eminent
clergyman reported to me in a letter a conversation he once had
with Miss Helen Dew, who, he said, knew Kilvert and understood
him. 'Mentioning to her that occasionally I was troubled about
Francis Kilvert's almost "inordinate affection", I asked her, "Do
you feel that he was a really good man?"'. She thought a little and
then she said, "Yes, he was a good man; if he had not been a good
man he would have been a very dangerous man".'

It is true that from time to time certain disturbing entries in
the Diary suggest that there was a darker side to Kilvert than he
cared to divulge. On one occasion he describes himself as 'an
angel satyr'. This phrase was apparently a single diary entry,
though William Plomer may have given it a false emphasis by
suppressing what preceded it and what followed it; it is not
characteristic of Kilvert to content himself with a one-sentence
entry. The full sentence reads

> An angel satyr walks these hills

– a sentence all the more striking because it is neither prepared for
nor explained.

On another occasion, speaking of Builth, which he had not
seen for ten years, and Aberedw, which he had first visited in
1865, he says

> O Aberedw, Aberedw, I never pass thy enchanted gorge and
> look up through the magic gateway of thy Rocks without
> seeming for a moment to be looking in at the gates of Paradise
> just left ajar. But there stands the angel with the flaming sword
> and I may not enter, and only look in as I pass the Gate.
>   (Vol. 3. 168)

The angel with the flaming sword may be Daisy's possessive
father, who had refused to consider him as a prospective son-in-
law, but in what sense can Daisy be associated with Aberedw?
Llanigon was a long distance away, and by 1875 Kilvert had

apparently recovered from his disappointment over Daisy.
Besides, St Michael is traditionally the castigator of sin and
wrong-doing, and though Kilvert calls himself a villain –

> Who would have believed that I could be such a villain?

Surely in his relations with Daisy he had been guilty of no more
than mild impropriety.

A third enigmatic passage occurs in Vol. 2. 356. He has been
spending the afternoon at Langley Burrell, reading *Memorials of a
Quiet Life* by Augustus Hare, who was his senior in his father's
school at Hardenhuish. The book stirs him in a peculiar way.

> As I sat there my mind went through a fierce struggle. Right
> or wrong? The right conquered. The sin was repented and put
> away and the rustle of the wind and the melodious murmurs of
> innumerable bees in the hives overhead seemed to me to take
> the sound of distant music, organs. And I thought that I heard
> the harps of the angels rejoicing in heaven over a sinner that
> had repented.

It is difficult to know the exact nature of the conflict which the
reading of the book provoked, but Hare himself refers in his
autobiography in the same oblique and euphemistic way to the
'underworld' of Hardenhuish school.

> The greater portion of Mr Kilvert's scholars – 'his little flock
> of lambs in Christ's fold' – were a set of little monsters. All
> infantile immoralities were highly popular – and – in such
> close quarters – it would have been difficult for the most pure
> and high-minded boy to escape from them. The first evening I
> was there, at nine years old, I was compelled to eat Eve's
> apple quite up – indeed the Tree of Knowledge was stripped
> absolutely bare.

There is no reason to think that things had changed by the
time Kilvert had reached the age when Hare came to Hardenhuish,

and he was probably involved in the same 'infantile immoralities', the memory of which troubled him so many years later in the vicarage garden at Langley Burrell.

In the same connection the following brief comments are to be considered. The first deals with the unexpected appearance in the hall at Bath where the Church Congress was being held of a beautiful young girl. Kilvert is immediately distracted by her.

> I watched her intently and as she bowed her fair head and knee at the Name of Names she assumed exactly the attitude and appearance of the angels that over-shadowed with their wings the ark and the Mercy seat. In the perpetual struggle between the powers and principles of good and evil the obeisance rebuked and put to flight an evil thought.
>
> (Vol. 2. 383)

A few days before this, writing about the dead Jane Hatherall, he says

> She loved me as I believe few have ever loved. Perhaps she loves me now . . . It may be that she is near me and sees me as I write. Oh Janie, dear Janie. This is all true. Pray for me, dear. I need it. Pray. Pray.

And on a third occasion, á propos of nothing, (unless young Frank Vincent the handsome young dragoon from Langley Burrell is uppermost in his mind) he writes

> Though I be tied with the chain of my sin yet let the pitifulness of Thy Great Mercy loose me.

We shall in all probability never know what Kilvert meant by these admissions and confessions. Perhaps the full diary contained more explicit revelations that were expunged by Mrs Kilvert, but since it is unlikely that much new material will come to light we must content ourselves with the meagre evidence at our disposal; and William Plomer once assured me that there was nothing in the passages he omitted that would seriously alter the opinion of Kilvert we receive from the selections he made. The passages quoted have been sufficient for some to confess themselves disturbed by certain elements in Kilvert's make-up, among them Mr H. S. Scarborough M.A. of Leominster, whose talk given to the Kilvert Society has not been widely publicised. Mr Scarborough is guilty of some errors and some misunderstandings, but there are several passages in his address that are very apt.

'When we have read and re-read the diaries, we begin to see that Kilvert is in many ways a puzzling person: we cannot easily understand him because he was far from understanding himself. He is a curious mixture of the ordinary and the extraordinary, the normal and the abnormal. We feel his charm and the graciousness of his nature at once, but the more closely we get to know him the more we are struck by odd, perhaps disconcerting, elements in his nature. As yet no one has properly explored his character, but such an exploration will be made before long. Kate O'Brien realised this when she said 'he lays his soul right open to the mockery, the cleverness and the portentous psycho-analytical wisdom of our age'.'

Mr Scarborough then goes on to discuss Kilvert's motives in keeping a diary.

'All commentators on Kilvert have paused to ask why he wrote his diary. He himself asked the question in a passage often quoted, and could find no satisfactory answer. He suggested that he did so either because so much in his uneventful life was too curious and beautiful to let perish, or because the diary might amuse others after his death. Neither motive is the whole explanation. Undoubtedly for nearly ten years the keeping of his diary gave him the greatest satisfaction life afforded. It did so because it satisfied a deep need that life left unsatisfied. What was this need? He was in one way a lonely man: he had a passion for beauty, for the poetry of existence, but lived among people who did not share it: he was thrown inward upon himself, and diarised to give his sensibility an outlet. He was in one way a self-centred man – not that he was selfish or disliked the company of others – quite otherwise – but his own feelings were of first importance to him, and in the pages of his diary he could let his feelings go.'

Mr Scarborough then proceeds to examine several 'peculiar features of (Kilvert's) writing, all of which I take to be signs of a violently repressed character.' He mentions Kilvert's dreams (which strike me as being no more bizarre than most dreams); the fascination that nakedness had for him, a fascination which put alongside our twentieth century obsession with pornography seems almost absurdly mild; his interest in flagellation, to which we shall return; and his passionate fondness for girls.

'Some find this fondness endearing, some find it amusing; but I find it frequently feverish in feeling, extravagant and unwholesome. Kilvert, nurtured on romanticism and endowed with lavish powers of feeling, created for himself an ideal of womanly beauty out of poetry he had read and out of sentimental daydreams. He was in his thirties bemused by this vision of a creature physically beautiful in a romantic way, and in character innocent, angelic, tender-hearted and pure; it was a completely adolescent conception, very like the dream-like half-insipid creatures of second-rate romantic poetry. This was his well-beloved, and he sought her and found her in every young feminine object that came within his sight. He never saw a girl or a maiden as she was; he saw her as the well-beloved and rhapsodized over this illusion of his. When he met little girls he poured out on them emotion which was rather his repressed sexual feeling than unsatisfied parental affection. He delighted to romp with girls, to fondle them, to nurse them, to kiss them. How often his remark of having gone ten miles for a kiss from a little child has been quoted as an example of his saintly innocent joy in childhood; but I cannot feel that it is this only.'

Many readers of the Diary have shared Mr Scarborough's uneasiness, and even William Plomer, who, alone among Kilvert scholars, had had access to all the surviving notebooks, speaks of 'certain peculiarities of his character'. Others, from prejudice rather than firm evidence, have suspected that he was the victim of a psychological disorder. It is true that Kilvert was inordinately attracted by little girls, but he was not alone in this respect. Paedophilia was almost as fashionable an eccentricity in the 1870's as homo-sexuality is in the 1970's.

It must be remembered that Kilvert was, at least before his health began to fail, an unusually robust and presumably virile young man, with easily aroused passions.

The moral code of his time, especially as it applied to the social class to which he belonged, his relative poverty and his calling – all imposed on him a chastity that must have been all the more difficult to sustain since, for the greater part of his ministry, he lived in a remote, almost mediaeval world where self-denial and sexual restraint were not the order of the day. The poorer people of Clyro and the neighbouring parishes were by no means puritanical in their sexual behaviour. Men kept concubines, infidelity was common, illegitimate babies were conceived and born under the very noses of the clergy. From this unconstrained behaviour Kilvert was debarred; and, to make matters worse, even harmless liaisons with the young women of his own class were difficult to form. Middle class parents watched jealously over their children. Mr Thomas of Llanigon was so possessive towards his daughters that all five died unmarried. A similarly jealous watch was kept over Ettie Meredith Brown, and possibly over Katharine Heanley.

The Victorian world was full of suspicious and possessive fathers, and equally full of underpaid and undervalued curates. The attitude of Mr Brontë towards Mr Nicholls and Charlotte was not an uncommon one. These taboos were all the more irksome to Kilvert because he was a naturally affectionate man, drawn to women as women were drawn to him. On one occasion he speaks, not with self-congratulation but bemusement, of his 'power of stealing hearts and exciting... love', of his 'strange and terrible gift'. This power often tempted him into indiscretions and placed him in what he would have called 'sinful' situations. The highly-charged language of the last few notes he made on his Cornwall holiday, for instance, leads one to suspect that he grew far more fond of Mrs Hockin than he felt was proper and that she had gone some way towards falling in love with him. There occurs in one of the unpublished parts of the Cornwall diary another of those oblique references to sin and temptation. On Sunday 24 July he records that they went to church twice. In the afternoon he and Mr and Mrs Hockin had coffee in the summer house. Nothing especial happens but Kilvert suddenly writes

Aside the devil turned & & – Ah – how intelligible.

It is only fair to say, however, that the full text of the Cornwall notebook throws no more light on Kilvert's possible passion for Mrs Hockin (apart from that almost insignificant aside) than the published extracts.

Kilvert was one of the most susceptible men in the world. 'In his middle thirties' wrote Plomer, 'he is in a state of almost continual bewitchment and emotional upheaval'; but he was condemned till very late in life to a bachelor existence. The only unclothed female figures he saw were the bodies of the little peasant girls who took their bath in his presence, and the voluptuous Victorian art-gallery nudes that excited him so much. It is true that in writing of his feelings for little girls Kilvert, as

Pearsall says in his *The Worm in the Bud*, in his description of the girl sleeping in the bedroom of Penllan, 'crosses the borderline from sentimentality into a more suspect area'. Perhaps in personalising the sun as he does Kilvert was incautious.

> He has stolen into her bedroom and crept along the wall from chair to chair till he has reached the bed, and has kissed the fair hand and arm that lies upon the coverlet and the white bosom that heaves half-uncovered after the restlessness of the sultry night, and has kissed her mouth, whose scarlet lips, just parting in a smile and pouting like rosebuds to be kissed, shows the pearly gleam of the white teeth, and has kissed the sweet face and the blue veined silky lashed eyelids and the white brow and the soft bright tangled hair, till she has unclosed the sweetest eyes that ever opened to the dawn, and risen and unfastened the casement and stood awhile breathing the fresh fragrant mountain air as it blows cool upon her flushed cheek and her half-veiled bosom, and lifts and ruffles her bright hair which still keeps the kiss of the sun.
>
> (Vol. 1. 173–4)

There is something disagreeable about the over-heated rhapsodies into which Kilvert is thrown on occasions such as these, and the other occasion recorded in the first pages of the second volume of the Diary. His long account of his petting and embracing the seven year old Carrie Britton ends

> I am exhausted with emotion.

At other times he draws close to what even William Plomer called an 'excessive interest in flagellation'. Probably the most offensive passage in the whole Diary is this; a little girl called Coates has been hoisted by Kilvert on to a swing. When she slipped her clothes got hitched on the swing and left her buttocks exposed.

> When I lifted the girl into the swing there were many aspirants for the seat, and in the struggle and confusion I

suppose I set her down with her clothes rumpled up and her
bare flesh (poor child) upon the board, and as her flesh was
plump and in excellent whipping condition and the board
slippery, they managed to part company with this result.

(Vol. 3. 218)

I would not cite this passage as evidence of 'an excessive
interest in flagellation', but the offending phrase 'in excellent
whipping condition' is distasteful, and in the context (there is not a
trace of viciousness in the account, which is characteristically
ingenuous) almost incredible.

Some of the disturbing lapses listed above may be accounted
for by the effect of prolonged celibacy on an unusually passionate
nature, but they may also be connected with two other factors – the
peculiar sense of sin felt by many over-conscientious Victorian
clerics, and by an immature over-romantic strain in Kilvert's
nature.

Lewis Carroll, to whom the diarist is often compared, writes in
the introduction to his *Pillow Problems* of 'nocturnal unholy
thoughts which torture with their hateful presence the fancy that
would fain be pure'; and Dr Jowett, whose moral integrity is
beyond question, once wrote about himself, 'Some passing vanity
or semi-sensuality is constantly interrupting me in prayer or in
serious thought . . . thoughts of evil, day-dreams, love fancies
that can easily find an abode in the mind.' It may be that when
Kilvert is referring to the satyric elements in his make-up and such
illicit emotions as the temptation that came over him in the garden
at Langley Burrell, and even at the Church Congress, he is merely
alluding to the all-too-human fantasies that troubled Carroll and
Dr Jowett from time to time – impulses which the Victorian
consciousness labelled as guilty and bestial, and of which, in his
role as a parson, he is expected to be exceptionally censorious.

Secondly it was a common habit of certain 'romantic natures
in the 19th Century to look upon themselves as men set apart from

the generality of mankind, a prey to socially unacceptable impulses and emotions. It was an attitude that many a 'byronic' young man assumed, an expression of their estrangement from a material and mercenary world. Although Kilvert was essentially a sociable person, he felt at times that he did not wholly belong to the bourgeois world into which he had been born. He speaks frequently of his need for solitude, and his longing for a more passionate and less inhibited world. As a poet manqué, as a cleric with poor prospects, as a rejected lover, as a passionate young man with no outlet for his deepest impulses and aspirations, and as a creative artist often out of tune with the complacent bourgeois families among whom he was compelled to move, he must, at times, have felt separate, alien, even guilty, and tempted to dramatise his own conflicts in cryptic byronic entries in the diary that he showed to no one.

Whatever the misgivings that Kilvert may have had about himself, whatever the half-understood impulses that aroused in him a feeling of guilt and sin, and whatever the 'peculiarities of character' that Plomer mentions in his introduction to Volume 3 of the Diary, the outside world seems to have found very little in his conduct to censure. In the eyes of some of the more privileged of his circle he was, of course only a curate with no particular talents or expectations. In a recently discovered letter written by young Lucy Ashe, daughter of the Squire, certain passages sound as though she is poking gentle fun at Kilvert's sentimental nature.

Mr Frank preached his farewell sermon last Sunday, part in the morning, and part of it in the afternoon. He is I think coming to wish us goodbye to day we must get 6 towels each for handkerchiefs would not be enough for such an affecting parting.

(August 1876)

It has been suggested, too, that the Bevan girls of Hay Castle were less interested in him than he was in them, and some of them were away at a ball in Ludlow when he called to say his final goodbyes.

Squire Ashe, however, who kept a careful eye on the parish he had once helped his father to run, and was always on the look-out for irregularities of conduct, was censorious only of the new practices which Kilvert and his father wished to introduce into the services; and both the Rector and his son were frequent guests at Langley House. Although advancement in the church came late to Kilvert, there is no evidence that the Bishop of St David's ever regretted having preferred him to the living of St Harmon; and Miss Newton, who was probably responsible for his coming to Bredwardine, and whose judgment of his character was no doubt based on what she had known of him as a curate in Clyro, valued him highly and was a kind friend to him. He may have been unacceptable as a prospective son-in-law to Mr Thomas and the Meredith-Browns (when he was a curate), but no objections were made to him (he was now the holder of a living) by Miss Rowland's father, who was the social equal of the Thomases and the Meredith-Browns. It seems as if it was not defects of personality but lack of expectations that Daisy's father and Ettie's mother objected to. Mr Venables, who was very close to his young assistant, was content to leave the parish, on occasions, in his sole care and would have welcomed him as his successor. The people of Clyro were excessively fond of him (his genuine surprise at the warmth of that affection makes his account of their reception of him when he revisited them all the more credible), and were never afraid to entrust their children to his care.

It is true that when we are trying to arrive at a just estimate of Kilvert's character we have little to go on apart from his own records; but there have survived some impartial testimonies that are worth quoting.

The first is an undated letter from a Mrs Amery of Cusop to William Plomer. The letter is among the Plomer papers deposited in Durham University Library.

Dear Sir,

I am writing to you to say how interested I have been in what you have written about Mr Kilvert which my mother knew well for it was at our cottage when he came back home from his wedding as there was several men to met him they took the horses which above althings were two Black Horses out from the carriage and got in the shafts and draged it to the vicarage it was raining pouring the day they came home and that was how he caught cold and died we always attended his grave for years till we left the parish it was a pleasure his wife used to visit us every year till she died and her niece which is living in Eastbourne she always used to take me on her lap and give me some of her tea. I have the photo of both Mr and Mrs Kilvert and a book of poems. They are people worth remembering if there more of there sort about the world would be better off the best always go first I have heard Mother telling us how he would visit every house in a fortnight. Well sir I won't bother to write any more now so will close hoping you have not heard the bit I have wrote you.

from M. Amey

To this letter Plomer added a note (dated 1948) 'Mrs Amey told me that whenever Kilvert had chicken for dinner he always cut off a good helping before he began it, and took this afterwards to some sick parishioners. She also spoke of his discretion. 'You could tell him anything and you knew it wouldn't go any further'.'

The second testimony is a note recently found in the Kilvert Society files. It is from one of the daughters of the Revd. David Vaughan of Newchurch.

I was born in Clyro and Mr Kilvert christened me in 1868. A few years later I remember him coming to our house. He was a tall man with a black beard. I had been running about a lot that day and Mother had put me to bed early, and I was to have a bowl of milk for my supper. I was sitting up in bed when the Rev Kilvert came. He picked me up and carried me round the room and then handed me my bread and milk. That's the nearest I've been to heaven and I've only to shut my eyes to live it all over again. I remember my mother telling me that all the people welcomed him to their homes for he always seemed to bring happiness with him.

The third testimony is to be found in the letter (already quoted in Chapter Eight) which Mr Jonathan Pugh of Berth, St. Harmon, sent to the first President of the Kilvert Society, and in which the claim is made that he was more tolerant in religious matters than some passages of the Diary Suggest.

The fourth witness is a Mr Cholmeley, the son of Adelaide Cholmeley whose wedding Kilvert attended at Findon.

He (Kilvert) was always very friendly and affectionate, and used to take me on his knee when I was a boy of nine or ten, a form of endearment which I considered undignified and unsuited to my age and structure . . . The last I remember of him was when he came on a visit to my uncle Marshall Heanley's farm near Skegness where I often spent my summer holidays. That would be about 1875 perhaps. There were two pretty and vivacious cousins there, Kate and Ellen Heanley to whom cousin Frank paid many delicate attentions, and to whom he indited a sentimental poem, something about Kathleen Mavourneen and Eileen Aroon. This made me laugh with all a hearty schoolboy's contempt for such weakness. The portrait of Frank that is in the *Listener* (the well-known official photograph) is exactly as I remember him, very sleek and glossy and gentle – rather like a nice Newfoundland dog. He must have left a pleasant impression on me to have stood out so clearly after a lapse of more than 70 years.

Perhaps the most balanced judgment on Kilvert's nature was made in a letter to me from Mr Charles Harvey who was one of the earliest Kilvert lovers and was able to consult, in the 1940's, many who still remembered Kilvert.

It was Havelock Ellis who, in his monumental 'Studies in the Psychology of Sex' first started to sweep away centuries of prejudice and traditional thinking by trying to establish more clearly what could reasonably be called 'within the normal'. I think myself that Kilvert emerges 'within the normal' if only just about so. Clergymen, especially celibate ones, have always been subject to conditions of living which expose them to additional stresses. Kilvert had a 'parsonic personality', and I have no doubt suffered from a form of neurosis which probably in these days would be correctly described as a 'psychological disorder', though not a serious one. Maybe we are all more or less psychologically disordered a part of (or even all) the time. But what, after all, do we mean by the expression? Who is sane, and who is not? Is there such a thing as absolute sanity any more than absolute truth?

Kilvert was sexually immature and the curve of his sexuality is almost as easy to trace from what he tells us in his diary as Pepy's is in his. I think that his psychological make-up was not so very unusual.

In the end we are left with the impression that several discerning readers of the Diary have expressed – the sense that this apparently most conventional of men was ultimately an enigmatic figure; and perhaps it is the unexplained and possible inexplicable puzzle of his character that constitutes one of the attractions of his Diary.

One last aspect of Kilvert's nature which few critics have ventured to examine has recently been explored by Father S. G. A. Luff in an illuminating essay in *The Clergy Review* (December 1979), upon which he subsequently enlarged in an address given to the Kilvert Society at Aberedw in 1980. Father Luff is the first critic to examine with any seriousness the spiritual side of Kilvert's nature. After commenting that the Diarist never devotes a paragraph to his theological opinions, his devotional practices or his spiritual thoughts, he goes on to say

"What thus appears a shortcoming in the Diary and in the Diarist does however express some essential quality in Kilvert the man and the priest. Spirituality for him was intrinsic to the mere fact, and the mere act, of living. Prayer was the breath of life, if by prayer you mean sensing the holiness of God in all that is best in creation and especially in man, and being prompted thereby to praise God . . .

(Kilvert) is not of course the first person to read divinity in nature, to 'turn a stone' or 'start a wing', but his sensibility to the universal sacrament is unusual. How many of us hear the wheat at night praising God, or in the droning of bees hear the music of angels over a repentant sinner? Few suspect that the cooing dove is 'making intercession for us with groanings that cannot be uttered'. Near Clyro he saw a blackbird dead in a gin fixed to a post – part of creation that 'groaneth and travaileth in pain'. He added: 'Somehow the suffering creature reminded me of the Saviour upon the Cross. I felt as if some sin of mine had brought him there'."

Father Luff's insights are so penetrating that they deserve to be quoted at greater length.

"The centrality of Communion and of Easter are expressions of Kilvert's religion which are evident in the Diary. Of Good Friday there was not much observance in his day: 'Good Friday has now become a holiday,' he wrote in 1870. All he could record was taking hot cross buns to five widows . . . It was Easter that made the diarist's pen sing. To be precise it was the Easter event that inspired this beautiful entry, for it was made on Quinquagesima Sunday at Bredwardine in 1878.

As I walked in the Churchyard this beautiful morning the fresh sweet sunny air was full of the singing of birds and the brightness and gladness of the Spring. Some of the graves were white as snow with snowdrops. The southern side of the Churchyard was crowded with a multitude of tombstones. They stood thick together, some taller, some shorter, some looking over the shoulders of others, and as they all stood up looking one way and facing the morning sun they looked like a crowd of men, and it seemed as if the morning of the Resurrection had come and the sleepers had arisen from their graves and were standing upon their feet, silent and solemn, all looking towards the East to meet the Rising of the Sun. The whole air was melodious with the distant indefinite sound of sweet bells that seemed to be ringing from every quarter by turns, now from the hill, now from the valley, now from the deer forest, now from the river.

There is a similar lyrical entry for Easter Sunday at Langley Burrell in 1876. He went out early on the common to see the lark rising and hear the bells from all around.

Suddenly the morning air all alive with the music of sweet bells ringing for the joy of the Resurrection. 'The Lord is risen', smiled the sun. 'The Lord is risen', sang the lark. And the Church bells in their joyous pealing answered from tower to tower, 'He is risen indeed.'

If spirituality means that limited capacity to see creation and life as God sees them, to weigh them by His values as far as we can, then Kilvert was a spiritual man. If it be Christian to have in heart and hold in mind the words of Jesus and apply them readily to every situation, then he is profoundly Christian. If a deep concern for the Eucharist as the central Sacrament of God's Dispensation be of great importance to stewards of the mysteries, then he was priestly. If the centrality of the Resurrection be a rediscovery of our time then he was ahead of his time . . . If a solicitude, seemingly unlimited, for others makes a good pastor, that is what he was."

Chapter Twenty
The Diary as Literature

The good diarist must, however, do more than illuminate his age
or paint a self-portrait. He must be able, under the pressure of deep
emotion and full involvement in his experience, to transform what
might have been a jejune report into passages of memorable and
stirring prose invested with the qualities of great imaginative
writing, and comparable in insight and memorability with the
triumphs of great fiction. Pepys's account of the Great Fire of
London, and Fanny Burney's record of her sad meeting with the
ailing George the Third in Kew Gardens remain with us like
fragments of great novels.

As a prose artist Kilvert lacks the consistency of Pepys or
Fanny Burney. At its worst his prose can be disappointingly
banal; and in this connection we must remember that William
Plomer chose to publish only the most interesting and vivid
chapters. His decision to publish extracts only involved, as we
have seen, the exclusion of several fine things; but on the whole he
seems to have chosen wisely. The Cornwall notebook contains
few passages, other than those selected by the editor, that are in
any way memorable; and the conventional nature of the account
lends substance to the critical comments made on Kilvert at his
least inspired by John Adlard in an article in the Michigan
Quarterly Review (*The Failure of Francis Kilvert*. Spring 1974).

Even the published parts of the Diary are not without their
longueurs. The Langley Burrell section exhibits a certain falling off

of urgency and excitement. Kilvert tends to fall back too
frequently on a mood of nostalgia and retrospection. His day-to-
day experiences fail to excite and stimulate him as his life at
Clyro had done: and when he is not excited his prose tends to
become limp. On occasions, too, when his concentration falters,
he tends to write self-indulgently, modifying and qualifying as he
goes, adding epithet to epithet till he has found the one that suits
him best, piling up clause on clause and phrase on phrase until his
sentences become top-heavy.

However, when all has been said about the limitations of the
diary as a literary form, and the short-comings of Kilvert's prose
when he is at his least attentive, the worst has been admitted. It is
true that he is often imprecise and repetitive, and too ready to fall
back upon the clichés of Victorian descriptive writing, but he can
just as often astonish us with the terseness and economy of his
prose.

> A group of people were sitting in the churchyard among the
> graves, and one woman was dressing a green grave with
> scarlet and white flowers near one of the vast black yews.
> The lurid copper smoke hung in a dense cloud over Swansea,
> and the great fleet of oyster boats under the cliff was heaving
> in the greenest sea I ever saw.
> I went round the premises late at night to see if the outhouses
> were locked up. All was still, and the white pig lying in the
> moonlight at the door of his house, fast asleep, with the moon
> shining on his white face and round cheek.
> At Vern Vawr a girl with green eyes was washing bright red
> potatoes in a bowl in the yard.
> A stout brown hare started out of the young plantation and
> ran down the slope as if she had an evil conscience about
> larches, the sun shining on her clean brown fur and white
> scut.

'In sentences like these we have the crystallisation, the design, the movement and the power of suggestion that are to be found in a good picture or poem,' says Plomer, and Richard Hoggart describes a similar passage as 'a beautifully attentive cameo, faithful and particular as a Bewick engraving.' Arthur Waley, who was a great Kilvert admirer, marked several passages in his copy of the Diary 'like a Chinese poem'. Dr A. L. Rowse compared the following passage to a Constable sketch.

It was a glorious evening, unclouded, and the meadows shone dazzling like a golden sea in the glory of the sheets of buttercups. The deep, dark river, still and glassy, seemed to be asleep and motionless, except when a leaf or blossom floated slowly by. The cattle by the mill plashed and trampled among the rushes and river flags and water lilies in the shallow places, and the miller Godwin in a white hat came down with a bucket to draw water from the pool.

What Plomer and Hoggart and Waley and Rowse are saying, in fact, is that at moments such as these Kilvert is transcending the common limitations of the diary entry, and is achieving something which is independent of the interest it may have as a sociological comment or an intriguing personal confession, a quality that raises the writing into the realm of pure literature. Passages such as these are often camouflaged by the even continuous flow of the diary narrative, but, once isolated (a poet critic such as Geoffrey Grigson is adept at uncovering them) they show through the texture of the day-to-day reportage like jewels.

Imagination, the quality which invests these, and other longer and more ambitious passages which might easily be isolated, is one of the elements which Miss O'Brien says the diarist may dispense with. If by imagination she means fiction, she may be right; but in a larger sense, she is mistaken. Even the diarist must choose, from the multitudinous elements that make up his total experience, what to him has been most significant and momentous. No less than the novelist, he needs to order his experience, to arrange the diverse elements of his living and feeling till he has found what to him is essential and paramount.

This selecting of experience may be termed 'imaginative' in a real sense; and certainly Kilvert often gives the impression of writing with the selectiveness of a poet or novelist. Sir V. S. Pritchett, probably the most perceptive of all Kilvert critics, draws our attention to this quality in Kilvert in his essay *A Curate's Diary* (*In My Good Books*. London 1942). He is speaking in this passage of the superiority of the diary to the novel or short tale in the field of characterisation.

> Where art is selective and one-sided, the diary dips its net daily, and brings out what is there. Take the Prodgers incident... She (Mrs Prodgers) came from Kington-St-Michael where droll things were always happening, and caused a lot of twittering when she insisted that she and the little Prodgers should be used as models in the design of the new stained-glass windows for the church. 'Suffer little children' was the subject, and Mrs Prodgers had edged her brood of sufferers well into the foreground of the picture. In a few lines there is the essence of a life-story.

It is in this last sentence that Pritchett draws our special attention to that process of selecting and emphasising that brings Kilvert close to the genuinely creative artist; and he goes on to provide a further illustration in the diarist's portrait of the tyrannical Squire Ashe of Langley Burrell.

> He (the squire) illustrates the aptitude of the diary form for collecting fragments day by day, for catching each day's contribution to the jigsaw of human character. The novelist must summarize, theorize and jump to conclusions; the diarist can take the more leisurely course of letting out character piecemeal... A vicar-baiter and a tyrant, the Squire ordered the tenor to be turned out of the choir, so spoiling the singing, but opposed 'with strong language' the

proposal to introduce a harmonium... The Kilverts won,
but the Squire would not pay a penny. This is not the end of
the squire. His portrait is perfected a few days later in the
midst of a later and very affecting description of a child's
funeral. Kilvert, familiar with rural sorrow, has a perceptive-
ness uncommon in literature. We can see the mother's
distracted face, her cries of guilt and helplessness, her hard
despairing eye. And then the afternoon sun shines in the
church and the birds begin to sing as if in honour of the dead
child, and Kilvert, as he reads the service, catches sight of
the Squire through the window. He is dressed in a white hat
and a drab suit, dashing fussily across the churchyard and
putting his stick in the grave to see that it is the right
depth...

Kilvert always has these compelling touches so that the
scene is never top-heavy with the emotion it arouses. His eye
and ear are acute; they seem to be roving over the scene and
to hit upon some sight or word which is all the more decisive
for having the air of accident. And in literature to convey the
chance effects of life without being bizarre is everything.

It is an exaggeration to say that Kilvert always takes the edge
off a threatening over-sentimentality, but it is true that over and
over again an account that teeters on the brink of over-statement,
and is in danger of being overloaded with sentiment, is rescued by
some touch of honest and accurate observation. A case in point is
the superb description of the Black Mountains under snow. He
tells how the cloud and mist rolled away from the mountain and
revealed a long rampart-line of dazzling snow.

I stood rooted to the ground, struck with amazement and
overwhelmed at the extraordinary splendour of this marvellous
spectacle... I wanted someone to admire the sight with me.
A man came whistling along the road riding upon a cart
horse. I would have stopped and drawn his attention to the

mountains but I thought he would probably consider me mad. He did not seem to be the least struck by or taking the smallest notice of the great sight...

(Vol. 1. 309)

Another is this little incident which occurred when he was walking to Aberedw with Morrell.

Near the whitewashed ugly abject-looking farm-house we heard a sweet voice singing, but the singer was nowhere to be seen. Presently on looking through the hedge we saw a crazy girl with a coarse ugly face under an old bonnet sitting on the grass singing to herself something like a hymn tune in a rich mellow voice, the words indistinguishable, perhaps there were none. When she saw us through the hedge she suddenly stopped singing and saluted us in a sharp abrupt tone...

(Vol. 1. 59)

A later assessment than Pritchett's can be found in Richard Fothergill's *Private Chronicles* (O.U.P. 1974). Dr Fothergill, one of the first academics to recognise the special literary qualities of the Diary, draws attention first to Kilvert's importance in what he calls the history of English sensibility, and then goes on to claim for him a 'literary earnestness' not generally ascribed to him. It is part of Dr Fothergill's thesis that the great diaries are often more carefully written than we assume, and to support his point he quotes a valuable comment made on Pepys by W. Matthews, one of the editors of the recently published complete diary.

The manuscript makes it fairly certain that Pepys's way of writing was far more complex than is usually assumed, and consequently his great diary is no simple product of nature thrown together at the end of each succeeding day. In part at least it is a product fashioned with some care, both in its matter and in its style... Entries are not always made daily but adhere to the convention of seeming so. They are composed from notes and rough drafts entered into the diary-volume with painstaking neatness in a fair copy state.

What Matthews says of Pepys is surprisingly applicable to Kilvert. He also was in the habit of making on-the-spot notes in a pocket book, and on occasions devoted considerable time to converting them into the final version. These final entries are fair-copy entries, with no erasures, crossings out or major corrections; and although the impression is given that the entries are made at the end of each day, there are indications, slight but positive, that although Kilvert adheres to the diary convention he sometimes makes several days' entries at one sitting; and on one occasion he speaks of the pains he took to find the correct word for a certain impression.

The special character of Kilvert's literary earnestness, says Fothergill, can best be understood by comparing him with another Victorian diarist whose work has come to light only in the post-war years. Munby's situation and interests are far more immediately arresting and unconventional than Kilvert's, but his mode of recording them is, in comparison, undistinguished. Once Munby's story is known and our curiosity about his situation satisfied there is little to tempt us to a re-reading. But the best of Kilvert is independent of the interest it may arouse as a sociological or psychological document. It has the self-sufficiency of good art.

Professor Hoggart, in spite of the complimentary tone of the greater part of his essay in *Speaking to Each Other* (Vol. 2.) declines in the end to rank him as highly as Fothergill does; and his qualified praise echoes Miss O'Brien's summing up.

I do not think (she says) that he was more than a potential writer of good prose. It always seems to have been hit or miss; an atmosphere, a memory, a mood, could control him and make him write as it dictated; but he could not control these masters – which only means that he never *learnt* to

write, but simply wrote; in the most alarming rushes, if that
was how he felt . . . or gently, objectively, humorously when
such states rule him . . .

It is true that in comparison with Pepys, Evelyn and Fanny
Burney, his diary is parochial and often pedestrian. He did not
have their advantage of moving in distinguished circles and in
close contact with eminent personages who were intrinsically
interesting. Nor did he have the good fortune that Dorothy
Wordsworth enjoyed of having a genius for a daily companion. In
addition his lack of intellectual curiosity, a certain emotional
immaturity, and a habit of feeding on inferior Victorian fiction –
all these shortcomings rob his writing of the more solid qualities
of his seventeenth and eighteenth century forbears. But even his
weaknesses turn on occasions to strengths. Miss O'Brien ends her
note on Kilvert with these words

> In the period in which he lived, with its influences of
> eloquence, tears and tenderness (Kilvert's habit of writing as
> the spirit moved him) was not a safe way to be a prose writer.
> Nor was there any safety – artistic or emotional – in Francis
> Kilvert . . . He got through, as a man and a writer, simply by
> the grace of God and the luck of the innocent.

This is a discerning comment, and Miss O'Brien's sense that
there is more in Kilvert than she can define is echoed by Professor
Hoggart. What Kilvert lacks in solidity and consistency he makes
up for by his magnanimity, his naïveté, his genuine concern for
people. 'He was the most charismatic of curates,' he says. 'A sort
of love flowed from his finger-ends'; and the Rev B. Humphreys,
at one of the commemorative services held by the Kilvert Society,
spoke of his 'continual lapsing into human affection', an
interesting phrase, illuminating his tendency to disregard the
accepted and conventional criteria of fine writing in the interest of
the human theme which was always his main concern. He is one

of the most objective and least dogmatic of men, and his prose, at its best, is as flexible as his personality, possessing an organic strength and vitality, that ability to modulate from mood to mood without incongruity which is the hallmark of a truly gifted writer. In the end one returns to the world that Kilvert immortalises for us. It is foolish to be too sentimental about it. For all its charm it had its darker side. It was after all, medical ignorance and the inability of a country doctor to deal with a condition that would now be cured by a simple operation that ended the diarist's life. But Kilvert, always appreciative and charismatic, constantly reminds us of the good things we have lost.

In Kilvert (says Professor Hoggart) the world slows down, and we realise how fast we have been running for years. Here everything is more sharply defined, and we can hear again how people speak, and see the detail of their movements, and those of nature, sharp and clear.

A personal but very stimulating study of Kilvert is to be found in *After Kilvert* (L. Le Quesne. O.U.P. 1978). Mr Le Quesne, who lived for a while in Ashbrook, the Clyro house in which Kilvert lodged, and had the good fortune to travel on the Hereford Hay and Brecon line before it was axed, is mainly concerned with the differences between Clyro in the 1870's and the 1970's, but in the course of his comparison he makes a number of penetrating comments.

Actually, it is the obscurity of the man that gives the Diary much of its appeal. The diary of a public man, of any man who has a reputation for something other than the diary itself, gives you only a new look into a past itself public, a past already known and shop-soiled. Kilvert's Diary has the rare quality of opening a window on a past otherwise totally unknown, a past that everybody would have assumed to be gone and forgotten beyond recall . . . A small window opens on that lost landscape, and you see it, clear and minute and secret and frozen and alive, like a landscape in the background of a Flemish Renaissance painting, a Patinir or a Breughel. These are the dead – not brought back to life again, but still living; there we are back in the lost past at the moment when it all happened.

There was a visionary in Kilvert somewhere; the touch here is something between Samuel Palmer and Stanley Spencer, and I think this capacity is the most truly original thing we are ever allowed to see in Kilvert, the deepest layer we ever reach... It has nothing to do with his religion... it was probably only vaguely sensed by Kilvert himself. Nevertheless it is my guess that it was some awareness of these as it were unsanctified powers stirring within him that led him to start the Diary...

A good claim can be made for ranking Kilvert as one of the most lively, likeable and entertaining of diarists, intrinsically far more readable than Woodforde or even Dorothy Wordsworth, and a far better writer than Munby. Nor has enough attention been paid to his humour. An illuminating and full study of his general characteristics can be found in *The Southern Marches* by H. J. Massingham; and A. L. Rowse has many fine things to say about him in several essays (in *The English Spirit, West Country Stories* and *Post Kilvert*, a review in Blackwood's, March 1979); but for a final comment we can do no better than return to Sir V. S. Pritchett.

Where Kilvert is superior to many of the novelists (of his age) is that he is writing straight from nature, idealising but never falsifying... His piety, like his sentiment, is firm but unprofessional. A being who feels, he does not go in for the muddy introspections which many diarists love, he has humour but he does not make insincere defensive jokes against himself. One likes him in the end... because, entirely without self-importance or self-consciousness, he is serious about himself. That supremely difficult art!

It is the special triumph of Kilvert's sincerity that he has conveyed and made credible his kind of feeling to a generation whose notions of love are totally alien to those of a bubbling young mid-Victorian curate . . . We have lost the art of rendering pure sentiment and the feeling for such a tenderness as Kilvert's. When we contrast the note and rhythm of our lives with those of Kilvert's we see there is more than a change of fashion between the generations. We perceive with a shock that it is we who are unnatural.

Appendix

The Surviving Letters of Francis Kilvert

So far only six of Kilvert's letters have been found.

1. 17 Dec. 1868. To Mr Venables, thanking him for some gift
    (Kilvert's birthday was in December). 'The unceasing
    kindness I have received ever since I have been here would
    alone be sufficient to induce me to do my best for this place. I
    hardly needed this new token of your readiness to overlook
    my deficiencies and to overrate what I have done. Acceptable
    and useful as the present is I value infinitely more the few
    lines which accompany it, showing that you are satisfied and
    pleased.'
    (Original in National Library of Wales).

2. 22 Dec. 1871. To Mr Venables from Raby Place, Bath
    (home of Kilvert's sister, Thersie, wife of the Revd W. R.
    Smith), referring to the impending retirement of Mr Venables,
    and Kilvert's own decision to leave Clyro. He declares his
    intention to stay at Clyro till the vicar retires (actually he left
    before Mr Venables) and says how sorry he will be 'to leave a
    place where I have spent seven such happy years.'
    (Original in National Library of Wales).

3-5. Three letters, written to Marion Vaughan, one of the daughters
    of the Revd David Vaughan of Newchurch, dated between

1873 and 1876, were left by the recipient to her daughter Gwen Hinksman, who in turn gave them to Mrs White, wife of the then Rector of Ombersley, near Worcester. Miss Hinksman, who in her later years became something of a recluse, declined to let the Kilvert Society see the letters, and Mrs White feels she has a duty to respect the wishes of her dead friend. She has, however, kindly allowed me to read the letters and make this summary of their contents.

Letter 3
8 Feb 1873. Written from Langley Burrell. It is a brief letter, expressing Kilvert's thanks to Marion for her photograph and sending his best wishes for her birthday and his own 'carte' and photograph. Mrs White thinks that the photograph is the well-known official photograph, the original of which is in Clyro Church. Kilvert tells Marion of a New Year's party he attended at the home of Sir John Awdry (presumably Notton House), at which there were no fewer than 150 guests. He also describes a Christmas party with a Christmas tree given for the children of Langley Burrell. It was attended by 60 children who each got 7/8 presents. He wonders if there was a similar Christmas Tree party at Clyro or Newchurch. (These events are also described in the Diary Vol 2. p 305-7).

Letter 4
4 Feb 1873. Also written from Langley Burrell. This is a longer letter, and deals principally with the running down of the *Northfleet* by the Spanish steamer *Murillo*. Kilvert is very indignant about the cowardly action of the Spanish captain in abandoning the wrecked vessel, and says, in most unchristian terms, that it is his dearest wish to see the rascally Spaniard hanged from his own yard arm! He is equally indignant about the current Miner's Strike, mentioning the hardships of the poor who are left without winter fuel and the sufferings of children in unheated houses, and inveighing

strongly against the iniquity of the Miner's Union in fomenting the strike and intimidating their fellow workers who wished to remain at work. He mentions with evident approval a proposal to import Chinese coolies to work in British mines. The letter is very illiberal in tone and almost vindictive in its condemnation of the strikers.
(The Diary account of these events is to be found in Vol 2. p 316 and 320).

Mention is made in this letter of a brother of Marion's whose family pet-name is Sellie, who has matriculated and is about to go to Oxford.

Letter 5
26 May 1876. Written from Oxford. Kilvert mentions that he is staying with an old college friend (Anthony Lawson Mayhew). It is a long letter describing some of the events recorded in the Diary (See Vol 3. p 315-320) – the beating of the bounds, and the ritualistic Oxford Movement service at St Barnabas, Oxford. The accounts given in the letter and the Diary are not identical. One does not get the impression that Kilvert was merely transcribing for Marion something he had already entered in his Diary. The letter supplements in some details the account given in the Diary, which may of course have been edited by William Plomer.

Perhaps it would be true to say that the final impression one receives from the letters is of a man whose nature is more conservative and whose prejudices (especially against Trades Unions, foreigners and the Oxford Movement) were stronger than the Diary implies.

6.   7 July 1879. From the Vicarage, Bredwardine, to Mary Powell of Brobury.

My dear Mary,
        I was very much pleased to have your letter and should

have answered it before – but I have been unusually busy. I
am glad to hear that you like your new surroundings and are
quite reconciled and happy. I often think of you when I am
walking to Brobury Church on the Sunday evenings and at
other times. Sometimes too I hear of you from Clara. Last
night the dear little Church was quite full and I was much
cheered in the morning by seeing three new faces at the Holy
Communion.

Your mother was not there yesterday. I hope she will
come next month. Yesterday morning was very wet. We have
had so many rainy Sundays this summer.

There has been much sickness lately among the children.
Little Sarah Stokes of Brobury was dangerously ill but is
better and one little girl Anne Williams of Craft y Webb
passed away on Friday night and will be buried tomorrow.
Miss Kilvert left us last Wednesday and it is very quiet and
lonely here without her. She is to be married on July 31st and
my own wedding is to be on August 20th.

It is a great pleasure to her to know that you are so
happily situated with regard to attendance at Church and I
know you are one that values the privilege. Do you remember
one evening when we were walking home together from
Brobury, we were talking about the good we might do those
round us by quiet influence and good example. As it was with
you here so I trust it will be with you now and wherever you
are and as you have begun so I believe you will go on bearing
witness for our Lord and master.
God bless you my dear Child.

Believe me to remain always your very sincere friend.
                              R. F. Kilvert.

The sister mentioned is Dora who kept house for Kilvert at
Bredwardine till her marriage to James Pitcairn. Her honeymoon
diary is published by the Kilvert Society in *Miscellany Two*.
This letter was kept by Mary Powell, whose family

emigrated to the United States, and was presented by her grand-daughter, Mrs Hurlbutt to the Kilvert Society at the Centenary Service in Langley Burrell Church. Mrs Hurlbutt travelled from Hawaii to attend the centenary celebrations.

Post-script

All our judgments on Kilvert – on the value of the Diary, the justice of the portraits of the men and women he describes, its literary value, even the portrait he presents of himself, must all be partial and provisional, since, for all that we know to the contrary, what he wrote in the lost parts of the Diary may have contradicted and would almost certainly have modified the impressions given in the published sections.

Some lost sections of the Diary may yet be recovered. The discovery of the few pages in his sister's hand at Langley Burrell is encouraging. The owner of the three unpublished letters may yet be persuaded to allow them to be transcribed. The mysterious owner of the third notebook may yet turn up. It is unlikely, however, that anyone will ever be in a position to publish the entire Diary. In the meantime it is unwise to be too dogmatic about Kilvert's career, opinions, beliefs and behaviour. All that is said about him may well have to be revised if by chance more of his missing manuscripts turn up. It is probably safe to say, however, that even on the limited evidence we possess, Kilvert must be reckoned among the best, most interesting and entertaining of our English diarists.

Bibliography

Selections from the Diary of the Rev Francis Kilvert. First published by Jonathan
Cape Ltd in three volumes. (1938, 1939, 1940).
Reprinted 1940.
New and Corrected edition 1960.
Reprinted with Index 1961.
Reissued 1969.
Reissued with illustrations 1977.
An abridged edition was first published in one volume in 1944.
Reprinted 1947, 1950, 1956.
Reissued 1960.
Reprinted 1973.
Penguin Books edition of abridged Diary. 1978.
American Edition. (ed. W. Plomer). New York. 1947.
Illustrated Children's Edition. (*Ardizzone's Kilvert*). J. Cape. 1976.
Folio Society Edition (*Journal of a Country Curate*). 1977.
Parts of the Diary have been translated into Danish by Anne Friis under the title of
Kilverts Dagbog (Martins Forlag. 1960).
Parts of the first volume of the Diary have been translated into Welsh under the title
of *Cymru Kilvert* by the Rev Trebor Lloyd Evans. (John Penry. Gwasg. 1973).

Critical Notices

W. Plomer. Introductions to three volume and single volume editions of the Diary.
W. Plomer. The Curate of Clyro (*At Home*. J. Cape 1958).
W. Plomer. Francis Kilvert and his Diary (*Essays by Divers Hands*. Royal
    Society of Literature. 1975).
H. J. Massingham. Kilvert of Clyro (Chapter 3. *The Southern Marches*. Hale.
    1952).
V. S. Pritchett. A Curate's Diary (*In My Good Books*. Chatto and Windus. 1942).
A. L. Rowse. Kilvert in Cornwall (*West Country Stories*. Macmillan. 1966).

A. L. Rowse. Kilvert's Diary (*The English Spirit*. Macmillan. 1966).

A. L. Rowse. Review of *After Kilvert* in *Blackwood's Magazine*. March 1979.

K. O'Brien. *English Diaries and Journals*. (Collins. 1943).

L. Le Quesne. *After Kilvert* O.U.P. 1978.

R. Hoggart. The Need for Love (*Speaking to Each Other*. Vol. 2. Chatto and Windus. 1970).

J. Adlard. The Failure of Francis Kilvert. (*Michigan Quarterly Review*. Spring, 1974).

D. T. W. Price. Priestly Life in the 1870's. (*Banner*. No date.).

R. Fothergill. *Private Chronicles*. (O.U.P. 1974).

J. M. Brereton. Curate of Clyro (*Blackwood's Magazine Sept. 1977*).

F. Grice. An Anglo-Welsh Community in the 1860's. (*Anglo-Welsh Review*. Spring 1977).

F. Grice. Kilvert and Folklore (*Folklore*. Autumn 1974).

B. Colloms. The Rev Francis Kilvert, Parson and Impressionist. (*Victorian Country Parsons*. Constable 1977).

S. G. A. Luff. The Priestly Life of Francis Kilvert. (*Clergy Review*. Dec. 1979).

Addenda

Anon. 'Deep in the Kilvert Country'. *T.L.S.* 19 Aug. 1960.

John Armitage. 'Chronicles of Kilvert's Country'. *Country Life.* 13 Sept. 1979.

Richard Cobb, "The view out of Kilvert's window", *New Society* (8 Feb. 1979), pp. 310–11 ill.

John Cornforth, "Kilvert's Parsonage, Wiltshire", *Country Life* 150 (30 Sept. 1971), pp. 800–04 ill.

J. P. Ferris, "A contribution from Kilvert", *Notes and Queries* 27 (Feb. 1980), p. 83.

Susan Hill, "Weekend with three clerics", *Daily Telegraph* (22 Oct. 1977), p. 11.

Kathleen Hughes, "Two Kilvert Letters", *The National Library of Wales Journal,* vol. XXII, p. (240).

Dafydd Ifans, "Kilvert at Aberystwyth", *The National Library of Wales Journal,* vol. XXII, pp. (234)–9.

Bernard Jones, "Kilvert's Diary: a poem identified", *Notes and Queries* 27 (June 1980), p. 215.

Brian Jones, "Relative Disaster", *The Guardian* (2 Feb. 1977), p. 16.

Howard C. Jones, "Ready to be snapped up" (Sale of Clyro Court and Cae Mawr), *Western Mail* (26 Sept. 1981), p. 11.

D. J. Lane-Griffiths, "Robert Francis Kilvert", *Cotteswold Naturalists' Field Club Proceedings* 35 (1966), pp. 34–8.

Betty Massingham, " 'Villaging' with Kilvert", *Illustrated London News,* 267 (Sept. 1979), p. 85, 87 ill.

H. J. Massingham, "A memory of Francis Kilvert", *Country Life* (1 Aug. 1947), p. 225, ill.

R. G. N(oppen), "Association with Kilvert: Hardenhuish Church", *Country Life* (3 February 1950), pp 319–20, ill.

V. D. Parkes, "Gentle Curate of Clyro", *Country Quest* (Summer 1962), p. 8.

J. H. B. Peel, "A Welsh hill Shepherd", *Daily Telegraph* (24 Nov. 1979), p. 15 ill.

J. W. M. Thompson, "Living in luxury", *Spectator* (7 June 1969), p. 754.

June Wilson, "Francis Kilvert's home country", *Country Life* (5 Sept. 1957), pp. 430–1, ill.

To be published in Spring 1982 – the full text of the Sandford Notebook – *The Diary of Francis Kilvert, April–June 1870,* (National Library of Wales).

Welsh Language Publications

Trebor Lloyd Evans, *Cymro Kilvert* (Abertawe: Tŷ John Penry, 1973).
(Selections from *Kilvert's Diary* translated into Welsh).

Trebor Lloyd Evans, "Y Gymru a welodd Kilvert", *Taliesin,* vol. 26, pp. 90–5.

Geraint Fychan, *Yr haul a'r Gangell* (Spring 1974), pp. 32–3. (Review of *Cymru Kilvert*).

Enid R. Morgan, *Yr hail a'r Gangell* (Winter 1975), pp. 30–4. (Review of *Cymru Kilvert*).

W. Islwyn Morgan, "Dyddiadur Francis Kilvert", *Yr Eurgrawn* 164 (1972), pp. 169–73; 165 (1973), pp. 27–31.

W. Islwyn Morgan, *Yr Eurgrawn,* 166, p. 48 (Review of *Cymru Kilvert*).

F. G. Payne, *Crwydro Sir Faesyfed– Y Rhan Gyntaf* (Llandybïe: Llyfrau'r Dryw, 1966), pp. 79–102.

Gomer M. Roberts, *Y Genhinen*, vol. 24, p. 52. (Review of *Cymru Kilvert*).

Robin Williams, *Taliesin*, vol. 28, pp. 122–3. (Review of *Cymru Kilvert*).

Publications of the Kilvert Society

(Publications Dept. Heulwen, Castle Gardens, Hay-on-Wye, Hereford).

Collected Verse of Francis Kilvert. Ed. O. Prosser.

Looking Backwards (on St Harmon, Kilvert's Homecoming, Funeral, etc). Ed. O. Prosser.

More Chapters from the Kilvert Saga. (Memoirs of Robert Kilvert, Emily Wyndowe, etc). Ed. H. Tanner and O. Prosser.

Kilvert and the Wordsworth Circle. R. I. Morgan.

A Kilvert Symposium. Ed. F. Grice.

Oswin Prosser Memorial Booklet. (Mr Venables's Diaries, The Solitary of Llanbedr, etc).

Further Extracts from Kilvert's Diary. Ed. O. Prosser.

Kilvert and the Visual Arts. R. Billingham.

Kilvert's 'Kathleen Mavourneen'. E. Farmery and R. B. Taylor.

Who's Who in Kilvert's Diary. F. Grice.

Walks in the Kilvert Country. M. M. Morgan.

Kilvert on Records. He, being dead, yet speaketh. Selections from the Diary made by Jerry Friar and read by Timothy Davies, who played Kilvert in the T.V. series. Saydisc Records, the Barton, Inglestone Common, Badminton, Glos. GL9 1BX.

The Other Francis Kilvert (Francis Kilvert of Claverton). F. Grice and Teresa Williams.

The Kilvert Society

The Society was formed in 1948 to foster an interest in the Rev Francis Kilvert, his work, his diary and the countrysides he loved.

The Hon. Sec. is:
E. J. C. West,
27 Baker's Oak,
Lincoln Hill,
Ross-on-Wye.

There is a Kilvert display in the Public Library, Hay-on-Wye, and a substantial Kilvert Archive in the Hereford Public Library.